How to Defeat

a

Superior

Opponent

How to Defeat a

Superior Opponent

by

Edmar Mednis

International Grandmaster

Summit Publishing
Los Angeles

First Edition: January 1989

ISBN # 0-945806-019

Typesetter:	*Marianne Zaugg*
Cover:	*Circle Box Design, P.O. Box 67A64, Los Angeles, CA 90067*
Photograph by:	*Fred Bunch, courtesy of USCF*
Diagrams copied by:	*Gert DeVries*
Proofreader:	*IM Jack Peters*
Consultants to the publisher:	*Gwen Feldman, IM Jeremy Silman*
Final Preparation:	*Marianne Zaugg*
Editor:	*Dodd Mitchell Darin*
Publisher:	*Summit Publishing, P.O. Box 67A48, Los Angeles, CA 90067*

To my mother

Preface

No matter how good you are, part of the time your opponent will be even better. Of course, if you are one of the world's top players, the number of those superior to you is small. If you are the reigning World Champion, then most likely no one is better than you. This book is not written for the benefit of the world's top players. They do not need my help.

But everyone else, from relative beginner through master, is continually faced with the prospect of sitting across the board from someone who, based on objective standards, must be rated the the superior player. What should you do to have the best chance of success? You do not want to lose and it would be so nice to win. When in the middle 1970's I decided to start writing chess books, the matter of choosing appropriate subjects became a very important one.

It seemed to me that a treatise on the practically very important topic of "how to defeat a superior opponent" would be of value to every chess player. How to go about it? This was the next concern. Of course, as a result of 25 years of personal tournament experience in battling those better than I, I knew what worked for me and what did not work for me. Moreover, I had much anecdotal information from other sources. Still, because of my educational background (Chemical engineering) and my scientific area of work (I was a chess professional!), I wanted a substantial and consistent source of material to base my conclusions on. After evaluating several alternatives, I decided to research all the games that Soviet grandmasters lost to foreigners in 1973. This allowed for a large number of beneficial characteristics: (1) in the aggregate, Soviet grandmasters were the world's strongest, (2) there was considerable diversity in the styles of the grandmasters, (3) the 68-game sample size was adequate and manageable. Moreover, besides the meaningful sample size, 1973 had other desirable characteristics. As you remember, in 1972 Bobby Fischer dethroned Boris Spassky as the World Champion. The Soviet functionaries took this defeat exceptionally hard and embarked on an aggressive program to reestablish Soviet chess supremacy. This meant greater opportunities, incentives and responsibilities for the Soviet players in international competition.Thus the sample offered an excellent opportunity to study very strong players at their most serious and best. Therefore I felt that the conclusions that I would draw regarding my objective of "how to defeat a superior opponent" would be firmly based.

Unfortunately, when I was doing the actual work, I allowed my imagination to run away from me. Rather than framing the results as I had intended, I decided on a catchy title, "How to Beat the Russians," and in the text also spoke about beating the Russians. Of course, I assumed that the potential reader would realize that the term "Russian" is used as a proxy for "superior opponent." But the end result was more confusion than clarity.

Therefore, I have now redone the material as I had originally intended it. The theme throughout the book is "how to defeat a superior opponent." Of course, there is some poetic license in this title also. All that I can really promise is to give meaningful advice on "how to play against a superior opponent." To gain a win, errors by the opponent are required. This is in the hands of our opponent and not in ours. BUT, if we do our part well, our risk of a loss decreases considerably and our chance of a win increases significantly.

Whenever a chess book is republished, the question arises as to how much of it must be redone. After all, every tournament adds at least a nuance to our knowledge of some opening variation. This means that to even try to stay up with our mass of knowledge explosion, each book should be revised at least annually. Obviously this is neither possible nor practical. What I have done is review in detail every part of my original 1977 manuscript. In general, my work has "stood the test of time," to paraphrase the title of one of Garry Kasparov's fine books. Where there has been something of significance to add, I have done so, and enclosed it in brackets so that the reader can immediately recognize it. Evaluating moves by question and exclamation marks is standard in chess literature. However, to ensure that the reader and author are on the same wavelength these are the presently accepted meanings:

!	=	a strong move
!!	=	a very strong move; a fantastic move
?	=	a bad move; a weak move
??	=	a horrible move; a blunder
!?	=	an enterprising move; a move worthy of consideration
?!	=	a dubious move, for theoretical or practical reason

In compiling information for this book, these standard sources were used: personal knowledge, personal contacts, and leading chess books and periodicals. When appropriate, direct credit is given in the text. In an undertaking of such scope, some errors of fact and interpretation are almost inevitable. The author accepts responsibility for all of these. Your assistance in bringing them to my attention will be appreciated.

As always, my deepest gratitude goes to my wonderful blonde wife Baiba, not only for typing the entire original as well as revised manuscript, but for never-ending physical and moral support.

This is my first book for Summit Publishing. I am very happy to be associated with Summit and its president, Dodd M. Darin.

New York, 1988   Edmar Mednis

Contents

Part 1   How to Defeat a Superior Opponent:

Opening Index

Sicilian Defense

Ruy Lopez

English Opening

How to Defeat a Superior Opponent

Principles, Explanations, Statistics:

Please follow the principles and guidelines given below whenever facing a superior opponent. Your results will improve significantly. The principles, in a rough order of their importance, are:

1. Play with confidence

Playing with confidence is the single most important principle. In any one-on-one competition-baseball batter vs. pitcher, tennis, table tennis-confidence is a prerequisite for success. If the batter is sure that he won't be able to hit the sharp curve, he won't; if the tennis player worries that he won't be able to return serve, he won't. Confidence in chess is even more important, because not only do you have time to worry before the game, but you have lots of time during the game to be a worrywart. Consider the following scenario: before the game you feel that you have no chance, soon after the start you feel uncomfortable and say to yourself, "I just want the game to last long enough to be honorable," then your superior opponent makes an error and you know that you stand better. But instead of rejoicing and thinking, "Now I've got you," you think: "No matter, I'll screw up again." With such an approach, is it any surprise that you do screw up?

The correct approach is as follows:

(1)   Before the game you feel good and confident. You are determined to do your best. You know that your opponent has lost games before to inferior opponents. (28% of the losses by grandmasters in this book were to non-grandmasters.)

(2a)   The game starts poorly for you. But you are determined to continue doing your best. You know that the superior player - being human - is quite capable of losing the thread of a position.

This happens, for instance, in Game 42, starting with White's 17th move.

(2b)   The game starts well for you. You are in good form and/or your superior opponent is having an off day or is underestimating you.

(3)   Either from (2a) or (2b) you now have the superior position. As the superiority of your position increases, so does your confidence, and you win in good style. Games 42 and 43 provide excellent illustration.

2. Don't do anything stupid

There is an army saying to the effect that "you want to live to fight another day." So also in the battle of chess. If you are going to commit suicide soon, your prospects for success are nil. Don't short circuit your chances for ultimate success by doing something stupid in the meanwhile. The three most important sources of stupid errors are the following.

Stupid choice of opening variation

Because your opponent has a higher rating than you, it is fair to expect that his overall chess knowledge is greater than yours. Therefore, also his knowledge of openings should be better. Why not surprise him with some variation that he knows nothing about? This is a reasonable thought, but in the execution of this plan, a stupid variation is chosen. After all, the superior player will be expected to be familiar with "good variations," so the only choice is a "bad variation," yes?. Of course, it is stupid to do this for both White and Black, but it is absolutely unforgivable when you are White. I will have more to say about this in Section 5.

Stupid move(s) in middlegame

You're playing normally enough when suddenly a plan or a combination fascinates you. Looking further into it you see that it does not work if the opponent responds correctly. But you like your move so much that you tell yourself that, after all, the chances are good that your opponent won't find the refutation. Isn't it simply stupid to think that something that you saw quickly, your superior opponent won't be able to find also?

Stupid behavior because of psychological reasons

It is so important to keep ourselves under rigorous discipline whenever we play. Even when we aim to play our best, there is no guarantee that we will come up with the best move. But when, because of psychological factors, we allow our mind to stop searching for the truth, disaster is just around the

2

corner. Of course, the superior player can also fall into this kind of self-induced trap. In 21% of the games in this book, psychological factors were a major cause of the loss. When you analyze Games 9, 16, 21, 52 and 55, you will see that the superior player loses drastically when he starts playing stupidly. What chance do you have when you behave similarly?

3. Play according to your style

There are very few truly universal players in the world. Paul Morphy, Alexander Alekhine, Boris Spassky, Robert J. Fischer come to my mind. Almost everyone else is better at some things than at others, be it violent attacks, clear attacks, deep opening preparation, "boring" endgames, positional maneuvering, clear positions, obscure complications etc. The only way you can expect to defeat a superior opponent is when you play your best. Of the 68 wins in this book, fully 51 (75%) were won because the victor played better.

You may be aware of what you consider certain weaknesses or dislikes in your opponent's style of play. Should you play in a manner that you are not comfortable with, but that you feel will cause your opponent to feel even more uncomfortable? Absolutely not! Always stick to your own likes! Your practical results will be better when you play according to your style and strengths. This means playing what you know, like, and have confidence in.

These principles apply equally to strong players. If a very strong player veers away from his style, results will be poor also. Game 47 is a perfect illustration.

Absolutely the worst thing that you can do is to crawl into a shell and somehow hope to survive. This is not a way to play for a draw, but a sure way to ensure a loss. Eternal vigilance is required in defending, because just a slight moment of carelessness is enough to cause the loss. Errors in carrying out an attack are much less frequent. In only 13 of the 55 applicable games (24%), was the attack misplayed seriously enough to lose the game. Losses from defensive errors were more than three times higher (76% vs 24%). If very strong players have so much difficulty defending, won't you do a lot worse?

4. Play the best moves

Competitive chess is a battle for the ultimate truth on the chessboard.

Even when playing your peers, you have no right to expect any gifts from your opponent. But when you sit down to face someone superior, you have to realize that the only chance for winning is to play your very best, from the beginning of the opening through the end of the endgame. It is up to you to win - the chances for a gift from your opponent are small. Only 11 (16%) of the games in this book were lost by "carelessness," i.e. blunders, and only 6 games (9%) by trying too hard to win.

Remember that your chances for finding the best move in a position are much better if you are familiar and comfortable with that kind of position, i.e. when you are playing in accordance with your natural style.

5. As White go for a sensible initiative

In international play, having the White pieces means starting off with a clear advantage. This is confirmed by overall statistics as well as by the course of the typical game between two grandmasters. The onus is always on Black to demonstrate (reach) full equality. The major part of White's advantage derives from being able to force his will onto the opponent. When added to the characteristic advantages that White can achieve in modern opening play, such as an edge in development or central superiority, this means that, as White, you can look forward to a pleasant situation on the board for a considerable time to come. This is largely because the lower-rated player does not have the discipline in playing the White pieces that the higher-rated player does.

It is now well recognized that all reputable main line openings lead to some advantage for White. Therefore there is no reason why the strategist should not feel satisfied at the end of a main line Ruy Lopez as he enters the middlegame, or as a Queen's Gambit Declined, Orthodox variation leads into the middlegame. The tactician should be equally happy as he starts the attack against Black's King in the Yugoslav variation of the Dragon Sicilian. After all, if at the start of middlegame action you still have the advantage, should you not feel confident of the future?

I am not saying that you should always play the most popular main line whenever facing a superior opponent. There is nothing wrong with doing this, but it is not the only correct approach. What you do want to do is to select, in accordance with your playing style, those variations which, based on our current knowledge of opening theory, allow White to retain at least some opening advantage. Do not count on your opponent misplaying a known

4

opening. Major opening successes, in terms of having a "won" position after the opening, will only occur as a result of your own original discoveries or your opponent's unjustified experiments. Enjoy them when they come, but don't expect them. Be satisfied with what grandmasters are satisfied with when they are White: a noticeable, even if slight, edge at the start of the middlegame. If you do select a modern sensible variation, you will be in excellent position to advantageously parry any unmotivated steps your superior opponent will take. Consult Games 23, 27, and 55 for proof.

The worst thing you can do as White is to throw away your inherent opening advantage by choosing a stupid variation. Look at what White does in the following two examples from my own recent play:

(1)   In T. Casagrande - E. Mednis, Lugano 1987, after **1 e4 c5 2 Nf3 Nc6 3 d4 cxd4 4 Nxd4 Nf6 5 Nc3 d6 6 Bg5 e6,** we have the start of the Richter-Rauzer attack in the Sicilian defense. The well established plan for White now is 7 Qd2 followed by 8 O-O-O. In the resulting variations, no clear way exists at present for Black to gain 100% equality. But when I asked the West German master after the game why he didn't play thus, he replied that I must surely know the variation better than he. This could well be so, but the bottom line is that White still stands better at the start of the middlegame. Instead of the normal 7 Qd2 White played the very infrequent and inferior **7 f4?!** and I went on to win as follows: **7...Qb6 8 Nb3 Be7 9 Qd2 O-O 10 O-O-O Rd8 11 Bxf6 Bxf6 12 h4 Qb4 13 Rh3 Bxc3 14 Rxc3 Qxe4 15 g4 e5 16 Rc4 Qg6 17 f5 Qf6 18 Kb1 d5 19 Rc5 h5 20 Na5 hxg4 21 Rxd5 Rxd5 22 Qxd5 Bxf5 23 Nxb7 Bxc2+,** White resigns.

(2)   In H. Rupacher - E. Mednis, Graz 1987, the Classical variation in the Sicilian Defense was reached after **1 e4 c5 2 Nf3 Nc6 3 d4 cxd4 4 Nxd4 Nf6 5 Nc3 d6.** White here has a large number of sound continuations: 6 Bg5, 6 Bc4, 6 Be2, 6 f4, 6 g3, 6 Be3. Instead the Austrian expert first strengthened my center by playing **6 Nxc6?! bxc6,** then threw away a valuable central pawn with **7 e5 ?? dxe5,** and thereafter entered a lost endgame with **8 Qxd8+?! Kxd8.** Having gained a sound pawn, I won the endgame without difficulty: **9 Bc4 e6 10 O-O Nd5 11 Ne4 f6 12 Bb3 a5 13 a3 Kc7 14 c4 Nf4 15 Re1 Nd3 16 Re3 Nxc1 17 Rxc1 Be7 18 Rd1 f5 19 Nc3 e4 20 Na4 Rb8 21 Ba2 c5 22 b3 Bd7 23 Nc3 Bc6 24 a4 Rbd8 25 Rxd8 Rxd8 26 Kf1 Bf6 27 Nb5+ Kb6 28 Re1 h5 29 Bb1 Rd7 30 Bc2 Bg5 31 Rd1 h4 32 h3 Bf4 33 Rxd7 Bxd7 34 Bd1 g6 35 Ke2 Be5 36 Na3 Be8 37 Nc2 Kc6 38 Ke3 Kd6 39 Na3 Bd4+ 40 Ke2 Ke5 41 Nb5 Bc6 42 Nc7 Bd7 43 Nb5 Bb2 44 Ke3 Bc6 45 Bc2 g5 46 Ke2 Be8 47 Ke3 Bh5 48 Kd2 Bd4 49 Ke1 g4 50 Kf1 gxh3 51 gxh3 Bf3 52 Na7 e3 53**

fxe3 Bxe3 54 Bd3 Bd2 55 Bc2 Kf4 White resigns.

When after the game I expressed my surprise to the Austrian expert at his choice of the "variation," he replied that I would be expected to know the normal lines better and that he felt that the endgame offered "some chances." Please note the dichotomy in White's approach: by playing e.g. 6 Bg5 e6 7 Qd2, White can definitely get "some chances" in a position where he has a slight advantage and is no material down. Isn't it simply madness to prefer, instead, a course of action which leaves him a clear pawn down in an endgame? Such an approach for gaining "some chances" carries a ridiculously high cost.

Please remember that in "must win" situations, it is not axiomatic to choose the sharpest or wildest variation. Consider all valid alternative approaches before selecting your choice. Garry Kasparov's thinking in preparing for his decisive last match game in 1987 against Anatoly Karpov is most insightful. After losing the 23rd game, Kasparov found himself a full point down and in need to win with the White pieces Game 24. Routine thinking could have suggested playing 1 e4 and after 1...e5, the wild King's Gambit with 2 f4, or after 1...c6 2 d4 d5, the extremely sharp advance variation with 3 e5 Bf5 4 Nc3 e6 5 g4. Instead, Kasparov chose a completely different approach and satisfied himself with a sensible, slight initiative after 1 c4 e6 2 Nf3 Nf6 3 g3 d5 4 b3. He won deservedly and retained his title. Kasparov's reasoning was that, against a sharp line, Karpov could be expected to search for the best move. However, in a quiet variation, Karpov would perhaps always see the image of the coveted draw in front of him and thus could be tempted to satisfy himself with the safest rather than the best moves.

6. As Black aim for a position of reasonable counter chances

In the previous chapter I discussed the advantages that White has at the start of play. They are real enough. Yet that is no reason to throw up our hands even before we start. In this book Black lost 39 games (57%). The bad news is that this is a lot. However, the good news is that Black won 29 games for a 43% success ratio. This shows that Black's prospects are real enough.

The major question is: what kind of an approach should you as Black use to improve your chances against a superior opponent?

First the don'ts:

(a) <u>Do not play a variation which is known to be dubious</u>

Black's disadvantage is real enough even when playing the "best" lines, so why handicap yourself even more by choosing something which is known to be inferior? The hope in using this approach is that our superior opponent will not be familiar with it and won't know what to do. But where is the factual basis for such hope? In the first place, since he knows more than I do, shouldn't he also know a lot about inferior lines? Moreover, the major advantage that the superior player has is his greater <u>understanding</u> of chess. Even if he is unfamiliar with your move/variation, the chances are that he will be able to come up with a good response.

(b) <u>Do not play a variation which is so inherently passive that you have to defend perfectly just to squeeze out a draw.</u>

Defending is always difficult, and even more so when your opponent is stronger than you. Aiming for positions that require 40-50 moves of careful defending is simply self-defeating. Your superior opponent will always know how to increase the pressure, and you will crack sooner or later. The superior player has superior "technique," i.e. the ability to know what to do when the position offers clear plans.

The best approach is something like a golden mean of the above unsatisfactory approaches. <u>Play a good sound variation where there are opportunities for counterplay.</u> In a sound variation, you will not be blown off the board. In a variation which offers prospects for counterplay, your superior opponent will not be able to only do "his thing," but will always have to worry also about your possibilities. Moreover, if the position will require him to make <u>non-routine</u> decisions, the chances are real that he may err. For a large number of specific success stories, study Games 10, 15, 18, 21, 31, 39, 42, 43, 51, 52, 54, 57, 62 and 66.

7. <u>Once you have the advantage, avoid all unnecessary complications.</u>

There are usually two steps to winning a game: first, getting a won position, and second, winning it. The grandmaster only has problems with the first step - the second part goes smoothly. It is the lower-rated player that is troubled by the second step. The major reason for his difficulties is that he feels both steps should be handled the same way. Nothing could be further from the truth. Often, to hope to get a won position, a substantial amount of risk must be tolerated. But, once the position is "won," take no more risks! This careful approach is <u>always</u> in order for everybody. Yet it is absolutely mandatory when you are trying to win a won position against a superior opponent. It is immaterial how you got your won position. Once you have it, play in accordance with the following principles:

- Establish and follow a clear plan.
- Don't allow counterplay.
- Avoid unclear or unnecessary complications.
- Be careful.
- Never be in a hurry, either with respect to time or number of moves. There is no extra prize for winning a game with lots of time left on the clock or for winning in 50 rather than 60 moves.
- Hold on to material advantage.
- When ahead in material, continually try to simplify the position by exchanging <u>pieces.</u>

Excellent examples of how to win won positions against very strong grandmasters are shown in the following games: 4, 5, 7, 9, 11, 19, 26, 27, 32, 34, 37, 41, 43, 44, 51, 52, 62, 67 and 68.

If the principles described above and executed in these games were good enough to defeat grandmasters, you can feel very confident that they will be more than good enough against your opponents.

8. Play an active strategic middlegame

To progress in chess, various skills are needed as prerequisites. One of these is familiarity with tactics. You have heard expressions of the sort "chess is 90% tactics." There is much truth to this, in the sense that you should look for (as well as be looking <u>out</u> for!) combinational possibilities throughout the opening, middlegame and endgame.Therefore a basic tactical arsenal is part of any strong player. There is no valid reason for you to expect your superior opponent will be weaker in basic tactics than you. A "game plan" which consisted of nothing but a series of tactical traps will not only lead to no scalps, but will end with your pieces disjoined throughout the board. The ultimate result invariably will be a most unpleasant loss.

At higher levels of play, tactics and strategy are usually enmeshed quite closely. Even then, what can be considered tactical errors cause only the minor part of losses. In only 25 of 66 applicable games (38%) in this book could errors in tactics be held responsible for the loss.

The very substantial majority of losses occur because of making strategic misjudgments in the middlegame. When the strategic requirements of a position are not obvious, more than one approach may seem to make sense. In fact, probably only one way is correct, but it is difficult to decide which could be the right way. Therefore, errors of judgment can occur very easily. If you have succeeded in establishing a position where the major bench marks are strategic in nature, your superior opponent no longer has the advantage of "more" knowledge or "more" experience. He has to solve a _new_ problem, and the chances are good that he will not be able to solve it under the practical consideration of the ticking clock. As study material the following games are suggested: 3, 4, 5, 6, 7, 9, 10, 11, 17, 19, 22, 32, 34, 35, 41, 47, 49, 67, 68. In them, a very strong grandmaster could not successfully cope with the strategic needs of his position. Your opponents are sure to have an even more difficult time under similar circumstances.

9. Expect that the major part of your successes will come in the middlegame

Your superior opponent is superior to you either in knowledge or experience or in both. Openings can be learned well enough from books or by very disciplined play and review. Therefore your chances in getting a won position in the opening are slight. In only 13 of the games (19%) in this book was opening play directly responsible for the loss. Similarly to openings, so too endgames can be learned well enough from books or by very disciplined play and review. Only 11 (16 %) of the games were lost because of endgame errors, and two of these were time control flukes.

Nearly two thirds (44 of 68 games or 65%) of the losses in this book came in the middlegame. Unquestionably, this is the area in which your superior opponent is most vulnerable. In the middlegame, deep strategic concepts, creativity, and original thought assume the greatest importance, whereas general technical knowledge and experience diminish in importance. Thus it is in the middlegame that the talented and less experienced player can compete effectively with his higher-rated opponent.

10. Use endgames for consolidating your advantage

Because your opponent will have greater technical knowledge of endgames or experience in endgame play or both, endgames are not a fruitful area for expecting successes against a higher-rated player. That is, do not expect to win equal endgames. As general policy, do not enter such endgames unless the draw is a very obvious routine matter. When there is the choice between an equal full-play middlegame and a full-play endgame, choose the former, for the reasons discussed in the previous section. Even worse for you is to voluntarily enter an inferior endgame from an inferior middlegame because your practical chances for survival are decreased considerably.

Yet do not look askance at all endgames. Look upon superior endgames with great enthusiasm. Once you have gained a significant advantage from the opening or middlegame, aim to enter a superior endgame. Superior endgames are always delightful because they offer fine winning chances with minimum risk of losing. Play them in accordance with the principles outlined in section 7. Review the recommended games from that section to learn "how to win a won endgame."

11. Always continue to fight on

Chess is so complicated a game and the nervous tension during a tournament game so high that errors are inevitable. This is true for the World Champion and all the way down to the rank beginner. A major difference between the world's top players and those clearly below them is not that the top players don't make errors (they actually make a lot), but their reaction to the error. The will to win is so strong in the top players that, instead of being fazed by their errors, they keep fighting on like tigers. A legend for the number of "lost" positions that he saved is U.S. grandmaster Samuel Reshevsky. When Shelby Lyman on his 1984 World Chess Championship TV show asked Reshevsky for his secret and what advice he could give for saving lost positions, the reply was: "sit tight and hope for a blunder." Both parts of the answer are very important. "Sit tight" means to do the best that can be done: prevent all of your opponent's threats while doing nothing which makes your own position worse. Yet there must be something in the future to make it worthwhile to put in all of this effort under unpleasant conditions. This "something" is the hope for an error by our opponent. Notice that you have no reason to "expect" an error. Such "expectations" can give you a false sense of optimism which can cause you to let your guard down. Moreover, if the expected error does not come (in a majority of cases it will not come), you will feel an unjustifiable letdown, and this can well affect your play in the next game. This is a particular danger if the next game is to be played later in the same day.

Yet the hope for a blunder gives us a valid reason for fighting on, while posing no psychological dangers if we are not successful. Blunders will occur enough times to make a difference in your score and ultimately your rating - as long as you are "still in the game." Particularly major blunders occurred in these eleven games, causing immediate losses of either a half point or a full point: 1, 29, 39, 46, 48, 57, 58, 60, 61, 63, 64.

Therefore never get despondent if an error has placed you in a poor position. Your superior opponent may well reciprocate with a major error of his own, as in the above examples. In addition to outright errors, the opponent may also lose the thread of the position,which as already mentioned, occurred in Game 42. Always remember that your higher-rated opponent is also human and can be affected by all the factors that can affect you. A particular reason for hope is if you have noticed that your opponent is having a bad tournament. This means that he is in poor form and can screw up your game too, as long as you put up the best resistance possible.

12. Don't get into time pressure

Time pressure is as much a menace to the tournament player as the black plague was to the general population centuries ago.There is no cure for it. As Garry Kasparov said in an interview with Shelby Lyman on the 1986 World Championship TV show: "Time pressure is simply something horrible. It prevents the mind from functioning. I may suddenly see that my Bishop has been moved to c4 and I cannot see any reason why it has moved there."

Grandmasters do suffer from this disease. In at least 18 of the losses (26%) was time pressure a significant factor. (Games 1, 2, 11, 12, 13, 20, 24, 28, 29, 33, 35, 38, 39, 46, 58, 61, 63, 64).

Therefore, if top players play so poorly in time pressure, your play will be even worse. Your chances of coping with time pressure when facing a superior opponent are nil. Therefore, don't get into time pressure.

To avoid time pressure, get in the habit of always saving time. Some guidelines for saving time are:

- Always get to the game on time.
- Go to the bathroom before the start of a game.
- Come prepared for the immediate opening play. Decide ahead of time what you will play for White and how you will respond when Black.

- Play the early opening efficiently. As a rule of thumb: take no more than 5 minutes for 5 moves; no more than 10 minutes for 10 moves.
- Save time by playing obvious moves and routine recaptures quickly.
- If a variation looks attractive and you've checked it through twice, go ahead and play it. If you're in good form, the variation will be good.
- Never procrastinate. If two moves check out to be equally good, play one of them quickly. Uncertainty is a necessary way of life for the chess player. Playing quickly at such moments will leave you with more time for later decisions.

The final guideline that I will leave you with is: as the time control approaches, leave yourself with no less than one minute per move. In particular, leave no less than five minutes for the last five moves and no less than two minutes for the last move.

√GAME 1

White: V. Hort
(Czechoslovakia)

Black: V. Antoshin
(U.S.S.R.)

Played at Budapest (Hungary) International Tournament, February 21, 1973, Round 8.

Reti Opening

The Czech grandmaster plans to go for a win by setting up a strategically sound but unbalanced position. Here, just a bit of carelessness allows Black to make a creative and vicious attack, and he gains a sound extra pawn in an endgame. The practical cost, however, is a huge expenditure of time, resulting in severe time pressure. To take advantage of this, White plays for complications by attacking Black's King, even though little material is left on the board. White's strong nerves carry the day when Black panics, blunders and suddenly finds himself facing an unstoppable mate threat. A gutsy win by White; a very unlucky loss for Black.

1	c4	Nf6
2	g3	c6
3	Nf3	d5
4	b3	

Hort plans to go for the win by establishing a sound, unbalanced, strategic, full-play middlegame. He sees no need to play 4 Bg2!?, which could allow Black to win and retain the c-pawn after 4...dxc4!?.

4	...	Bg4

Black chooses the most active and modern continuation. With this move, Black shows his readiness to exchange his light squared Bishop for White's Knight at f3 at the proper moment. This reduces White's control over the key d4 and especially e5 central squares. Other theoretically sound approaches for Black are 4...Bf5 and 4...g6 followed by 5... Bg7.

5	Bg2	Nbd7
6	Bb2	e6

A logical central and developmental move. There is also the opportunity for a sharper approach: 6...Bxf3!? 7 Bxf3 e5 8 d3 Bc5 9 e3 Qe7 10 O-O e4, with Black having full and sound equality in Andersson-Vaganian, Hastings 1974/75, which was drawn in 29.

7	O-O	Bd6
8	d4	

8 d3 followed by 9 Nbd2 seems logical to keep the central diagonal open for the dark squared Bishop and to reinforce the e4 square. With the immediate 8...Bxf3! 9 Bxf3 O-O Black can prevent White from gain-

ing anything, since after 10 Nd2 a5 the passive location of White's Knight on d2 does not allow much opportunity for action. This point was well demonstrated in Ribli-Geller, Round 13 (Black's dark squared Bishop was on e7 and White had not played c4); Black easily equalized and drew in 31 moves.

8 ...	O-O
9 Nbd2	Qe7

A dual purpose move: preparing a potential central advance by means of ...e5 and enabling ...Ba3 exchanging White's Bishop on b2.

10 a3

Preventing the second of Black's plans. At the start of this round, both Hort and Antoshin have 4-3 scores and are anxious to improve their tournament standing. After the text move, the middlegame offers more strategic play than would follow after the exchange of the dark- square Bishops. The disadvantage is that White gives up a full tempo for development, and this is just sufficient for Black to equalize . According to theory, White's most accurate continuation is 10　Re1. After 10...Ba3 11 Qc1! Bxb2 12 Qxb2, White has a slight advantage because of his greater central space.

10 ...	e5!

This liberating advance estab-lishes approximate equality.

11 cxd5	cxd5

Black must retain central influence. 11... Nxd5? 12 e4! Nf6 13 Qc2 with White better, is therefore inferior.

12 dxe5	Nxe5

Black's active piece placement compensates for his isolated pawn at d5. White's safest approach is 13 Nxe5 Bxe5 14 Bxe5 Qxe5 15 Nf3. But this offers little in the way of winning chances, so White plays...

13 Nd4?!

Hort does not overlook the rejoinder but judges it harmless. It turns out to be anything but that.

13 ...	Nd3!
14 Bc3?!	

Continuing to rate Black's 13th as harmless. After the safe 14 Qc2!, Black's advantage, if any, is minute.

| 14 ... | Rac8 |
| 15 Qc2 | |

What now, Knight?

| 15 ... | Nxf2!! |

A most brilliant, creative, sound sacrifice whose deep point appears as late as move 22. The practical difficulty is that the preparation and execution of such sacrifices requires time-consuming thought. Too often serious time trouble results, which then spoils everything that has been achieved.

16 Kxf2

The King ventures out because 16 Rxf2 fails to 16...Qe3 17 Rc1 Bxa3 and Black regains, with interest, his sacrificed material.

| 16 ... | Rfe8! |

The quiet first point. The obvious threat is 17...Qe3+ and White's response is the only reasonable one.

| 17 Qd3 | Bxe2!! |

A second brilliant sacrifice whose primary purpose is to gain time for...Ng4+.

18 Nxe2

18 Qxe2 allows the same move, 18...Ng4+!, and after 19 Kg1 (19 Qxg4? Qe3 mate) Qxe2 20 Nxe2 Rxe2, White's position is so awkward that he loses back even more material than he gained.

| 18 ... | Ng4+ |
| 19 Kg1 | |

19 Ke1? is punished by 19...Rxc3! 20 Qxc3 Qxe2 mate and 19 Kf3? by 19...Rxc3! Nxc3 (20 Qxc3 Qxe2 mate) 20...Nxh2+ 21 Kf2 Bc5+ followed by mate.

| 19 ... | Qxe2 |
| 20 Rf3?! | |

At first glance, this is a satisfactory answer; however, Black sees far more deeply than White. It may be more difficult for Black to handle the sharp 20 Qxd5!?, after which the position remains exceedingly complicated. For instance, Black can win back most of the sacrificed material with 20...Bc5+ 21 Kh1 Nf2+ 22 Rxf2 Bxf2! and still maintain a strong attacking formation. The situation is unclear, however. Clearly unsatisfactory for White is 20 Qxe2?, which transposes into the note after White's

18th move.

| 20 ... | Qxd3 |
| 21 Rxd3 | Rxc3!! |

The third brilliant sacrifice of the game.

| 22 Rxc3 | Be5! |

This elegant follow up is the ultimate point of Black's play. Any attempt to save the Rook allows 23... Bd4+, so ...

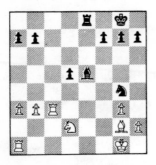

23 Rd3?!

White has had enough of the complications and is satisfied to enter a pawn-down, opposite color Bishops endgame. This gives White fair drawing chances. Even so, the complicated 23 Rcc1! (but not 23 Rac1? Bd4+ 24 Kh1 Nf2+ 25 Kg1 Ne4+ 26 Kh1 Nxc3) seems like the right move. Black does have a perpetual check in hand after 23... Bd4+ 24 Kh1 (24 Kf1?? Nxh2 mate) Nf2+ 25 Kg1 Ne4+ 26 Kh1 !! but attempts for more may well give less.

| 23 ... | Bxa1 |
| 24 Rxd5 | Ne3 |

Starting here Black, despite (or possibly because of) great time pressure, ignores the safety of his King. He has clearly won the battle, but ultimately he loses the war. A nice safe move here is 24...Nf6! which keeps White's Rook away from the seventh rank. Black does not need to rush matters, the important thing is to get safely to move 40.

| 25 Rd7 | Nxg2 |
| 26 Kxg2 | g6 |

Objectively this is playable, but it needlessly weakens the f6 and h6 squares. This proves decisive at the end. The good, safe move is 26...h6!.

27 Nc4

27 Rxb7?? Re2+ and Black wins the Knight.

27 ...	b5
28 Nd6	Re3
29 Nxf7?!	

White, speculating on Black's time pressure, plays for an attack against Black's King. The move carries definite hazards for White but in the end leads to a win. The sound way to go for a draw is to exchange all Queenside pawns starting with 29 Nxb5! The resulting position in which Black has a 3 pawn versus 2 pawn advantage on the Kingside is a theoretical draw.

29 ...	Rxb3
30 Rxa7	Bd4!
31 Nh6+	Kh8

Again playable but dangerous. Much safer and stronger is 31...Kf8!. Then after 32 Rxh7 Rxa3!, Black's b-pawn is a very dangerous threat.

| 32 Rd7 | Be3? |

Attributable to time pressure. Obviously correct is 32...Bb2!, which not only keeps the f6 square protected but also ensures winning the pawn on a3.

| 33 Ng4 | Bc1?? |

Protecting against a nonexistent threat (34 Nxe3) and ignoring the real one (34 Nf6). 33...Bg5 may not be fully satisfactory after 34 h4 h5 35 Ne5 followed by 36 Nxg6+,but Black can still keep equality after 33 ...Kg8! 34 Nf6+ Kf8 35 Nxh7+ Ke8.

Then, because of the threat to the pawn on a3, White seems to have nothing better than to take a perpetual check after 36 Nf6+, etc.

34 Nf6

And so the combination of the King in the corner and the weakness of the f6 square leads to an unstoppable mate on h7. Tragic !

34 ...	Rb2+
35 Kh3	
Black Resigns	

GAME 2

White: V. Antoshin
(U.S.S.R.)

Black: G. Sax
(Hungary)

Played at Budapest (Hungary) International Tournament, March 1, 1973, Round 14.

Grunfeld Defense

White uses a rather obscure opening system and emerges with a clear spatial and developmental advantage. But, by being too greedy, he throws away his pluses to gain a rather inconsequential pawn. As compensation, Black gets good squares for his pieces. Soon a position results in which White can do nothing with his extra pawn. The position remains in balance, until White plays to win with a ridiculous Queen retreat, instead of accepting the draw by repetition of moves, and soon suffers a painful loss. Black storms in with his pieces and opens lines in front of White's King; suddenly there is no defense to mate.

This game demonstrates excellent practical middlegame play by the youthful Sax, who deservedly punishes White for trying to win with stupid moves.

1 d4

Antoshin, a strategist, generally opens with the strategic 1 d4.

1 ...	**Nf6**
2 c4	**g6**
3 g3	

The fianchetto of the light squared Bishop is a popular, sound, flexible approach. The centrally sharpest move is 3 Nc3.

3 ...	**Bg7**
4 Bg2	**d5**

With this move, Black establishes the Grunfeld Defense, named after Ernst Grunfeld, who demonstrated its playability in the early 1920's. The Grunfeld, Black's most unbalancing response to d4, is a popular weapon when Black is playing for a win. In this defense, Black invariably allows White to build a strong center, hoping eventually to attack and annihilate it. If this does not turn out successfully, Black may be smothered. Instead of the text move, Black can also choose 4...d6 leading to the King's Indian Defense, or 4...c5, which often leads to the Benoni Defense or the Yugoslav variation of the King's Indian. An interesting example of what can happen when both sides are satisfied with a draw occurred in Round 1, Antoshin - Adorjan (after 4...c5) : 5 Nf3 Qa5+ 6 Bd2 Qb6 7 Nc3 cxd4 8 Na4 Qd6 9 Bf4 Qb4+ 10 Bd2 Qd6 11 Bf4 Qb4+ 12 Bd2 draw!, because of the three-fold repetition of position.

| 5 cxd5 | Nxd5 |
| 6 e4 | |

This continuation has gone out of style because such sharp advances have been shown to be too early for White to adopt. The normal and popular approach now is 6 Nf3 followed by 7 0-0.

| 6 ... | Nb4! |

Sharpness is required to take advantage of White's incomplete development. Black's move has two tactical points: (1) 7 Ne2? loses a pawn after 7...Bxd4 8 Nxd4 Qxd4 9 Qxd4 Nc2+ followed by 10...Nxd4; and (2) 7 Qa4+? fails to 7...N8c6 8 d5 Nd3+ 9 Kf1 (or 9 Kd2 Nxb2!) Nxc1 10 dxc6 b5! 11 Qc2 Bxb2!!.

6...Nb6 is too passive, and White gets a nice if small advantage: 7 Ne2 0-0 8 0-0 e6 9 Na3!.

7 a3

Chasing the Knight where it basically wants to go. 7 d5 is more logical, but Black obtains full counterchances with 7...c6!.

7 ...	N4c6
8 d5	Nd4
9 Nc3	0-0
10 Nge2	Bg4

In combination with the next move this is a rather artificial concept which allows White to achieve a significant central superiority. The correct and book move is 10...c5! to fortify the powerfully placed Knight. After 11 0-0 e5, Black's chances were at least equal in Donner-Keres, Beverwijk 1964.

| 11 0-0 | Bf3?! |

And here 11...Nxe2+ 12 Nxe2 c6 is a better approach.

12 Bxf3	Nxf3+
13 Kg2	Ne5
14 f4	Ned7
15 Be3	

With strong, simple moves, White achieves a significant advantage in development and in central space. He stands better.

15 ...	c6
16 Qb3	Nb6
17 dxc6?!	

This premature dissolution of the central tension throws away nearly all of White's advantage. He does win a Queenside pawn, but Black's compensation is sufficient. The strategically correct approach is 17 Rfd1! followed by 18 Rac1, with a clearly superior position.

17 ...	Nxc6
18 Rfd1	Qc8!
19 Bxb6	

Here 19 Rac1 has no meaning because of 19...Na5 followed by 20...Nac4. So White takes the pawn.

19 ...	axb6
20 Qxb6	

Leads to nothing. The more patient 20 Nd5! Qe6 21 e5 still allows White to retain a slight edge.

20 ...	Na5!

From now on the game becomes increasingly Black's, though White never seems to realize that things are changing. Black wins the game by patient, purposeful strategy, combining throughout attack and defense. His compensation for the pawn rests on a number of imperceptible factors: White's somewhat loose Kingside, pressure and attacking chances against White's Queenside, and a good diagonal for the dark-square Bishop. Equally important is that White has no opportunities either for active play or to realize his Queenside pawn advantage.

21 Qf2	Qc4

22 Rd5	e6
23 Rc5	Qa6
24 Rd1	Rfd8!

Black is unafraid to exchange a pair of Rooks since he will obtain control of the d-file.

25 Rxd8+	Rxd8
26 e5	

To close off the Bishop's diagonal is logical. However, there is a cost attached to it: White is now weaker along the a8-h1 diagonal. This weakness will be decisive.

26 ...	Bf8
27 Rb5	Nc4
28 Qf3	Rd7!

A position dynamically in balance. Black protects his b7 pawn and threatens 29...Nd2 30 Qe3 Qc6+.

29 Kh3!

Looks awkward but is required to prevent Black's Queen from getting to c6 with check.

29 ...   Be7!

An excellent practical move. Black improves the position of his Bishop and awaits further developments. Now 29... Nd2 30 Qe3 Qc6 can be parried by 31 Nd4!.

30 a4

Neither important nor harmful.

30 ...   Kg7!

One more excellent waiting move, forcing White to decide what to do. Such a tactic is very annoying when the opponent (such as White here) is in time pressure.

31 Qe4

White has no way to strengthen his position, so he correctly threatens to chase away the Knight.

31 ...   Nd2
32 Qe3   Nc4

Black has nothing better than to repeat the position since 32...Qc6? is again met by 33 Nd4.

33 Qe4   Nd2
34 Qh1??

An act of sheer madness: in order to play for a win White puts his Queen on the worst square of the board and thereby allows Black's pieces to achieve total domination. Such action is explainable partially by White's time pressure but mainly by psychological factors. At the start of this round Antoshin had a respectable 7-6 score and, with White, was looking forward to improving it at the expense of young Sax, who at that moment was in last place. Sax is now a grandmaster, but at the time he had just become an international master. Nevertheless, he calmly and logically demonstrates the folly of White's approach. This game illustrates what happens when obviously stupid moves are played in an attempt to win.

34 ...   h5!

Opening the h-file is deadly.

35 b3?

35 Qg2 has to be better, and after 35...h4 36 gxh4 Rd3+ 37 Ng3. Black's strongest after 35 Qg2 is 35...Qa8! preparing for play on the h-file.

35 ...   h4!
36 Qg1?!

36 gxh4 fails to 36....Rd3+, since 37 Ng3 leaves the other Knight hanging. 36 Qg2 still has to be better.

36 ...   Qc6!

Thank you for the diagonal!

37 Qg2	Nf3
38 Qf2	

38 Kg4 allows 38...Nxe5+!.

38 ...	hxg3
39 hxg3	Rd8!

On the way to the open h-file.

40 Kg4	Nd2!
White Resigns	

White is still up the Queenside pawn but has no defense to Black's threat of 41...Qh1! followed by 42...Qh5 mate. If 41 Qe1 or 41 Qg1, Black mates with 41... Qf3+ 42 Kh3 Rh8.

GAME 3

White: A. Planinc
(Yugoslavia)

Black: Y. Balashov
(U.S.S.R)

Played at the Wijk aan Zee (Netherlands) International Tournament, January 1973, Round 13.

Ruy Lopez (Steinitz Deferred Variation)

Satisfied with his tournament standing and facing an impulsive attacking player, Balashov elects to defend a strategically cramping variation. The decision proves quite incorrect. Rather than engage in premature attacking sorties, White follows a strategy of playing clearly, simply and well. Black is ground down without opportunities for counterplay.

1	e4	e5
2	Nf3	Nc6
3	Bb5	

The world famous Ruy Lopez, a deadly weapon in the hands of a Fischer or Karpov. Who hasn't heard of it and what more is to be said about it? Just one brief comment may be in order, though. Despite first appearances, the "Ruy" is much more of a strategic opening than a tactical one. The Bishop move puts clear pressure on the e5 square and in particular the e5 pawn. However, the threat is not immediate: e.g., 3... a6 4 Bxc6 dxc6 5 Nxe5?! Qd4, and Black wins back the pawn and has an excellent position. Yet on a longer range basis, the Ruy Lopez is a most effective "Black center threatening" opening.

3	...	a6
4	Ba4	d6

The most common move of course is 4...Nf6, and we'll see it first in Game 13. The text forms the Steinitz Deferred Variation, an improved version of the basic Steinitz (3...d6). The interpolation of the moves 3...a6 4 Ba4 gives Black considerably more defensive flexibility. An obvious illustration is the "Noah's Ark" trap: 5 d4 b5 6 Bb3 Nxd4 7 Nxd4 exd4 8 Qxd4? c5 9 Qd5 Be6 10 Qc6+ Bd7 11 Qd5 c4, and Black wins a piece.

5 0-0

One of Robert J. Fischer's many, many contributions to opening theory is the demonstration that the immediate castling is not only completely playable, but is in fact White's most flexible approach. Here White's most unbalancing continuation is 5 Bxc6+, and 5 c3 often leads to variations similar to 5 0-0.

5	...	Bd7

The sound move. The

dangerous looking 5...Bg4 6 h3 Bh5
(now 6 ...h5!? is more common) 7 c3
Qf6?! was deflated pretty well in
Fischer-Geller, Bled 1961, after 8
g4! Bg6 9 d4 Bxe4 10 Nbd2 Bg6 11
Bxc6+ bxc6 12 dxe5 dxe5 13 Nxe5!.

6 Re1   Nge7

Theoretically playable, but in
practice quite passive. The strategic
idea is for the Knight to go to g6,
where it guards the e5 square. The
practical problem is that Black will
have no meaningful chances for
counterplay. Somewhat more active
are 6...g6 and 6...Nf6.

7 d4   Ng6
8 c3   Be7
9 Nbd2

Note White's healthy play:
sound development toward the center.

9 ...   0-0

Both Keres and Tal feel that
9...h6 to be followed by 10....Bg5 is
more accurate.

10 h3!

A good preemptive move to
prevent a ...Bg4 followed by ...Nh4.

10 ...   Re8

Once more protecting e5. After
the game, Balashov criticized this

move and suggested 10...Bg5 instead. Although Black's dark-
square Bishop remains quite passive
throughout the game, to exchange it
off for a Knight paradoxically gives
White the two Bishop advantage to
go with his greater center influence.
Black's problem simply is that he has
chosen a sound but very passive
buildup.

11 Bb3!

Black's last has weakened the
f7 square; so that's where White
points his light -square Bishop.

11 ...   Nh4

This exchange does not lighten
Black's load. Perhaps a shade better
is 11...Bf6 or 11...Bf8.

12 dxe5!

An opportune moment to liquidate central tension. White is sure to
obtain a superior, risk-free position.

12 ...   Nxf3+?!

Balashov suggests 12...dxe5 as
more accurate. If then 13 Nxh4 Bxh4
14 Nf3 Bf6, and Black is a move
ahead of the game continuation.

13 Nxf3   dxe5

But not 13...Nxe5? 14 Nxe5
dxe5 15 Qd5, and White wins material.

14 Bd5!

The opening phase is over and and White has emerged with basic but important advantages: the more active light-square Bishop, pressure against the e5 pawn, and pressure against the f7 square. On the other hand, Black can do nothing to White. Some pluses, no minuses: White has an ideal practical situation.

14 ...	Bf6
15 Qb3	

The attack against the f7 pawn is real, whereas that against the b7 pawn is not. Thus it is useful to precede the text move with 15 b4!, thereby expanding White's space on the Queenside.

15 ...	Qe7
16 Be3	

The Queen is trapped after 16 Qxb7?? Reb8 17 Qxc7 Ra7.

16 ...	Rab8

Black has no meaningful way to improve his position; e.g., after 16...Nd8 White expands on the Queenside with 17 a4, and 16...Na5 allows White a favorable endgame after 17 Qb4! Qxb4 18 cxb4 Nc6 19 a3!.

17 Qc4	b5
18 Qe2	Nd8
19 b4!	Be6
20 Bc5	Qd7
21 Red1!	

GM Planinc gives a perfect demonstration, the first one in this book, of "how to defeat a superior opponent:" play strategically clear, healthy moves. Such an approach is doubly useful for practical play since the chances for winning are excellent, and the dangers of losing minimal. After the text move White commands the d-file.

21 ...	Bxd5
22 Rxd5	Qc6
23 Rc1!	

Again, crystal clear strategy: with Black's Queen on the c-file, White prepares to open that file for his other Rook with c4; he will then have strong pressure against Black's backward c-pawn.

23 ...	Nb7

23...Ne6 is no improvement: after 24 g3! (not 24 Nxe5? Nf4!) Nxc5 25 Rxc5, White will soon have doubled Rooks on the c-file.

24 c4!

After careful preparation White executes his first sharp advance in the game. Even so it comes only on the Queenside, is purely strategic, and does not threaten Black's King. Nevertheless, Black's positon is nearly critical.

24 ...   Rbd8?

Now Black's position becomes critical. 24...bxc4 25 Rxc4 Qe6 offers slender chances for defense.

25 Be3!

Clears the c-file for the c1 Rook and thereby threatens 26 cxb5. Thus Black must capture something.

25 ...   bxc4

Will lose quickly. No better however, is 25...Rxd5 26 cxd5 Qd7 27 Rc6! Ra8 28 Qc2 Bd8 29 Nxe5.

26 Rxc4   Qa4
27 Rxc7

The first well deserved fruit.

27 ...   Qxb4

No matter what Black does he will be at least a pawn down. For instance, 27...Nd6 28 Bc5 or 27...Rxd5 28 exd5 e4 29 Rxb7 exf3 30 Qxf3.

28 Qxa6   Qxe4?!

Leads to the loss of the Knight. Also of little long term use is 28...Nd6 29 Bd2! Qb1+ 30 Rc1 Qb8 31 Ba5.

29 Rd2!!

If now 29...Rxd2 30 Nxd2 followed by capture of the stranded Knight. Thus Black must protect it.

29 ...   Rb8

With the slender hope of 30 Ba7? Nc5!! 31 Bxc5? (31 Qf1 is about even) Rb1+ 32 Kh2 Qf4+ 33 g3 Qxf3 and it is Black who wins.

30 Rb2!
Black Resigns

The thematic piling up on the Knight wins it for nothing. Pointless is 30...Nc5 31. Rxb8! Rxb8 32. Rxc5 (or 32. Rc8+ or 32. Qc8+), etc. If 30...Re7 White has the tactical 31. Qxb7! Qxb7 32. Rbxb7!. Black would not have needed to fear these variations if he had played 9...h6!?.

GAME 4

White: Y. Balashov
(U.S.S.R.)

Black: A. Saidy
(U.S.A.)

Played at Tallinn (Estonia) International Tournament, February 27, 1973, Round 6.

Sicilian Defense (Closed Variation)

The American international master completely outplays his opponent in a strategic masterpiece. Whereas White can't decide what to do on the Kingside, Black very thematically gets his play going on the Queenside. He opens the b-file and penetrates with his major pieces. The exchange of Queens is of no help to White and soon Black starts to win material. The rest is an efficient mop-up operation.

1 e4   c5

The first of many, many - a total of twenty - Sicilians in this book. The Sicilian is by far the most unbalancing of Black's replies to 1 e4. In effect, Black ignores White's sharp, active first move in order to start fashioning his own play on the Queenside. Such an approach is double edged because Black runs the

risk of being mated before he can accomplish anything on the Queenside. Nevertheless, the Sicilian is Black's primary weapon when he must win. In the latter stages of his 1972 match against Fischer, Spassky selected it exclusively. Generally play is tactical, the major consideration being the speed of either side's attack. In this game, however, strategic considerations soon dominate. Overall the Sicilian is a successful defense for Black in this book: of the twenty decisive games, Black wins nine.

2 Nf3   d6
3 Nc3

In place of the usual 3 d4, but the text has little independent meaning or value.

3 ...   a6

An invitation to the Najdorf variation after 4 d4 cxd4 5 Nxd4 Nf6. 3...Nf6 is also good.

4 g3

A strategic decision more logical in the abstract than in practice. White enters a closed variation in which he expects Black's 3...a6 to be a waste of time. However, the position is not very useful for White either since the early development of the Knights has robbed the c- and f-pawns of a central role. In addition, Black's third move will prove to be quite helpful later on.

| 4 ... | Nc6 |
| 5 Bg2 | Bg4!? |

Introduced into modern tournament practice by Fischer, which already makes it worth a closer look. The strategic idea has two points: to clear the Queenside for quick action and to establish control of the key central square e5. Black does have to allow White the two-Bishop advantage, but the closed nature of the position makes this relatively unimportant.

| 6 h3 | Bxf3 |
| 7 Qxf3 | |

Hort-Fischer, Palma de Majorca Interzonal 1970, continued 7 Bxf3 g6 8 d3 Bg7 9 a4 e6 10 Bg2 Nge7 11 0-0 0-0 12 Be3 Qa5 with full equality for Black, who went on to win in 72. Balashov's move is of equivalent value.

| 7 ... | g6? |

(This careless move met a devastating refutation in Biyiasas-Timman,Wijk aan Zee 1979: 8 e5!! dxe5? (The minor evil is 8...Bg7) 9 Qxc6+ bxc6 10 Bxc6+ Qd7 11 Bxd7+ Kxd7 12 Na4!, and White exploited the Black pawn weaknesses on c5 and e5 to win convincingly on move 35. Instead of 7...g6?, with the careful 7..Nf6 Black could expect equality.)

| 8 d3?! | Bg7 |
| 9 0-0 | Nf6 |

With 9...e6 and 10...Nge7, Black could follow in Fischer's footsteps. His move is also O.K.

10 g4

White quite correctly starts activity on the Kingside, which is where his opportunities lie.

| 10 ... | Rc8 |

Black must exhibit necessary precaution. The immediate 10...b5?? is a losing blunder because of 11 e5!.

| 11 Ne2 | b5 |
| 12 Bd2 | Nd7! |

Both sides have completed their initial development. Black has not yet castled, but since White has no immediate threats against Black's King, Black can do so at his convenience. With the text move, Black opens the Bishop's diagonal and establishes firm control of the d4 and e5 squares. Chances are in balance.

13 c3?

But this unbalances things in Black's favor by giving him a readily attackable object. Correct is the non-weakening 13 Rab1.

13 ... b4!

Black knows where his chances lie: along the to-be-opened b-file and against the Queenside pawns. His execution of the strategic objectives is very impressive.

14 Qg3 Qb6
15 f4

White's last attacking move in the game.

15 ... 0-0
16 Kh1 bxc3!
17 bxc3 Rb8!

b-file, here I come!

18 Qe1?!

The critical moment in the game. Basically White had two choices: to go ahead with his Kingside attack, thereby handing over the Queenside to Black, or to try to minimize the danger there by adding defensive power, as he does with the text move. The tournament standings significantly influenced the course and result of this game. At the moment Balashov was undefeated and had a good 3-2 score,

whereas Saidy had only one win in five decisive games. Thus Black is quite ready to play chess, that is, to find out what the position offers, whereas White prefers not to take undue chances and risk a loss. Returning the Queen, however, will have *no winning* chances; the difficulties of defense remain. Such a passive approach invariably gives poor results.

Saidy correctly suggests that White should try to work up an attack with 18 h4, 19 Bh3, 20 g5 etc. Black is better of course, but at least White has some chances. In the game he has none.

18 ... Qb5!
19 Qb1 Qb2!

So that when White exchanges, Black's Rook gets to the seventh.

20 Qc1 Rfc8

Protecting the Knight and thereby negating the threat of 21 e5. Throughout Black's play is careful and incisive.

21 Rd1 Rb6
22 Bf1 Rcb8

b-file here we come!

23 Qxb2

What else?

23 ... Rxb2

The exchange of Queen's has not lightened White's task. Black's Rooks control the open file; one Rook is even on the seventh. Black's Bishop and Knights have excellent objects to attack on the Queenside. In theory, White's position may be barely tenable, but in practice such joyless positions almost always are lost.

| 24 Be1 | Rc2! |
| 25 Rdc1 | |

Doubling on the seventh must be prevented.

| 25 ... | Rxc1 |
| 26 Rxc1 | Rb2 |

Exchanging a pair of Rooks has not helped White much. Black's Rook towers over White's, and Black's Knights are ready to move in for the kill. Note the impotence of White's Bishop pair.

| 27 Ra1 | Nb6 |
| 28 a4 | |

Otherwise after 28...Na4 and 29...Rc2 the c -pawn is lost. However, Black immediately takes advantage of the weakened b3 square.

28 ...	Na5!
29 Kg1	Nb3
30 Ra3	a5!

Not giving White the chance for a bit of air after 31 a5. Despite severe time pressure, Black's strategy and execution are impeccable.

31 Bf2?!

Allowing further Knight penetration. 31 Kf2 is better.

| 31 ... | Nd2 |
| 32 Ra1? | |

Leads by force to a loss of material. Therefore 32 Be1 has to be better.

32 ...	Rb1!
33 Rxb1	Nxb1
34 d4	Nxa4
35 e5	c4!

Fixing White's pawn on c3 and thereby accentuating its weakness.

| 36 exd6 | exd6 |
| 37 d5 | |

Otherwise Black plays 37...d5

and protects his c-pawn.

37 ...	Nd2!

After 37...Nxc3 (either) 38
Nxc3 Nxc3 White has 39 Bxc4.
Therefore Black plans to exchange
White's Bishop on f1 first and then
go after the c-pawn.

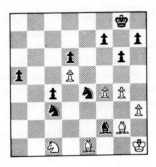

38 Bg2

Desperation. There is nothing
left for White.

38 ...	Nxc3
39 Nc1	Nde4
40 Be1	Bd4+
41 Kh1	Bf2
White resigns	

Two pawns down and with more
to come: e.g. 42 Bxc3 Nxc3 43 Bf1
Be3 44 Ne2 Nxd5, etc. It is time to
concede.

GAME 5

White: J. Timman
(Netherlands)

Black: Y. Balashov
(U.S.S.R.)

Played at Sochi (U.S.S.R.) International Tournament, September 1973, Round 4.

King's Indian Defense
(Samisch Variation)

White has a slight edge all the way through. The decisive strategic elements are a better Bishop and some space advantage. White builds on these until cracks appear in Black's position. With superhuman defense Black may eventually have drawn, but White's patience, perseverance, and good play bring him a deserved win.

1	d4	Nf6
2	c4	g6
3	Nc3	Bg7
4	e4	d6

Black selects the King's Indian Defense, a relatively modern concept. It came forward in full force only after World War II mainly as a result of creative contributions by Soviet analysts and practitioners. The King's Indian is another unbalancing counter to 1 d4, though not so unbalancing as the Grunfeld. White

has a considerable advantage in space; however, Black has a flexible, sound position and plans to undermine White's center by means of an early... c5 or... e5. If the undermining effort is not successful, White will retain a tangible and meaningful spatial advantage. All in all, the King's Indian is a fighting defense, giving Black good winning, and excellent losing, chances.

5 f3

White chooses the Samisch variation, named for the German grandmaster who introduced it into modern tournament practice over sixty years ago. The Samisch is at present considered to be among the very best methods against the King's Indian. Despite first appearances, the Samisch is actually a positional, strategic variation. White believes that, with his c-, d-, and e-pawns out in full, his center influence is more than sufficient, if only he takes steps to support and stabilize it. 5 f3 obviously supports the e-pawns and allows 6 Be3 without having to worry about Black's ...Ng4. Another popular approach for White is the so-called Normal Variation starting with 5 Nf3 and 6 Be2. (Our first example of this is Game 21, Korchnoi-Ghitescu, Bath 1973).

5 ...   0-0

By far the most popular and flexible move. For the unusual 5...b6 see Game 31, Polugaevsky-Szabo, Hilversum 1973.

6 Be3   e5

Historically the most common method: Black immediately and directly challenges White's d-pawn. But as this game shows, it has the long term strategic disadvantage of locking in Black's dark-squared Bishop. More popular now, therefore, are systems with 6...Nc6 or with 6...b6, 7...a6, and then 8...c5.

7 d5

Forced and forcing. 7 dxe5 instead leads to an even endgame, and 7 Nge2 blocks the Bishop on f1.

7 ...   c6

Attacking White's outpost is the most consistent approach, even though White is bound to retain a considerable space advantage, anyway. A reasonable alternative is Uhlmann's 7...Nh5 followed by 8...f5.

8 Qd2

A good, flexible approach, once played almost exclusively. Among other plans, White gets ready for Queenside castling. Currently in fashion is the even more flexible and developmental 8 Bd3, followed by 9 Nge2 and 10 0-0.

8 ...   cxd5
9 cxd5

9 Nxd5 only looks good; in reality White's center influence is lessened. After the text move, we have the basic position in this subvariation. White has a number of strategic pluses: more space, as a result particularly of his d-pawn on the fifth rank; play against Black's Queenside, possibly along the c-file; and the better dark-square Bishop, since Black's is hemmed in by his e-pawn. It is usually in White's interest to exchange the light-square Bishops (Black's good Bishop) to accentuate the advantage of the one which remains. Black's counterplay is based on attacking the base of White's center pawn chain by means of ...f5. Overall White's objective is to minimize Black's counterplay and develop his own advantages.

9 ...   Na6

Aiming at c5 without blocking the Bishop on c8 (as 9...Nbd7

would). The text move and 9...a6 are equivalent in value.

10 Bb5!

A theoretical and strategically meaningful novelty. White develops his light-square Bishop, thereby enabling further development with 11 Nge2. White also makes it harder for Black to develop his Queenside since now 10...Bd7 leads to a Bishop exchange desirable for White. A good theoretical novelty is of extra value against superior opponents for two reasons: (1) it tends to take away the value of their superior opening knowledge; and (2) by surprising them in their own backyard, it has undisputed psychological effect. (Does he really know more than I? etc). After the known 10 Nge2 or 10 Bd3 Black can equalize more easily.

10 ...   Nh5

Here the Knight is actively but somewhat loosely placed. Better perhaps is 10...Ne8!?.

11 Nge2   f5
12 exf5!?

A double-edged capture which strengthens Black's center and decreases White's center influence. On the other hand, Black's forced recapture with the pawn (12...Bxf5? or Rxf5? loses a piece after 13 g4) definitely loosens Black's Kingside and

White's pieces are well situated to exploit that looseness. After 12 0-0 Nf6! Black has definite pressure against the e4 square and is in a position to recapture on f5 with his Bishop, if he so desires.

12 ...   gxf5
13 0-0   Nc7?!

This Knight is not able to get to a useful spot via this route. Timman suggests 13...Nc5 14 b4 Nd7 as a better approach.

14 Bc4   Nf6
15 a4!

Necessary to prevent Black's counterplay. The immediate 15 Bg5?! allows 15...b5! (16 Nxb5?? Nxb5 17 Bxb5 Qb6+ wins a piece for Black).

15 ...   Kh8
16 Bg5!

An annoying pin. If now 16....Qe8, then Black's Queen Knight has no place to go.

16 ...   Nce8
17 Ng3!   f4

Handing over full control of e4 to White, but the coming 18 Bd3 would force it anyway. The looseness of Black's Kingside is quite apparent now.

18 Nge4   h6

19 Bxf6!

The Knights are of more value here. In particular White would willingly trade three pairs of minor pieces in order to be left with a Knight against Black's locked-in dark-square Bishop.

19 ...	Nxf6
20 Bd3	a6
21 g4!	

Black has not even completed his Queenside development, but White with his pieces well placed, is ready to expand his space on the Kingside. If Black lets the pawn be, White will play Kh1 and then prepare to play on the Kingside, Queenside, or both, for he then has a clear advantage everywhere. And if Black captures, ...

21 ...	fxg3 e.p.
22 hxg3	Nxe4
23 Nxe4	Bf5!?

Playing to exchange his light-square Bishop for the Knight and thus avoid the disadvantage of his Bishop on g7 versus the Knight. This is Black's most logical, strategic approach.

24 Kg2

Black's Queen now finds a good location on b6. Unfortunately this cannot be prevented by 24 Qe3?! because of 24...Qa5!.

24 ...	Bxe4
25 Bxe4	Qb6
26 Rh1	

With the threat of 27 Rxh6+!.

26 ...	Rf6
27 Rac1	Raf8
28 Rc4	

White looks better, but what are the strategic reasons? White obviously has the active Bishop and chances against Black's weakened Kingside and along the open c-file. On the other hand, Black has no opportunities to attack White. This does not mean that White's task of realizing his advantages is easy, however. Black has quite sufficiently protected everything attackable. Sophisticated maneuvers are required to get Black to misplace his pieces, but this takes time. Thus White very practically elects to undertake nothing substantial until time control on move 40: he simply ensures that at adjournment he'll still have all the present advantages.

28 ...	a5
29 Qc3	Kg8
30 Rh4	R6f7

Combinations played from a position of weakness are seldom good: Here 30...Rxf3? fails to 31 Bxf3 e4 32 Rg4! exf3+ 33 Kf1.

31 b3	Rf6
32 Qd3	Kh8
33 Rh5	Kg8
34 Bh7+	Kh8
35 Be4	Kg8
36 Bf5	Kh8
37 Rch4	Qc5
38 Rc4	

38 Bg6 leads to nothing after 38...Kg8, so White maintains the status quo.

| 38 ... | Qa3? |

Black should do the same with 38... Qb6!. The text is a tempting infiltration into White's position but the Queen proves impotent as a lonely general caught behind the enemy lines. By itself the Queen can do nothing offensively, and its absence as a defender will soon be felt.

39 g4!	Qb2+
40 Kg3	Qa1
41 Qe3!	

At once preventing all checks by Black and taking up a more effective attacking location.

41 ...	Qd1
42 Be4	Kg8
43 Rh2!	Rf4
44 Rhc2!	

This sealed move threatens 45 Rc1, trapping Black's Queen. This gives White time to penetrate along the c-file.

44 ...	Qa1
45 Rc1	Qb2
46 Rh1!	

The immediate 46 Rc8 allows 46...Bf6! and suddenly Black has the threat 47...Bh4+!. After the text move, White has forced Black's Queen onto the seventh rank where it has much less scope than on the eighth.

46 ...	R8f6
47 Rc7	Rf7
48 Rxf7	Rxf7

If 48...Kxf7, then 49 Qb6! is very strong.

| 49 Bf5 | Rf6 |
| 50 Rc1! | |

The exchange of a pair of Rooks has benefited White since his remaining Rook can now develop extra power along the c-file by going after either the seventh or eighth rank; then Qb6 may follow.

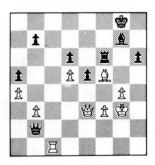

50 ...   e4!?

Positionally Black's prospects are hopelessly bleak, so he tries to get some breathing room with this sacrifice. If now 51 Bxe4 Rf8! and Black is threatening 52 ...Be5+. But White can time the capture of the e-pawn better.

51 f4!   Rf8
52 Rc4!

Prepares to take off the e-pawn efficiently and, equally important, prevents Black's...Bd4.

52 ...   h5
53 Rxe4   hxg4

53....h4+?! just loses the pawn: 54 Kxh4 Qh2+ 55 Qh3 Qf2+ (or 55...Bf6+ 56 g5) 56 Kg5, and it is White who is attacking!

54 Bxg4   Bh6

Such an attacking move is tempting but turns out poorly. The reason in hindsight is clear: the attack doesn't amount to anything, and the Bishop will stand quite badly for defensive purposes. The only practical chance is 54...Qc3!; then after 55 Qxc3 Bxc3 Black has ...Bb4, which protects the d-pawn and generally keeps the Bishop in an active spot. White's technical difficulties in achieving the win would be considerable. Things are much easier after the text move.

55 Rc4   Qf6
56 Qe6+   Kh8
57 Qxf6+   Rxf6
58 Be6

Note that in this endgame Black's Bishop has a significantly less useful location than above. White's active pieces, in combination with the passed f-pawn, must lead to a certain win. Timman's technique is very convincing.

58 ...   Rf8
59 Kg4   Kg7
60 Re4   Kf6
61 Kf3!

To deny Black's Bishop, after an eventual f5, access to the e3 square.

61 ...   Re8
62 Re2   Re7
63 Rh2   Bg7
64 Rc2!   Bh6
65 Rc8

Compared to the position after White's 58th move, White's Rook is more active here, Black's less so. As a result Black has no satisfactory way to protect his d-pawn.

65 ...	b5
66 Rh8	Kg7
67 Rg8+	

Saving time to reach the control on move 72.

67 ...	Kf6
68 Rh8	Kg7
69 Rd8!	

White used 30 minutes for this move in order to be completely sure of the coming complications.

69 ...	bxa4
70 bxa4	Rb7
71 Rxd6	Rb4
72 Rd7+	Kg6
73 Rf7!	

Protects the pawn on f4 and clears the way for the advance of the d-pawn. The loss of the a-pawn is immaterial here.

73 ...	Rxa4
74 d6	Bg7

Leads to a prosaic finish. The end after 74...Rd4 75 d7 a4 76 Rf5! Bg7 (to get to f6) 77 Bd5 !! is prettier.

75 f5+	Kh6
76 f6	
Black resigns	

The Bishop is lost: 76...Bh8 77 Rf8, etc. Timman considers this the best game of his life.

GAME 6

White: J. Smejkal
(Czechoslovakia)

Black: Y. Balashov
(U.S.S.R.)

Played at Sochi (U.S.S.R.) International Tournament, September 1973, Round 14.

English Opening

Black mixes several strategic ideas in the opening and gets a fair amount of indigestion. White saddles Black with a number of uncompensated positional weaknesses. While under an unpleasant squeeze, Black makes a middlegame error and the strategic pressure becomes unbearable. Soon White wins material, and Black resigns when he must give up even more. A clear, logical, strategic, no-risk effort by White- excellent for defeating "a superior opponent."

1	c4	e5
2	Nc3	d6

Theoretically a playable move but not too popular in practice. The reason is that Black sets his central pawn formation very early and thus deprives himself of flexibility in this regard. More common is to develop a Knight with 2 ...Nf6 or 2 ...Nc6.

3 g3

A quiet, sound approach. Centrally more active is 3 Nf3, which we'll see in Game 27, Uhlmann-Lutikov, Leipzig 1973. The sharpest is 3 d4!?, made possible by the passive nature of Black's second move. After 3...exd4 4 Qxd4 Nc6 5 Qd2, White follows up with 6 b3 and 7 Bb2 and has a slight central advantage.

3 ...   Bg4?!

Unquestionably a novelty, but it does not have a sound strategic basis. Such experimentation hardly ever gives positive results. The Bishop's position on g4 has a number of deficiencies, and what does it accomplish here? Black should imitate White by playing 3...g6, with an eventual ...f5 in mind. Such an approach would give meaning to the deferral of the King Knight's development.

4 Bg2

Gains a tempo by attacking the pawn on b7 - the first minus of Black's third move.

4	...	c6
5	Nf3	Nf6
6	0-0	Nbd7
7	d4!	

White's nice, harmonious centrally developed position confers a small but safe edge.

7 ...   Be7

Black adds an element of the Old Indian to his pawn formation. Because of 4...c6, 7...g6 followed by 8...Bg7 is now disadvantageous since Black's d-pawn may be weak. The position after Black's 7th move reveals that he's mixed several opening systems. This will make it very difficult for him to come up with a meaningful plan.

8 h3

What now, Bishop?

8 ...   Bh5?!

The retreat does not work out well. Therefore 8...Bxf3 is best, even though White is left with a sound two-Bishop game.

9 Nh4!

A creative method of taking advantage of the newly created weakening of the f5 square. Black should now further retreat the Bishop to g6.

9 ...   0-0?!
10 Nf5   Re8?!

Too mechanical. Still best is 10 ...Bg6 to force the Knight to declare its plans.

11 d5!

White's pieces are well posted for this central advance, which ensures White new gains.

11 ...   cxd5?!

Leads to new weaknesses, for which nothing is gained in exchange. 11...Qc7 is also faulty because of 12 dxc6 bxc6 13 Nxe7+ Rxe7 14 Nb5!, and Black's d-pawn is gone. The minor evil is 11...c5. After 12 Qd3, followed by 13 e4, White has a significant space advantage in the center. However, the closed nature of the position does not allow this to be immediately realized.

12 Nxd5   Nxd5
13 Bxd5

In strategic terms this position is very favorable to White. White's light-square Bishop has a marvelous central diagonal, whereas Black's dark-square Bishop is tied to protecting Black's backward and weak d-pawn. In addition Black has chronically weakened the d5 square. White has gained much and given nothing.

13 ...	Qc7
14 b3	Bf8
15 Bg2	Rad8
16 Bb2	

The Bishop has no future here. As Smejkal points out the immediate 16 Ba3! would save White a move.

16 ...	Nc5
17 Qd2	f6
18 Rfd1	

Applying pressure to the backward d-pawn.

18 ...	Bf7
19 Ba3!	

And now the Queen Bishop, too, is pointing in the right direction.

19 ...	Qc8
20 Ne3!	

Black's last chased the Knight where it wanted to go anyway. White's control over d5 is now absolute. Black is completely without play, whereas White can further strengthen his position before undertaking definitive action.

20 ...	b6
21 Rac1	f5

Unquestionably weakens the Kingside. It can hardly be criticized, however, since Black needs room to breathe.

22 Nd5	h6
23 Kh2	Re6?

Black's position, though rather without prospects, is possibly tenable. But the text allows tactics that produce a strategically devastating exchange. The best way to keep the status quo is 23...Ne6.

24 Bxc5!!

Exchanging Black's best minor piece so that all of Black's strategic deficiencies remain. The problem with 23... Re6? is that the "logical" 24...dxc5 fails to 25 Nf6+, and White wins the exchange.

24 ...	bxc5

Equivalent to 24...Qxc5.

25 e4!

With no danger of a Black Knight getting to d4, White can readily weaken that square to launch an attack against Black's Kingside, particularly the light squares.

25 ...	g6?!

25...Ree8 has to be a shade better than this new weakening.

26 Qc2!	fxe4
27 Bxe4	Kg7
28 Rd3!	

Going immediately for Black's chronic weakness, the d-pawn. Throughout the game, White's general approach consists of crystal-clear strategy. About the only overt tactical possibility occurred on the note to White's 24th move, and that was the moment at which White's permanent strategic superiority was ensured.

28 ...	Be7
29 Rcd1	Bf6?!

The Bishop stands awkwardly here. The abject 29 ...Bf8 is better.

30 Nc3!

Threatening 31 Bd5 to exchange Black's good Bishop and make White's Knight the much superior minor piece. At the moment that threat also includes winning the d-pawn, and Black's reply does nothing about it. Black could prolong resistance only with 30...Qb8.

30 ...	Be7?!

31 Bd5	Rf6
32 Ne4	Rf5
33 Bxf7	Rxf7
34 Nxd6!	

The Knight is beautiful, but a pawn is a pawn, especially here where the d-pawn serves to support both the c-pawn and e-pawns.

34 ...	Bxd6
35 Rxd6	Rxd6
36 Rxd6	

With an attack on the g6 pawn, thereby forcing Black's reply.

36 ...	Rf6
37 Rxf6	Kxf6
38 Qd2	
Black resigns	

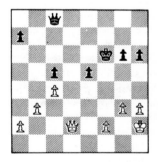

White threatens both 39 Qxh6 and 39 Qd6+. Black resigns because he must lose additional material; e.g., 38...Qf5 39 Qd6+ Kg7 40 Qxc5, etc.

GAME 7

White: R. Knaak
(East Germany)

Black: Y. Balashov
(U.S.S.R.)

Played at Leipzig (East Germany) International Tournament, October 1973.

Modern Benoni Defense

The characteristic situation in this opening is that White has superiority in the center while Black's chances lie on the Queenside. Some carelessness on Black's part allows White's Queen Rook to penetrate Black's Queenside, and this means that White's chances are superior across the board. When, out of frustration, Black weakens his Kingside, White uses sharp play to establish a very convincing attack against Black's King. To stem the tide, Black acquiesces to some material inferiority, but White is not to be denied. He executes the technical part faultlessly and demonstrates that Black's last twenty moves are in vain. Overall, the course of the game is an excellent illustration of the value and logic of playing a good, healthy opening system with which one is familiar. That official theory does not give its highest rating to this system is of secondary practical importance.

1 c4	g6
2 d4	Bg7
3 Nc3	

Now after 3...d6 we could anticipate the King's Indian and after 3 ...Nf6, either the King's Indian or Grunfeld. But with his text move, Black shows that he has something else in mind.

| 3 ... | c5 |

This flank counter signifies the onset of the Benoni (the usual move order is 1 d4 Nf6 2 c4 c5 3 d5), for White's next is pretty much forced because 4 Nf3?! cxd4 5 Nxd4 Nc6 leads to an excellent position for Black.

4 d5	d6
5 e4	Nf6
6 Bd3	

This and the following form a rather unusual but fully playable setup against the Benoni. It is a method which Knaak knows, likes, and has succeeded with. These considerations are more important than theory's ruling that White's most promising approach is 6 Nf3.

| 6 ... | 0-0 |
| 7 Nge2 | |

Here too, 7 Nf3 is possible.

| 7 ... | e6 |
| 8 0-0 | exd5 |

9 cxd5

After 9 exd5 the pawn formation is rather symmetrical, the chances rather even. After the text move we get the characteristically unbalanced pawn formation of the Modern Benoni. White will seek to take advantage of his extra pawn in the center by trying to get in the central advance e5. Black, on the other hand, has a Queenside extra pawn and will aim for a pawn advance there. The White King Knight is theoretically misplaced because it will not be able to directly assist in the e5 advance. But the Knight will find a useful spot on g3 where it will efficiently protect the e5 pawn and thus minimize Black's counterplay against that important point.

9 ...   Nbd7

Obviously to overprotect e5. There also are other logical moves. An immediate 9 ...a6 generally leads to play similar to that in this game. In Beyen-Tal, 1972 Skope Olympiad, Tal was successful with 9...b6!? followed by ...Ba6. 9...Na6 seems somewhat less useful. In Knaak - Cobo, Camaguey 1974, White achieved a slight advantage with 10 h3 Nc7 11 a4 b6 12 Bg5 Qe8 13 f4.

10 h3	Re8
11 Ng3	a6
12 a4	Rb8
13 f4	Qc7
14 Be3	c4

15 Bc2

The previous moves were easy to follow. White started his play in the center, and Black took steps to contain White's central activities, while starting to fashion his own play on the Queenside. The chances are *dynamically* roughly balanced; however each side must play almost perfectly to retain this balance.

15 ...   b5?

In strategic terms this is already the losing move. To get in ...b5 is of course logical, but as played Black allows White's Queen Rook to penetrate Black's Queenside devastatingly. White's Queen Bishop must be cut off from Black's Queenside, as Timman- Ljubojevic, Amsterdam (IBM) 1975 demonstrated: 15 ...Nc5!, and now after either the game's 16 Bd4?! or the more accurate 16 Qf3, Black achieves full counterplay with 16...b5.

| 16 axb5 | axb5 |
| 17 Ra7 | |

Since 17 ...Rb7? now fails to 18 Nxb5, White's Rook dominates both the Queenside and part of the seventh rank.

17 ...	Qd8
18 Qd2	b4
19 Na4	

Note how useful White's King Knight is now on g3, where it protects the e-pawn.

19 ...	Bb7
20 Bf2	Ba8
21 Bb1!	

An excellent nothing move. White ensures that Black cannot play...b3 with a gain of time and says to Black, "Can you come up with a reasonable move now?" In cramped, lifeless positions- like Black's here- it is most difficult to play when no direct threats are involved. Black needs a "pass" move which is at least semi-useful. Something like 21 ...Re7 may fit the bill here. Instead ...

| 21 ... | h5? |

At least partly out of frustration, Black feels that he must do something here and threatens 22 ...h4. But the move just seriously weakens the Kingside. Note that White's previous move set it up. Today Rainer Knaak is a grandmaster, but at the time of this game he was still a 20 year old youngster. Nevertheless, he handled the position like a real trooper.

| 22 e5! |

From now on he plays the position with all his youthful vigor and energy.

| 22 ... | dxe5 |
| 23 f5! | |

The clear weakness of the g6 square as a consequence of Black's 21...h5? is the rationale behind White's central break, culminating in a pawn sacrifice.

| 23 ... | e4 |

The White King Bishop's diagonal must be shortened.

| 24 fxg6 | fxg6 |
| 25 Bd4! | |

Except for the Queen Knight, nearly all White's pieces are trained in the direction of the Black King. White threatens 26 Qg5, since then 26...Kh7 is refuted by 27 Bxf6 Bxf6 28 Rxf6. Black has no satisfactory defense. If now 25...Nxd5, simplest is 26 Bxe4. Black's try is neither better nor worse.

| 25 ... | Bxd5 |
| 26 Rxd7! | |

The active location of the Queen Rook enables this fairly routine combination, whereby White wins two pieces for a Rook.

| 26 ... | Qxd7 |

Or 26...Nxd7 27 Bxg7 Kxg7 28 Qxd5.

| 27 Bxf6 | e3 |
| 28 Qc2 | |

The g6 square is obviously weak. Another advantage of 21 Bb1! is that the Queen can be placed on the Bishop's diagonal.

| 28 ... | Bf7 |

The weak spot must be protected. There is no time for 28... e2 29 Nxe2 Rxe2 30 Qxe2 Qxa4 because of 31 Qe5!, and Black will not be able to protect all of his weak spots.

| 29 Bxg7 | |

And now 29...Kxg7? is refuted by 30 Nxh5+ gxh5 31 Qh7+ Kf8 32 Bg6, so, in order to deflect the King Knight, Black must throw away his passed e-pawn.

29 ...	e2
30 Nxe2	Kxg7
31 Nf4	

White has the clear material advantage of two Knights for a Rook and pawn and again menaces g6. There is no direct defense, and 31 ...b3 leads to a mating attack by White after 32 Qc3+. Thus Black settles for a lost endgame-no bargain either.

31 ...	Rb5
32 Nxg6	Qd4+
33 Kh1	b3
34 Qc3	Qxc3
35 Nxc3	Rb6
36 Nh4	

Now White has two Knights for a Rook. Black does have some chances in his extra Queenside pawn, but with sufficient care on White's part nothing should come of that. And White is very careful.

36 ...	Rbe6
37 Kh2	Re1
38 Rxf7+!	

An effective exchanging combination. White gets rid of the Bishops because his has little immediate scope and sets up an endgame of two impregnable Knights against a single Rook. The whole concept goes well with the general principle "when material ahead, exchange pieces."

| 38 ... | Kxf7 |

39 Bg6+	Kf8
40 Bxe8	Kxe8
41 Nf3	Rc1
42 Nd2	

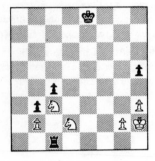

Wins the c-pawn and destroys any hope Black may have. Even so the care with which White handles the remainder of the game is impressive. First he makes the position of his Knights and b-pawn impregnable and then maneuvers his Knights step by step to more active locations, without neglecting the defense of the b-pawn.

42 ...	Rc2
43 Nxc4	h4
44 Ne4!	Ke7

44 ...Rxc4? 45 Nd6+ and 46 Nxc4. Thus with the help of tactics White stabilizes his Knights.

45 Ned2!	Kf6
46 Kg1	Kg5
47 Kf1	Rc1+
48 Kf2	Rc2
49 Kf3	Rc1

50 Ne3	Rc8
51 Ne4+	

After 52 Nxb3?! Rb8 Black wins back the b-pawn. White has absolutely no reason to allow such an exchange. The corollary to "when material ahead, exchange pieces" is "when material ahead, do *not* allow the *routine* exchange of pawns." The hope in superior endgames is to queen a pawn; the more pawns there are, the easier it is to do.

51 ...	Kg6
52 Nd5!	Rc2
53 Nf4+	Kf5
54 Nd3	Rc6
55 Nec5	Rd6
56 Nc1	Rd2
57 N1d3!	Kg6
58 Ke3!	Rc2
59 Nxb3	Kg5
60 Nd2	
Black resigns	

With Black's last hope, the b-pawn, gone, there is nothing to do but give up.

GAME 8

White: S. Kagan
(Israel)

Black: D. Bronstein
(U.S.S.R.)

Played at Petropolis (Brazil) Interzonal Tournament, August 6, 1973, Round 10.

Sicilian Defense (Najdorf Variation)

Bronstein unwisely plays into a variation which is a specialty of his opponent. After suffering through an inferior opening and middlegame he gets nothing more for his efforts than an inferior endgame. Kagan plays the endgame consistently and well; in due course he transforms the advantage of Queenside passed pawns into the win. Another good example in which a well-prepared opening, followed by consistent strategic play, is rewarded with a Russian scalp.

1 e4	c5
2 Nf3	d6
3 d4	cxd4
4 Nxd4	Nf6
5 Nc3	a6

The Najdorf Variation! Whoever has heard of chess has heard of Bobby Fischer, and nearly everyone who has heard of Fischer has heard of the Najdorf Variation of the Sicilian Defense. The variation is named after Argentine Grandmaster Miguel (Misha) Najdorf, who was the first top-level player to demonstrate its playability. Very early in his career Fischer chose the Najdorf as his defense to 1 e4, and until his 1972 match with Spassky, it remained essentially his only defense to 1 e4. But what is good for Fischer is not always good for everyone else! Black's other popular 5th moves, 5... Nc6, 5...e6, 5... g6, can all be explained and justified by normal opening considerations, such as development or control of the center. But what does 5...a6 do? Well ,it takes the b5 square away from White's King Bishop and Knights and makes an *eventual* ...b5 possible. Still that is very little considering how active White's position is in the Sicilian. The point of the Najdorf is to challenge White in the strongest manner possible to an unbalanced fight. Such an approach fits Fischer's fight-to- the-end style perfectly. The theoretical justifications for the variation derive from an apparently inexhaustible series of tactical counterchances unearthed by Fischer and his legion of followers.

But this variation is not for the amateurs, who will quickly come to grief in its muddy waters. One must be a hard-studying professional. Bronstein has a very broad opening repertoire which includes the Najdorf, but his selection of it is a serious psychological error. We'll have more on that in a minute.

6 g3

Long out of fashion. In fact, at present the only steady user is the Israeli IM. *(In the 1980's the U.S. Grandmaster Sergey Kudrin has made 6 g3 his major weapon against the Najdorf.)* The strategic point is to achieve a solid setup, somewhat similar to that reached after 6 Be2 e5 7 Nb3 but with the King Knight placed more flexibly on e2 and the fianchettoed King Bishop acting at long range on the d5 square. By far the most popular move is the sharp 6 Bg5, which we'll first see in Game 30, Timman-Polugaevsky, Hilversum 1973. The positionally active 6 f4 arises in Game 29, Sax-Polugaevsky, Hilversum 1973. Other popular moves are the sharp 6 Bc4 and the positional 6 Be2.

6 ...   e5?!

With this Black enters the Najdorf proper. Objectively the move is fine, so the ?! marks are meant only for this specific instance. The choice is wrong because (1) Kagan is probably the world's leading expert on it, and so Bronstein is playing into his opponent's strength; and (2) even though Black was forewarned about it (for instance, in Round 8 against Reshevsky, Kagan had already played thusly), he apparently had done no preparation for it, for he obtains a clearly unsatisfactory position out of the opening. What of the strategic tradeoffs in 6 ...e5? Black chases the Knight away from its active central location and achieves some control of the d4 square. On the other hand, Black's d-pawn is rendered backward and the d5 square is permanently weakened. In the course of this game, the disadvantages are clearly the more apparent.

Of course, Black could ignore 6 g3 and continue 6...Nc6 or 6...g6. In Kagan-Csom, Sao Paulo 1973, which followed the Interzonal, Black successfully employed a Scheveningen like formation with 6 ...e6.

7 Nde2   Nbd7

About equivalent is 7...Be7 8 Bg2 Be6 9 a4!, as in Kagan-Reshevsky, Round 8. A slight plus for White resulted after 7...Be6 8 Bg2 Nbd7 9 a4 Be7 10 0-0 Rc8 11 h3, in Holmov-Petkevich, U.S.S.R. Club Teams 1976. Premature is 7 ...b5? 8 a4! b4 9 Nd5!, with advantage to White.

8 a4!

But here, it's necessary and useful to prevent Black's ...b5.

8 ...   Be7
9 Bg2   0-0

Can't be bad, but immediate Queenside development is Black's

most promising route to equality: 9
...b6! 10 0-0 Bb7 11 Nd5 Nxd5 exd5
Rc8!.

10 0-0   Rb8?!

The idea behind this move is
strategically deficient. 10...b6 is correct.

11 h3

Prepares Be3 and enables an
eventual g4. Kagan knows these
types of positions well.

11 ...   b5?
12 axb5   axb5
13 Ra7!?

Another good, and possibly
better, move is 13 b4!, fixing Black's
b-pawn. As in game 7, the opening of
the Queenside favors only White, for
he controls the a-file and, at the
moment, even has a Rook on the
seventh. In addition, Black has an
isolated, weak b-pawn, a backward
d-pawn, a permanent weakness on

d5, and absolutely nothing to show
for these deficiencies. Overall White
is clearly better and can look forward
to a number of favorable fields of
action: Queenside, center, Kingside.
But most important is that White is
familiar with and comfortable in
these kinds of positions. At the time
of the game, Kagan was in last place
(he finished the tournament in a tie
for last), whereas Bronstein was
among the leaders. Yet the self-as-
surance with which White handles
the game could easily indicate that
the roles were reversed!

13 ...   Bb7

Here and later Black plays too
passively. Necessary is 13...b4! 14
Nd5 Bb7 (14...Nxd5 15 Qxd5 Nc5
also looks playable) 15 Bd2 (15
Be3!) Nxd5 16 exd5 Qb6 17 Ra4
Ba6! 18 Rxb4 Qc5, and Black had
positional pressure for the pawn in
Mestel-Balashov, European Team
Championship, Moscow 1977.

14 Be3   Nb6
15 b3   Nc8

Chasing the Rook away at the
cost of misplacing the Knight. Moreover, Black's b-pawn is now awkward to defend.

16 Ra2   Qd7
17 Qd3   Bc6
18 Nd5!   b4

Otherwise 19 Nb4. The pawn is

even weaker on b4 however.

| 19 Qd2 | Bd8 |
| 20 g4! | |

Expanding his space on the Kingside and creating a useful place for the King Knight on g3. White is better all across the board. Do note how patiently he plays to increase his advantage. Unless the position requires sharpness- which this obviously does not- such an approach is very practical.

| 20 ... | Qb7 |
| 21 Ng3 | Nxd5 |

This does shield the d-pawn but gives up more space and frees e4 for White's pieces.   Still there is no constructive continuation.

| 22 exd5 | Bd7 |
| 23 Rfa1 | |

A little intermezzo on the a-file. Nothing comes of it, but there is no harm done. Black is too passive to be able to undertake anything of value.

23 ...	Qc7
24 Be4	g6
25 Bh6	Re8
26 Kh2	Bf6
27 Rg1	

Black has to play on the Queenside- his traditional area in the Sicilian- and the center is semi-blockaded, although White does have

spatial advantage there. Thus in due course White is able to create realistic attacking chances on the Kingside, traditionally his strongest field of play. Black is sentenced to much long, unpleasant defending.

27 ...	Qd8
28 Ra6	Bh8
29 Nf5!	

Obviously the Knight is inviolate (29 ...gxf5?? 30 gxf5 + etc.) and so one more piece has become actively placed.

| 29 ... | Qc7 |
| 30 h4! | |

Continuing the attack.

| 30 ... | Bb5 |
| 31 Raa1 | Qc3?! |

For some reason, this move has gotten an "!" in a number of chess publications. Black, with a weak b-pawn and a chronically   weak d-pawn, willingly enters a much inferior ending. After the Queen exchange, White's b-pawn becomes passed. The middlegame for Black is inferior, but the chances for an opponent to err in this stage are considerably higher. An inferior ending is easy to lose and offers no hope to win. A reasonable middlegame move is 31...Ne7.

32 Qxc3	bxc3
33 Ne3	Bf6
34 Bg5!	

White goes quickly to work on Black's weak c-and d-pawns. He doesn't need to worry about the resulting doubled g-pawns, especially since they help to hold back Black's Kingsde pawn majority.

34 ...	Bxg5
35 hxg5	Nb6
36 Nd1!	Rec8
37 Rg3	Be2

The only move, otherwise Black loses the c-pawn for nothing. The g4 pawn does not equal the c-pawn here, but it is better than nothing.

| 38 Nxc3 | Bxg4 |
| 39 Nb5 | Bf5 |

Again the only try, since White was threatening both 40 Nxd6 and 40 Rxg4.

40 Nxd6!

A play for passed pawns!

| 40 ... | Bxe4 |
| 41 Nxe4 | |

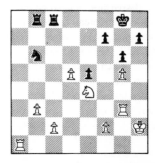

Black can reestablish material equality in two ways, but the strategic deficiencies remain. If now 41 ...Rxc2 White can choose to attack with 42 Nf6+ Kg7 43 Rf3, followed up by 44 Kg2 and 45 Rh1, or to activate his passed d-pawn with 42 d6. As played, however, Black allows White to retain connected passed pawns on the Queenside.

| 41 ... | Nxd5 |
| 42 c4 | Nf4? |

The Knight is too far from the scene of action, the Queenside, here. Only with the blockading 42...Nb4! are there some chances for successful resistance.

43 Ra7!

It's obviously quite useful to have command of the seventh rank.

43 ...	Rb6
44 Rc3	h6
45 c5	Re6
46 b4!	

Passed pawns must be pushed! White consistently follows this sound endgame principle. Foolish instead is 46 gxh6 because of 46 ...g5!, when Black's Kingside pawns are mobilized and his Rook is able to bother White's King.

46 ...	hxg5
47 Rca3	

There is more than one way to play such a position, while still keeping in mind the strategic requirements. 47 Nxg5 is O.K. With the next move White tries to hasten his passed pawns by exchanging one defending Rook.

47 ...	Kg7
48 Ra8	Ree8
49 Rxc8	Rxc8
50 b5!	

Passed pawns must be pushed!

50 ...	Ne6
51 c6	Rb8
52 Nd6	e4
53 Ra7	Kf6
54 c7	

Wins the Knight all right, but leads to considerable technical difficulties since White's pieces become awkwardly placed. IM Kaplan gives

54 Rb7! Rd8 55 Nxf7 followed by an early b6 as a considerably simpler and surer win.

54 ...	Nxc7
55 Rxc7	Ke6
56 Nb7	f5
57 b6	Kd5
58 Kg2	

White is a Knight and passed b-pawn ahead, but it is difficult to do anything with them. Black has to move his King very carefully so that White gets no opportunity for a Knight fork. Correct therefore is 58 ...Ke6! 59 Rc6+ (59 Nc5+ Kd6 60 Nd7? fails to 60...Rxb6) 59...Kd5! 60 Rd6+ Ke5 61 Rd7 Kf4!, and it is not really clear how or whether White can extricate his Knight without losing the b-pawn.

58 ...	Kd4?!
59 Rd7+	Kc3?

59...Ke5? also fails because of 60 Nd6!: 60 ...Rxb6? 61 Nc4+. However, 59...Kc4! still leaves some drawing chances after 60 Nd6+ Kc5 61 Nf7 Rxb6!.

60 Nc5!	Kc4

Too late now. Of course 60 ...Rxb6? allows 61 Na4+.

61 Rc7!	Kb5

Or 61...Rxb6 62 Nd7+.

62 Nd7

Winning easily. If the Rook
moves away, the b-pawn moves
forward. Even so it is impossible to
explain why Black does not resign.
White is short of time, but not *that*
short .

62 ...	Rxb6
63 Nxb6	Kxb6
64 Rg7	Kc5
65 Rxg6	Kd4
66 Rxg5	e3
67 fxe3+	Kxe3
68 Rxf5	

Black Resigns

GAME 9

White: V. Hort
(Czechoslovakia)

Black: D. Bronstein
(U.S.S.R.)

Played at Petropolis (Brazil)
Interzonal Tournament, August 12,
1973, Round 14.

Queen's Gambit Declined, Slav Defense

Hort decides on a sly method of
countering Bronstein's own special
variation. The choice turns out to be
excellent since Bronstein is not at all
comfortable in the normal waters.
First White achieves a nice central
superiority, then the two Bishops,
then the d5 square, and then a pawn.
The material advantage gets exploited in an instructive passed-
pawn endgame. The game is an excellent example of the effectiveness
of playing away from a strong
opponent's strength.

| 1 d4 | d5 |
| 2 c4 | c6 |

This, one of the two sound ways
to reinforce Black's pawn on d5, is
called the Slav Defense. The more
common method, 2 ...e6, leads to
various positions in the Orthodox
Defense, and we'll see a number of

them in this book later on. Theoretically playable, but currently un-
popular, is to acccept the gambit with
2 ...dxc4.

| 3 Nc3 | Nf6 |
| 4 Nf3 | dxc4 |

Giving up the center here leads
to variations of the Slav proper. The
playability of the Slav rests on the
point that recovery of the gambit
pawn by White entails certain slight
disadvantages. If Black doesn't want
to give up the center he can play 4
...e6, which usually leads to various
Meran positions. Our first example
here will be game 20, Rukavina-
Korchnoi, Leningrad 1973.

5 a4

The only meaningful way to
recover the pawn. However, the
positional cost is a slight weakening
of the Queenside and the loss of a
tempo for development. But there is
nothing else. 5 e4?! leads to a dubious gambit after 5 ...b5 6 e5 Nd5, and
5 e3 b5 6 a4 does allow the eventual
recovery of the pawn but under circumstances where there is no advantage.

5 ...   Bg4!?

One of a number of Bronstein's
creative innovations. The usual theoretical move is 5 ...Bf5 to directly
hinder White from getting in the
central advance e4. That is how Hort

defended as Black against Portisch in Round 11, and he drew in 27. What is the point of Bronstein's move? To gain counterplay as a result of the pin on the Knight, or, if the Knight moves away, on the e-pawn. The move came as no surprise to Hort since Bronstein had been employing it successfully for years. Indeed in Round 4 Bronstein had obtained a 24-move draw against Keres with it.

6 e3!?

But this move surely surprised Bronstein! The normal theoretical continuation is 6 Ne5 Bh5, and then either the positional 7 g3, as Keres played, or the sharp 7 f3. With the text move, however, Hort voluntarily allows the pin and ignores what Black is doing. He aims for the usual Slav positions fully realizing that he may arrive a tempo down. He hopes that Bronstein will be ill at ease in them.

6 ...	e6
7 Bxc4	Nbd7
8 h3	Bh5
9 Qe2	Bb4

A standard maneuver in the Slav. The Bishop finds a secure home here and seeks to prevent or minimize indirectly the effect of White's pawn on e4.

10 0-0	Qe7

Black aims for ...e5 as quickly as possible.

11 e4	e5
12 d5	

To break the pin with 12 g4 is too dangerous because of 12 ...Nxg4! 13 hxg4 Bxg4, when Black has two pawns and an excellent attack for the piece. Thus White must push on by.

12 ...	a5?!

Bronstein has a penchant for this move in "his variation," but here it seems rather pointless. Correct is 12 ...h6 to give the Queen Bishop a convenient square at h7 and prevent a potential Bg5 by White.

13 Rd1!

White logically and consistently strives to support his strong point, the passed d-pawn.

13 ...	0-0?!

Too routine or careless. This was the last chance for 13...h6!.

14 g4!

But unlike the position after Black's 11th move, here it is safe enough since White is a couple of defensive moves ahead.

14 ...	Bg6
15 Nh4!	

The correct way to play the position. After exchanging Black's Queen Bishop, White will have a clear spatial advantage, a strong point on d5, and the two Bishops, whereas Black will have nothing to counter these pluses. Faulty instead is 15 Bg5?! h6 16 Bh4 Bh7, with Black having at least full equality.

15 ...   cxd5?!

As a general principle, central tension should not be resolved unless something is gained in exchange. Here Black permanently hands over control of the d5 square to White without any countergain. Black's position is somewhat lifeless, but a normal move like 15...Rfd8 to keep the status quo (suggested by GM Gheorghiu) is in order.

16 Nxg6   fxg6?!

Bronstein would be the first to realize that the capture toward the center is positionally correct: 16

...hxg6. Then after 17 Nxd5 White has a small but safe and enduring advantage. To allow this doesn't seem practically advisable to Bronstein, so he tries to mix things up by opening the f-file. Strategically, however, this is unsound, and it is he who gets mixed.

17 Bxd5+!   Kh8

In line with his previous move. After 17...Nxd5 18 Nxd5, White has a colossal Knight on d5.

17 Bxb7!

White has to take what Black is forced to give; otherwise Black will be all right.

18 ...   Rab8
19 Bd5

White has a sound extra pawn, and it is up to Black to demonstrate what he has for it.

19 ...   Nc5
20 Bg5!

Developing while attacking.

20 ...   h6
21 Bh4   Ne6
22 Bxe6   Qxe6?

After this Black's cause becomes hopeless. The zwischenzug 22...Bxc3 is imperative, since then, after 23 bxc3 Qxe6, Black doesn't have to worry about a White Knight arriving on the d5 square. Black then has reasonable chances to hold a draw since White has a number of weaknesses in his position, and this makes the realization of the pawn advantage technically very demanding.

23 Nd5!   Bc5

23 ...Nxd5 24 Rxd5 is no better.

24 Bxf6!

Closing off the f-file, establishing a Knight on d5, and winning another pawn. Black is theoretically lost. However, the consistent accuracy of White's play is very impressive.

24 ...	gxf6
25 Qd2	Kg7
26 Qxa5	

Why not? White now has two Queenside passed pawns.

26 ...	Bd4
27 Qc7+	Kh8
28 Rac1!	

With Black in severe time pressure, Hort sees that active play is the best method to underscore the many weaknesses in Black's position. If Black now plays the normal 28 ...Rxb2, White has 29 Rc6 Qf7 30 Qd6! followed by 31 Rc7 and the attack must be decisive. Therefore Black searches for salvation in a lost endgame, but this is hardly to be recommended.

28 ...	Rfc8?!
29 Qe7!	Qxe7
30 Rxc8+	Rxc8
31 Nxe7	Rc2
32 b4!	

White's pride is the connected passed pawns, and they must be retained. By comparison, White's f-pawn and Black's g-pawn are, at the moment, of little significance.

32 ...	Kg7

Of course 32 ... Rxf2?? is met by 33 Rxd4!.

33 b5!

Passed pawns must be pushed.

33 ...	Ra2
34 Nd5	Rxa4
35 b6!	

Black has recovered a pawn, but White is still ahead a strong, advanced passed b-pawn.

| 35 ... | Ra2 |
| 36 Rb1! | |

Rooks belong *behind* passed pawns. After this move it is clear that White's b-pawn will cost Black his Bishop.

36 ...	Rxf2
37 Kh1	Rf3
38 b7	Ba7
39 Kg2	

An immediate 39 b8= Q Bxb8 40 Rb7+! is equally winning.

39 ...	Rf2+
40 Kg3	Re2
41 b8=Q	Bxb8
42 Rb7+	

By taking the Bishop off with check White is able to save his e-pawn.

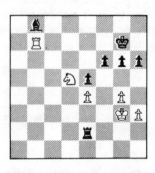

42 ...	Kf8
43 Rxb8+	Kf7
44 Rb7+	

Black resigns

GAME 10

White: S. Furman
(U.S.S.R.)

Black: R. Calvo
(Spain)

Played at Madrid (Spain) International Tournament, December 13, 1973, Round 14.

Catalan Opening

By playing accurately and actively, Black emerges from the opening with ready equality. When White hesitates in the center, Black quickly establishes his clear superiority over both the center and Queenside. The superiority gained as a result of strategic play is transformed into a full point by means of sharp tactics against White's weakened Kingside. A perfect blend of strategy and tactics, in which the former is used to set up the decisive combinational motifs.

1 Nf3	d5
2 d4	

Despite starting off with the Reti, White quickly jumps at the opportunity to establish a Queen's Gambit Declined, a rather safe opening. In the previous round, Furman gained an important victory against Uhlmann in a long tough endgame and in this, the next to last round, is tied for first place with his "pupil" Anatoly Karpov. He evidently isn't in the mood for a tough fight, however, and this psychological factor is significant.

2 ...	Nf6
3 c4	e6
4 g3	

Instead 4 Nc3 enters the normal channels of the QGD. With the text move White opts for the Catalan, a sound opening but against which Black has known methods of equalization, especially if White has already played d4.

4 ...	Nbd7!?

Black selects an interesting and an effective order of moves. The conventional continuations are 4 ...Be7 and 4 ...dxc4.

5 Bg2	dxc4
6 0-0	

Safe and routine. The active 6 Qa4, leading to play similar to the main variations, is preferable.

6 ...	c5!

Because White ignores Black's Queenside, Black is able to initiate freeing activity there.

7 Na3

Again quite harmless. More

active is 7 Qa4 or 7 dxc5.

7 ...	Nb6!
8 Nxc4	Nxc4
9 Qa4+	Bd7
10 Qxc4	b5!

Looks weakening, but Black correctly sees that with Black's development of the Queenside essentially complete, White has no way to take advantage; moreover, Black obtains a definite spatial advantage on the Queenside.

11 Qd3

Tempting the c-pawn forward turns out quite fine for Black. Perhaps 11 Qc2 is sounder.

11 ...	c4!
12 Qc2	Bc6

Black has established a sound 3 vs. 2 pawn majority on the Queenside, and White has an extra pawn in the center. To obtain prospects of meaningful play, White must be able to make use of his central pawn. His next move contesting the e4 square, is good.

13 Bg5	Be7
14 a4?!	

The accurate move order is 14 Bxf6! Bxf6 15 e4.

14 ...	a6?!

With the immediate 14 ...Be4! Black could transpose into the text game. After Black's 14th, the chances are dynamically balanced. Black has his Queenside pawn majority; White, if he plays resolutely, has an opportunity of an active pawn majority in the center.

15 Rfd1?

This routine move does nothing for the needs of the position. The only logical approach is to give up the two Bishops with 15 Bxf6! Bxf6 16 e4. White then has a good central presence and chances for a full-play middlegame.

15 ...	Be4!

Yes! Black now has advantages both in the center and Queenside, whereas White has nothing.

16 Qc1	0-0

Castling is one of the objectives of opening play. Of course, another saying goes "castle only when you have nothing better to do." Black castles ten moves later than White, only after achieving his strategic goals. On the other hand, White castled on move 6 and achieved nothing.

17 Ne5

What else?

17 ...	Bxg2
18 Kxg2	h6
19 Bf4?!	

In cramped positions, the defensive side benefits by an exchange of pieces. The right approach, therefore, is 19 Bxf6!. Apparently White is not aware of his position's deficiencies.

19 ...	Rc8
20 f3?!	

Hoping to get in e4, but the move turns out to be nothing but a Kingside weakness. Opening the a-file with 20 axb5 is absolutely required to gain some breathing room for the Queen Rook.

20 ...	Nd5!
21 Bd2?!	

Last chance for 21 axb5!.

21 ...	b4!

The first use of tactics to further

a strategic aim: to advance the Queenside pawns.

22 Be1?!

Such passivity is doomed to fail. White had to try the gutsy 22 Nxc4!?. Calvo gives then 22 ...b3 23 e4 Nb6 24 Ba5 Rxc4 25 Bxb6 Qc8 26 Qe3 Rc2+ 27 Rd2 Bb4 "with advantage to Black;" even so White is in better shape here than in the game.

22 ...	c3!
23 b3?!	

There is really nothing good to suggest, but giving Black a protected passed c-pawn can't be right.

23 ...	f5!
24 Bf2	Bg5
25 e3?!	

Now the floodgates will burst. 25 f4 is a must. White didn't want to weaken e4, but the King is more important than a central square...

25 ...	c2!!

Black has used fine strategy to outplay his opponent and achieve a marvelous position. Starting here, he shows admirable tactical sharpness and transforms his superiority into a win. Positionally speaking, the text move looks quite risky since the safe protected passed pawn becomes a far-advanced passed pawn with an uncertain future. However, it is the start of a devastating Kingside attack.

26 Rd3   f4!!

Continuing to strike when the iron is hot. If now 27 gxf4 Bxf4 28 exf4 Nxf4+ 29 Kg1 Nxd3 30 Nxd3 Rxf3 and White is in shambles. So...

27 Nc4	**fxe3**
28 Bxe3	**Nxe3+**
29 Nxe3	**e5!**
30 h4	**Qf6!**

Every Black move contains a threat. There is no defense; e.g., 31 hxg5 Qxf3+ 32 Kh3 hxg5! followed by 33...Rf6 (or 33....Rc6) and then 34 ...Rh6+. And after 31 f4, annihilation follows by means of 31... Bxf4 32 gxf4 Qxf4. White's text move leads to a unique position!

31 Nd5	**Qf7**
32 hxg5	**Qxd5**
33 gxh6	

There is nothing. If 33 Qe3 Rxf3! 34 Qxf3 e4, etc.

33 ...   e4!

One more active shot - the last one required.

34 hxg7	**exd3**
35 gxf8=Q+	**Rxf8**

What an unusual sight! White is even a pawn ahead, but the unsafe King and Black's far advanced pawns obviously guarantee Black a win. The passed pawns are decisive in the variation after 36 Qe3 Qxf3+ 37 Qxf3 Rxf3 38 Kxf3 d2.

36 Qh6	**Qxf3+**
37 Kh2	**Rf6**

Obviously the end is very, very near.

38 Qh4	**Kg7**

Or 38...d2! 39 Qg5+ Kh7 40 Qxd2 Rh6+.

39 Re1	**Qf2+**
40 Kh3	**Qxe1**
White resigns	

GAME 11

White: L. Szabo
(Hungary)

Black: Y. Geller
(U.S.S.R)

Sicilian Defense
(Dragon Variation)

The Hungarian GM demonstrates an excellent practical choice of opening variations. Rather than indulge in sharp unclear tactics-something his opponent apparently counted on- he prefers a strategically clear position in which White can count on a minute advantage. White ultimately gets an advantage of a two-to-one Queenside pawn majority. It should not be enough to win, but Black's defensive task is unpleasant and he fails to do his best. As a result, White gets a passed pawn and a demonstrable technical win. The game further exemplifies the logic behind the "much to gain, little to lose" approach.

1	e4	c5
2	Nf3	d6
3	d4	cxd4
4	Nxd4	Nf6
5	Nc3	g6

With this move Black establishes the Dragon Variation, a sound, logical opening. The fianchettoed King Bishop will bear down effec-tively on his central diagonal and the King will be ready to castle. The only very slight theoretical minus is that ...g6 weakens the Kingside and gives White's h-pawn an attackable object after h4 and h5. This is exactly the factor that White tries to exploit in the most modern and popular subvariations. Even though the Dragon is not Geller's primary weapon, he is a recognized authority on it. As a matter of fact, he was *the* author of the section on the Dragon in the *Encyclopedia of Chess Openings*.

| 6 | Be3 | Bg7 |
| 7 | Be2!? | |

Forty years ago everybody played thusly, but over the last twenty or so years *the method* has become the Yugoslav Attack with 7 f3, 8 Qd2, 9 Bc4, followed by 0-0-0 and a Kingside pawn storm. The variations here have become very long (easily twenty moves and more), complicated, and ever-changing. Geller can be expected to be thoroughly up-to-date. Therefore Szabo prefers a change of pace. He steers the game into the "old" variation, whose major benchmarks are strategic rather than obscurely tactical. In this way he risks considerably less against a theoretically well-prepared opponent. The "old" variation may not even be inferior to the Yugoslav Attack.

| 7 ... | Nc6 |

8 0-0   0-0

White has a slight central superiority because his e-pawn is on the fourth rank, whereas Black's d-pawn is only on the third. Theoretically speaking, if Black can get in ...d5 without incurring disadvantages, he is sure of full equality. He does "threaten" 9...d5 now, to which White's most analyzed response is 9 Nb3. However, after 9 ...Be6 Black gets good development and White's chances for an advantage are quite problematical. Therefore White tries...

9 Qd2

Not as "bookish" as 9 Nb3, but at least as good.

9 ...   d5

And so Black gets in this freeing push with good chances for theoretical equality. In practice, however, the resulting positions are rather lifeless for Black and offer scant hope for anything more than a laborious draw. Theoretically no worse and practically more promising are 9...Bd7 and 9...Ng4.

10 exd5	Nxd5
11 Nxc6	bxc6
12 Rad1!	

In conjunction with the following move, this strengthens White's play significantly. White stands clearly superior after 12 Rfd1 Be6 13 Bd4 Nxc3? 14 Qxc3 Bxd4 15 Rxd4 Qb6 16 Rb4 Qa5 17 Rc4!, as in Mednis-Drakert, 1955 New York State Championship. However, Black saves a full tempo and obtains approximate equality with the correct 13...Bxd4! 14 Qxd4 Nxc3! 15 Qxc3 Qb6, as in Mednis-O'Keefe, 1956 U.S. Open Championship.

12 ...   Be6

By far the soundest response. After 12...Bxc3?! 13 bxc3, Black's Kingside will miss the King Bishop; after 12...Bf5?!, White has 13 Nxd5! with greater power than in the game (Smyslov-Denker, Groningen 1946); after 12...Qc7 13 Bd4 e5 14 Bc5 Rd8 15 Ne4 Be6 16 Qg5 (analysis by Gufeld), White is also better.

13 Nxd5!

This paradoxical capture allows White to retain a slight edge. Black's center appears to be strengthened, but this will be true only momentarily. Instead, the routine 13 Bd4 can be met by the maneuver from the Mednis-O'Keefe game, 13...Bxd4! 14 Qxd4 Nxc3 15 Qxc3 Qb6, and Black's good development gives him equality.

13 ...   cxd5

After 13...Qxd5 14 c4!, White has the advantage of the superior Queenside pawn formation.

14 Bf3   Qc7

The d-pawn can't be protected, so Black must counter against White's pawns. 14...Bxb2? is faulty because of 15 c4! and 16 cxd5, with a big plus for White.

15 Bxd5   Bxd5
16 Qxd5   Qxc2

This is better than 16 ...Bxb2?! 17 c4, when after 18 c5 White will have a sound passed c-pawn. In the game, White has a harder time establishing a passed pawn.

17 Rd2

The opening phase has been completed, and White has the tangible advantage of the Queenside pawn majority. Black's extra Kingside pawn cannot forcibly be made passed, whereas White has realistic chances to do so on the Queenside. Overall, of course, White does not have all that much since Black's position is unques-

tionably defensible. But in a practical game White's "something" is worth a lot more than Black's "nothing."

17 ...   Qc7
18 b4!

To be of any benefit, the majority must be mobilized.

18 ...   Rad8
19 Qe4   Rxd2
20 Bxd2   Qd7
21 Be3   Rc8
22 a4!

Continuing, with the help of tactics, to mobilize the pawn majority. After 22...Qxa4?! 23 Qb7!, White will win Black's a-pawn and obtain a passed b-pawn. Black's response is quite correct.

22 ...   a6!
23 a5   e6
24 Bc5   Qb5!
25 h3!

Up to here, both sides have played excellent chess, from both theoretical and practical points of view. Black has stopped, for the foreseeable future, the further advance of White's Queenside pawns. On the other hand, White does still have his majority and a position generally without risk. With the sound practical text, White gives his King an escape hatch so that he won't ever have to worry about back-rank mates. White is not going to force or overextend anything; he'll play good moves and, if Black defends perfectly, the game will end in a draw.

25 ...   Rd8?!

Black clearly takes a step in the wrong direction. Control of the d-file is not at issue since Black can undertake nothing there. It is time to try to break White's formation with 25 ...Bf8!. But Black is so transfixed by the beauty of his Bishop on the "Dragon diagonal" that he doesn't want to part with it. Yet the beautiful Bishop has nothing to do on his diagonal.

26 Rc1!   h5?

Now things get serious since White gets the c-file for his Rook. It is imperative to return the Rook: 26 ...Rc8!.

27 Bb6!   Rd5
28 Kh2

A move that comes in fantastically handy at the end!

28 ...   Bf6?!

By now Geller is in time pressure, and good moves are hard to find under such circumstances. The text makes matters worse by allowing White a favorable Rook exchange. Perhaps 28...Be5+ 29 f4 Bd6 is a better defense. In any case, Black's position is nearly critical.

29 Rc5!

The exchange of the Rooks breaks the blockade of the b5 square and thus enables White to get his Queenside pawns going. Szabo plays the resulting endgame with great energy and accuracy.

29 ...   Qd7

This way Black at least gets a passed pawn. 29...Rxc5? 30 bxc5! is completely hopeless.

30 Rxd5   exd5
31 Qf4   Be7
32 Bd4!   Bd6

The threat was 33 Qh6!, and 32 ...Qd6 is met by 33 Be5 Qxb4 34 Qh6!.

33 Be5   Bxe5
34 Qxe5   d4

Allows an immediate advance

of White's b-pawn. But even after the preferable 34...Qb5 comes 35 Qd6!, threatening 36 Qb6!, and Black is lost.

35 b5!

A beautiful way to reach the strategic objective of a passed Queenside pawn. Now 35...Qxb5? allows 36 Qxb5 axb5 37 a6, and White queens with check. And little better is 35...axb5 36 a6 d3 (or 36...Qa7 37 Qxb5, followed by 38 Qb7, etc.) 37 Qb8+ Kg7 38 a7 d2 39 a8=Q d1=Q 40 Qh8 mate! So Black pushes on.

35 ...	d3
36 bxa6	d2
37 Qb8+	Kg7
38 a7	d1=Q
39 a8=Q	

Four Queens make this situation unusual. White again threatens the same mate as given in the previous note, so Black must exchange a pair of Queens.

39 ...	Q7d6+
40 f4	

Black resigns

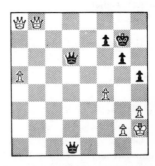

Actually Black was unable to complete his 40th move before his flag dropped and he lost on time. This was a humane ending to the game, since after the forced 40 ...Qxb8 41 Qxb8, White's extra passed a-pawn promises a theoretical win which is not that difficult for a grandmaster to demonstrate.

GAME 12

White: P. Biyiasas
(Canada)

Black: Y. Geller
(U.S.S.R.)

Played at Petropolis (Brazil) Interzonal Tournament, August 6, 1973, Round 10.

Sicilian Defense

Geller does well enough against an unusual setup by White and has at least full equality as the middlegame is reached. However, White defends well to hold the game in balance, and Black must accept an approximately even double Rook endgame. Searching for winning attempts, Geller gets into serious time pressure and compounds his difficulty by choosing a rather complicated variation. With three moves to go both sides have horrible hallucinations, and Black oversteps on move 40. A loss caused by being overeager to win an even position.

$$
\begin{array}{lll}
1 & e4 & c5 \\
2 & Nf3 & d6 \\
3 & Bb5+ &
\end{array}
$$

Formerly thought to be a harmless amateur check, this move acquired a solid reputation in tournament practice in the 1970's. From a developmental point of view, White

quickly clears the Kingside for castling and is then ready for rapid central action. And there is a logical strategical point also. After the exchange of Bishops, White can get a Maroczy type of pawn formation (c4 and e4), thereby limiting Black's potential counterplay from either ...b5 or ...d5. Note that, as a result of exchanging his King Bishop, White doesn't have to worry about having a bad Bishop in the Maroczy formation.

$$
\begin{array}{lll}
3 & \dots & Bd7
\end{array}
$$

The normal response. There is no reason to allow a pin with 3...Nc6, and 3...Nd7 is a bit unsound, though well suited to a risky attempt at winning.

$$
\begin{array}{lll}
4 & Bxd7+ & Qxd7 \\
5 & 0\text{-}0 &
\end{array}
$$

The immediate 5 c4 is most common here, though the text is perfectly O.K.

$$
\begin{array}{lll}
5 & \dots & Nc6
\end{array}
$$

Or 5...Nf6.

$$
\begin{array}{lll}
6 & b3?! &
\end{array}
$$

The IM and Canadian Champion is a resourceful player who does not, however, pay much attention to opening theory. *(Peter Biyiasas is now a grandmaster and plays for the*

U.S. Chess Federation.) The fianchetto of the Queen Bishop has nothing to do with either the strategic or developmental requirements of the position, and it allows Black to effortlessly get at least equality. The modern approach is 6 c4!, with a nice slight plus for White.

6 ...	Nf6
7 Re1	g6

O.K., but since Black will soon play ...e5, the Bishop will be rather dead here. More effective is 7...e5! 8 c3 Be7 9 d4 0-0 10 dxc5 dxc5 11 Qxd7 Nxd7, as in Suba-Ghitescu, 1973 Rumanian Championship (by transposition), with some endgame advantage for Black who is better developed.

8 Bb2	Bg7
9 c4	

So White does set up a Maroczy pawn formation but loses considerable time in misplacing the Queen Bishop. A more logical follow up to White's 6th is 9 d4, with approximate equality.

9 ...	e5!

Prevents any play White could have in the center, and deadens White's Bishop. Black now has a slight edge because he will be able to develop some play on the Kingside, whereas White is ill-placed to do anything on the Queenside. This is just the reverse of the situation usually true in the Sicilian, but the blocked center changes the scene drastically. White's central bastion e4 is to be attacked by Black's ...f5, whereas Black's c5 should be attacked by White's b4. Black is closer to realizing his plan than White is.

10 Nc3	0-0
11 d3	Nh5

Black is obviously ready for play along the f-file with ...f5, whereas White has prepared nothing on the Queenside. Black's a shade better, but White's position is quite defensible. From now up to move 38 White plays perfect chess, doing whatever the position requires.

12 Nd5!	Ne7!

The dominating Knight must be eliminated. 12...f5?! is premature because of 13 exf5, and the centrally desirable 13...gxf5? fails to 14 Nxe5!. After 13...Rxf5 14 Nd2!,

White has full control of the important e4 square.

13 Bc1!

White realizes which is the proper diagonal for this Bishop. Somewhat late, but not too late!

13 ...	Nxd5
14 cxd5	Nf4
15 Bxf4	exf4
16 Rc1	Rae8
17 Qd2	f5

Black gets in this thematic advance and stands slightly better.

18 Ng5!

The threat of 19 Ne6 forces the following exchange, whereby White's pawn formation is improved.

| 18 ... | fxe4 |
| 19 dxe4 | |

After 19. Ne6?, very strong is 19...f3!.

| 19 ... | Qg4 |
| 20 Nf3 | |

Forced, since 20 Ne6? again allows 20 ...f3. After the text move Black still stands a shade better because of his Kingside chances. Most exact now is 20...Be5!, which would blockade White's e-pawn and prepare a pawn advance on the Kingside.

| 20 ... | Qh5?! |

The Queen gets in the way of its own pawns here. *(As already mentioned above, the correct approach is 20 ...Be5!, and if 21 h3 Qd7! (22 Ng5? f3!).)*

| 21 h3 | b6 |
| 22 b4! | |

So White starts his thematic Queenside play - late, but not too late!

| 22 ... | Be5 |

A required blockading move. After the immediate 22 ...g5?! White establishes strong counterplay with 23 bxc5 bxc5 24 e5!.

| 23 a4! | g5! |

More thematic play by both sides.

24 Nxe5	Rxe5
25 f3	Qg6
26 Kf2!	

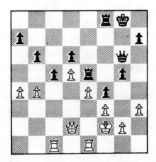

White gets his King out of the way of Black's coming pawn storm. White is able to neutralize Black's threats on the Kingside and create some play on the Queenside. The position remains in dynamic balance.

| 26 ... | h5 |
| 27 Rh1 | Qg7 |

27 ...g4!? 28 hxg4 hxg4 29 Rcg1 is double-edged, but if Black is hell bent to win, that is a logical approach. It is surely more effective than Black's try later on in the Rook endgame.

28 bxc5	bxc5
29 Qc3	Rb8
30 Rb1!	

White is ready to obtain an advantage on the Queenside, so Black must acquiesce to an even double-Rook endgame.

30 ...	Ree8
31 Qxg7+	Kxg7
32 Ke2	

Both sides correctly centralize their Kings.

32 ...	Kf6
33 Kd3	Ke5
34 Kc4	Rh8

The endgame is even, and considering his time shortage, Black's soundest approach is to offer a draw.

At the moment Geller was only half a point out of first place and a draw with Black would not really be unsatisfactory. Nevertheless, he had decided that a win against the youthful Canadian was a must. The result was a very unpleasant loss caused by seriously overestimating the condition of his own nerves.

35 a5!

What now, Black?

35 ...   Rhc8

Preparing the following unclear sacrifice. A safety first move is 35 ...a6, and after 36 Rb6 Rxb6 37 axb6 Rb8 38 Rb1 Rb7, we have a successful double blockade for a draw.

36 Rhg1!

Accurately anticipating Black's plan, White protects his g-pawn, which Black could possibly be attacking with an eventual ...Rc2.

36 ...   Rb4+?!

Objectively this move is O.K., but it leads to no advantage, and it is quite foolish, almost madness, to make it in time pressure. A waiting move or maneuver such as 36...Rd8, following by ...Re8, ...Rf8 etc., is in order to reach the safety of the time control on move 40.

37 Rxb4   cxb4+

38 Kb5??

Completely overlooked by Black in his calculations. Instead Black anticipated 38 Kxb4 Rb8+ 39 Ka3 Rb5 40 Ka4 Rb2, and he has reached the time control. Even so, the chances here are about even. Black has compensation for the pawn but no more. The text, though unexpected, is based on a hallucination which gripped both players not only during the game but apparently thereafter.

38 ...   Kd4??

Black is too unnerved to think clearly. Correct is the obvious 38 ...b3! and White is lost. White no doubt intended 39 Ka6 b2 40 Rb1, but overlooked the devastating strength of 40 ...Rb8!! 41 Kxa7 Rb4. White's King is a captive on the edge of the board, his Rook can't move and Black wins easily by infiltrating with his King; e.g., 42 a6 Kd4 43 Ka8 Kc3 44 e5 dxe5 45 d6 Kc2 46 Rxb2+ Kxb2 47 d7 Rd4, etc. In his notes to the game Geller gives 39 Kb4! as drawing against 38 ...b3, but that must be also based on some hallucination. Obviously after 39 ...b2 40 Rb1 Rc2 White's position is hopeless after either 41 Kb5 Rxg2

or 41 Kb3 Rxg2.

39 Ka6!

Going after the a-pawn is very strong in this position.

39 ...   b3
40 Rd1+!

Black overstepped the time limit and lost.

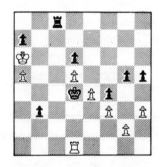

White's last move also came as a surprise to Black, and as he was searching for a reply, his flag fell. The proper response is the retreat 40 ...Ke5 ! Then after 41 Kxa7 Rc4! (given by Geller in his notes to the game) 42 Kb6 Rb4+ White is somewhat better, but Black's active Rook placement should allow him to hold the draw.

GAME 13

White: Y. Geller
(U.S.S.R.)

Black: L. Portisch
(Hungary)

Played at Portoroz (Yugoslavia) Playoff Match Tournament to select qualifiers for Candidates matches, September 10, 1973, Round 5.

Ruy Lopez
(Breyer Variation)

A game Geller loses rather than Portisch wins. Employing a theoretical opening novelty, White enters the middlegame with a slight but clear advantage. Continuing resolutely he wins a pawn by move 26. For the next 60 moves he remains a pawn ahead. However, because of time pressure, he does not play most accurately in the first session, and the material advantage subsequently turns out to be insufficient to win. But Geller refuses to accept the obvious and drives himself so hard that he loses control of the situation, unexpectedly oversteps the time limit, and loses. A tragic example of self pressure. Portisch delivers an excellent demonstration of how to hold a draw, but the other half point is a gift from Caissa.

1	e4	e5
2	Nf3	Nc6
3	Bb5	a6
4	Ba4	Nf6
5	0-0	Be7

Entering the labyrinth of the "closed" variation. The "closed" is by far the most modern way of defending the Ruy. Black prepares to castle and will then try to defend the e5 central post. The other main variation is the "Open" with 5...Nxe4, and we'll see that in Game 22. It is not at all clear that Black has an easier time defending in the former than the latter. The reason for the popularity of the closed variation is simply that when Black currently allows the Ruy, he looks forward to a slow, strategic, maneuvering game rather than a sharp tactical one. The closed variation offers this; the Open does not.

6	Re1	b5
7	Bb3	d6
8	c3	0-0
9	h3	

An immediate 9 d4, though playable, allows the pin 9...Bg4. The text move prevents the pin - at the cost of a tempo - and ensures that White will be able to proceed with the d4 central advance without being bothered by Black. What can Black do about White's coming 10 d4, which will put pressure on Black's e-pawn and establish a central superiority for White? Well, there is no way to prevent White's d4, so Black should satisfy himself with setting up the most useful formation to minimize the strength of the advance.

9 ...   Nb8

What kind of a move is this? When the young amd talented Hungarian Master Breyer suggested this retreat in the 1920's his " reward" was long derisive laughter. How can such a retreat be logical? But there are two sound reasons behind it. First, the current position of the Queen Knight prevents the c-pawn from being used centrally. When the Knight goes to d7 (the Queen Knight is required to protect the e-pawn after White plays d4), the c-pawn is ready to advance. Second, the Black Queen Bishop has little to do on its present diagonal and also would have little scope on b7 with the Queen Knight on c6. But with the Queen Knight on d7 the fianchettoed Bishop has a nice central diagonal. Are there any disadvantages to Black's plan? Yes, the obvious: the maneuver costs two tempos. The Tchigorin Variation, 9 ...Na5 10 Bc2 c5, has been Black's most popular defense since the early 1900's but it has the strategic drawback of leaving the Queen Knight out of play on the edge of the board. Other reasonable moves for Black are 9 ...h6, 9 ...Be6, and 9 ...Nd7.

10 d4   Nbd7
11 c4

When the Breyer became popular in the mid-1960's, this was White's main weapon. Actual practice over the last ten years has shown that Black's position is too sound to be stormed successfully by such positionally brutal means. Even so, Geller has remained partially true to this move. White's strongest continuation is the logical developmental 11 Nbd2!. The second time Geller was White against Portisch in this play-off he did play thus, obtained a won position, but then allowed Portisch to escape with a draw. We'll see 11 Nbd2! in Game 61, R. Byrne- Tukmakov, Leningrad 1973.

11 ...   c6!

Note how well the c-pawn now helps Black's position on both Queenside and center.

12 Qc2?!

Geller's novelty, a successful one in this game. Objectively speaking, however, it is difficult to see the point of placing the Queen here. The main line long, long ago (i.e., 1960's!) was the sharp 12 c5 Qc7! 13 cxd6 Bxd6 14 Bg5 exd4! 15 Bxf6 gxf6 (15 ...Nxf6?? 16 e5 wins material for White), and now after either 16 Nxd4 Nc5, as in Gligoric- Petrosian, Los Angeles 1963, or 16 Qxd4 Ne5, as in Fischer-Portisch, Santa Monica 1966, Black's active pieces and the two Bishops are sufficient compensation for the weakened Kingside. Such a conclusion is not obvious, but extensive master practice has shown it to be so. Nevertheless, White has nothing better than 12 c5. The problem is simply that 11 c4 is too prematurely sharp to pose objective problems for Black.

12 ...   a5?!

A brave but positionally unmotivated sortie. In Tal-Timman, Sochi 1973, contested a few days after this game, Black played the sound developmental 12 ...Bb7! and after 13 Nc3 b4 14 Ne2 exd4! 15 Nexd4 g6! 16 Ne2 Nc5 already had a slight advantage (the game was drawn in 68).

13 a4

This too, is overeager. White obtains better opportunities to take advantage of Black's weakened Queenside with 13 a3!

| 13 ... | bxc4 |
| 14 Bxc4 | d5! |

15 Bd3

In his analysis Geller rates Black's position as equal after move 14. Even so, to spend over an hour on the text move is excessive. Clearly, after 15 exd5 cxd5 16 dxe5 dxc4 17 exf6 Nxf6 (or 17 ...Bxf6) 18 Qxc4, Black's two Bishops and White's weakened Queenside give Black full compensation for the pawn. So what else does White have but the text? The time wasted here will be worth a lot later on.

15 ...	dxe4
16 Bxe4	Nxe4
17 Qxe4	Bb4?!

Geller criticizes this and instead recommends 17 ...Nf6! 18 Qxe5 Bd6 feeling that Black's Bishops and open lines compensate fully for the pawn.

18 Bd2   Bxd2?

This move, which furthers White's development and leaves Black with weak Queenside pawns, is the real reason for Black's coming difficulties. Szabo has correctly pointed out that after the correct 18... exd4! White's advantage is quite minor.

| 19 Nbxd2 | exd4 |
| 20 Qxd4! | |

But here White's advantage is major: he is ahead in development, has a well-placed Queen, and will be ready to start menacing Black's isolated a- and c-pawns.

20 ...	Nf6
21 Rac1	Bd7

The exchange of Queens loses the c-pawn by force.

22 Nc4

Perfectly O.K., though 22 Ne5!? to prevent Black's next may be a shade better.

22 ...	c5!?

Correctly exchanging one of his weak pawns.

23 Qxc5	Bxa4
24 Nfe5!	

24 Nb6?! Nd7! leads to nothing. Now, however, 25 Nb6 is the threat.

24 ...	Rb8

Leads to the loss of the a-pawn, but there is nothing good to recommend. If 24 ...Nd7 25 Nxd7 Bxd7 26 Red1 and Black is stuck in a most unpleasant pin.

25 Qa3!	Bb5

Instead 25 ...Rb4? is refuted by 26 Nxa5! Qxa5 27 Nc6!.

26 Nxa5

And so White has won Black's remaining Queenside pawn, is a sound pawn ahead, and will remain at least a pawn ahead for the rest of the game. But for the missing pawn, Black's position is satisfactory, so his practical chances for a draw are reasonable. Nevertheless, with accurate, matter-of-technique play, White should be able to win. However, a shortage of time, caused by thinking excessively in the opening phase, begins to rear its unwelcome head.

26 ...	Qb6
27 b4	Rfe8
28 Qc3!	Re6
29 Nec6	Rbe8
30 Rxe6	Rxe6
31 Qc5?!	

Exhanging Queens is logical both from the standpoint of the position and White's time pressure, but this is not an accurate way to accomplish it because Black's Rook can reach an active behind-the-pawn location. Correct is 31 Nd4! Re8 32

Qc5!, and after 32...Qxc5 33 bxc5, White's Rook is well placed behind his passed pawn.

31 ...	Qxc5
32 Rxc5	

Here 32 bxc5?? loses a Knight.

32 ...	Re1+
33 Kh2	Ba4
34 b5?!	

A logical move in time pressure, but the pawn is rather exposed here. To prevent Black's coming h-pawn advance with 34 f3! h5 35 h4! is better. White should then still win in due course.

34 ...	Rb1!

Black's Rook is ideally placed *behind* the passed pawn. This allows Black to watch both the b-pawn and White's King.

35 Nd4	h5
36 Rc8+	Kh7
37 Rb8	h4!

The pawn severely limits the White King's activity and even gives Black certain chances for a mating attack.

38 Rb7	Kg6?!

The King is awkwardly placed here. Correct is the active 38...Ne4! 39 Rxf7 Nd2!, and the threat of 40

...Nf1+ forces White to allow the drawish position after 40 g3 hxg3+ 41 fxg3 Bxb5, etc.

39 Nac6!	Ne4
40 Ne5+	Kf6
41 Ng4+	

The game was adjourned here, with Geller sealing his 41st move. It was resumed two days later so the players (and their seconds!) had enough time to analyze. After the match tournament, Portisch stated that he was sure of having qualified for the Candidates matches when he couldn't find a win for White in this position. Black has a sufficient bind on White's Kingside, and so White is eventually forced to exchange his b-pawn for Black's h-pawn.

41 ...	Kg6
42 Ne5+	

Black can defend against this. After the game Geller suggested 42 b6!? as worth trying.

42 ...	Kf6
43 f4	

White now threatens 44 Rxf7 mate, so Black has no time for 43... Ng3??.

<blockquote>

43 ...   Bb3!
44 Nef3!

</blockquote>

The h-pawn must be eliminated; otherwise White is in great danger of being mated. For instance, 44 Nxb3? Ng3 and the best White can hope for is a draw after 45 Ng4+ and 46 Nf2.

<blockquote>

44 ...   g6!

</blockquote>

Taking away f5 from White's Knights.

<blockquote>

45 Nxh4   Bd5
46 Rc7

</blockquote>

As frustrating as it is, there is no way for White to prevent his b-pawn from eventually being lost. Thus if 46 Rb6+ Ke7 47 Nhf3 Nc3!, and now 48 Ne5 is foiled by 48 ...Rb2!.

<blockquote>

46 ...   Rd1

</blockquote>

Satisfactory, but even more exact is 46... Rb4! 47 Nhf3 Nd2‡.

<blockquote>

47 Nc2   Rb1
48 Ne3

</blockquote>

The b-pawn cannot be saved.

<blockquote>

48 ...   Rxb5
49 Nf3   Be6
50 Nd4

</blockquote>

White's chances to win this ending are scant, but Geller is nonetheless determined. Such impractical determination is psychologically motivated. He began the play-off disastrously, having lost twice to Polugaevsky and drawn once with Portisch. Having had a "won" game from early on, Geller couldn't accept any other result. Under such unhealthy pressure strange things can happen.

<blockquote>

50 ...   Rb4
51 Nxe6   Kxe6
52 Rc4

</blockquote>

The exchange of Rooks can't be the way to success. But Black's Rook and Knight are placed quite well, so keeping Rooks on also offers no real hope. The problem is simply that the position is too dry for a win.

<blockquote>

52 ...   Rxc4
53 Nxc4

</blockquote>

The pawn formation is rather symmetrical, except that Black is missing his h-pawn. Otherwise

Black stands well, and with accurate and logical play, Portisch is able to hold the position for a draw. However, something unbelievable happens at the very end!

53 ...	Kf5

But not 53...g5? 54 fxg5, and White has a passed h-pawn and fantastic winning chances. Black does want to exchange pawns, but only on his terms. This means a symmetrical exchange, such as f-pawn for f-pawn, Black's g-pawn for White's h-pawn, or Black's f-pawn for White's g-pawn. The last thing that Black wants to allow is a passed pawn.

54 g3	Nc5
55 Kg2	Nd3
56 Kf3	Nc5
57 Nd6+	

As the course of the game shows, it is insufficient for White to play with only his King and Knight. To begin to use the pawn majority with 57 g4+! is necessary and correct. This gains space for White, and an eventual ...f5 can be met by g5!; Black's g-pawn may then become a real weakness.

57 ...	Ke6
58 Ne4	Nd7!

A good defensive spot for the Knight. At the moment, there is nothing to attack in White's camp;

thus "attacking" Knight moves such as ...Nd3 serve no purpose. Exchanging Knights leads to a normal lost King + Pawn endgame.

59 Ke3

Black's reply cannot be prevented since 59 g4 is also met by 59 ...f5!, with an attack on the Knight.

59 ...	f5!

This paralyzes White's pawn majority since a later g4 can be easily parried by the symmetrical pawn exchange, and all that White has achieved is a symmetrical and drawn Knight + 2 pawns vs. Knight + pawn endgame. As it turns out, this is the last pawn move in the game. The game was adjourned with Black having sealed this move. After a four hour break, it was resumed for another two sessions of play.

60 Ng5+	Kf6

Black's King is going to stay near the weakened g-pawn. There is little point in the aggressive 60 ...Kd5.

61 Kd4	Kg7!
62 Ne6+	

62 Kd5?! leads nowhere: 62 ...Nf6+ 63 Ke6? Nh5, and White's g-pawn is lost.

62 ...	Kf7

| 63 Nc7 | Nf6 |
| 64 Nd5 | Nd7! |

Black has achieved what looks like an impregnable defensive formation, and he is not about to depart from it except for the best of reasons. Thus he eschews 64...Ne4?! 65 g4! Nf2 66 g5! Nxh3 67 Ke3!, and Black's Knight is trapped and may well go lost.

65 Nc7	Nf6
66 Nd5	Nd7
67 Nc3	Nf6
68 Ke5	Nh5!

Note how the lack of White's g4 gives Black's Knight more scope.

69 Ne2	Ke7!
70 Kd5	Nf6+
71 Ke5	Nh5
72 Kd4	Nf6
73 Ke3	Nd5+
74 Kf3	Kf7!
75 Nc1	Kg7!

Black is more than happy to keep the status quo.

76 Nd3	Kf7
77 Kf2	Kg7
78 Ne5	Nf6
79 Ke3	Kh7
80 Nd3	

Over the last twenty moves, White has not made any progress. He refrains from 80 g4 because of 80...Nd5+ 81 Kf3 fxg4, etc. He can't get himself to concede the draw.

80 ...	Kh6
81 Ne5	Kg7
82 Nc4	Kf7
83 Kf3	Nd5
84 Ke2	Kg7
85 Kd3	Nf6
86 Ke3	Kf7

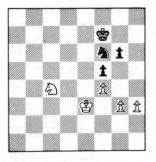

White overstepped the time limit and lost.

As White was playing 87 Kf3, his flag fell, and he had to be forfeited. How could such a thing happen in such an easy position? The explanation is almost unbelievable. As a result of a massive block-induced no doubt by nervous overexertion-Geller had marked move 84 (instead of the correct 88) on his score sheet as the end of the time control. Thus with the "time control" over, he paid no attention to the clock until he was forfeited. Tragically, this very half point prevented Geller from reaching the 1974 Candidates matches.

GAME 14

White: J. Smejkal
(Czechoslovakia)

Black: R. Holmov
(U.S.S.R.)

Played at Luhacovice (Czechoslovakia) International Tournament, May 1973.

English Opening

White comes out of the strategic opening with a free position, having a space advantage on the Queenside and no weaknesses whatever. In trying to build on these, he chooses a double-edged pawn advance on the Kingside. This creates a dynamically balanced situation, and when Black doesn't respond with sufficient energy, White achieves a clear superiority in space and position. Though in considerable time pressure, Smejkal maneuvers purposefully and by adjournment is ready to penetrate Black's camp. Some pretty motifs with passed pawns seal Black's fate.

1 c4	Nf6
2 g3	e5
3 Bg2	c5

A controversial decision. Black establishes a strong central position with a particular grip on the d4 square. The cost, however, is a permanent weakening of the d5 square. Normal moves here include 3 ...Nc6 and 3 ...g6.

4 Nc3	Nc6
5 Nf3	

White plans to complete his development before thinking about anything else. More incisive is 5 d3! h6 (otherwise 6 Bg5 puts great pressure on the d5 square) 6 a3! followed by 7 Rb1 aiming for an early b4. In this way White should be able to retain his first-move advantage.

5 ...	d6
6 0-0	Be6
7 d3	h6

Again 8 Bg5 must be prevented.

8 a3	d5?!

In trying to eliminate the hole on d5 even before he has completed his Kingside development, Black is clearly overeager. White is now able to take advantage of Black's uncastled King to obtain a solid initiative on the Queenside. The patient 8 ...Be7 is in order and only after 10 Rb1 d5!. Then Black is O.K.

9 Qa4!

With the threat of 10 Nxe5. 9 ...d4? is refuted by 10 Nxe5! dxc3 11 Nxc6 Qd7 12 Qb5!. Thus Black must protect the e-pawn.

9 ...	Bd6
10 b4!	0-0

All captures are worse; e.g., 10 ...cxb4 11 axb4 Bxb4?! 12 Nxd5 Nxd5 13 cxd5 Bxd5 14 e4 Be6 15 Nxe5!, or 10 ...dxc4 11 bxc5! (11 ...Bxc5?! 12 Nxe5).

11 b5	Ne7
12 cxd5	Nexd5
13 Bb2	Nb6

13 ...Nxc3 just makes it easier for White to apply pressure: 14 Bxc3 Nd7 15 Nd2! Nb6 16 Qc2 Qe7 17 a4.

14 Qc2	Rc8

If 14 ...c4?!, 15 d4! with substantial advantage for White (Minev).

15 Nd2!

The opening phase has ended and White has space advantage on the Queenside, a fantastic diagonal for his King Bishop, and good poten-

tial for his Queen Bishop on the central diagonal. Black's e-pawn is awkward to protect. Overall White has a safe and comfortable plus.

15 ...	Qe7
16 Na4!	

Gaining more space on the Queenside and opening the Queen Bishop's diagonal. 16 a4? is faulty because of 16 ...Nbd5! and the Knight gets the important b4 square.

16 ...	Nxa4

Now after 16 ...Nbd5 17 Nc4! Black has problems keeping both his e-pawn and b-pawn protected.

17 Qxa4	Bb8
18 Nc4	Bd5
19 e4!	

A major and correct positional decision. White locks in his King Bishop and weakens his d-pawn and d4 square. His compensation is the two Bishops and a significant space advantage. The following exchange is forced since 19 ...Be6? drops the e-pawn.

19 ...	Bxc4
20 Qxc4	Rcd8
21 Bh3?!	

White is already in incipient time pressure. The Bishop is not safe here and the move just wastes time. White has two logical methods to capitalize on his greater space. The first, suggested by Smejkal, is to improve the location of the Kingside pieces with 21 Rfd1, 22 h4, 23 Bh3, and then to continue the Queenside expansion with a4, a5, etc. This is slow, but Black is very cramped and has no meaningful counterplay. The other, sharper approach is to play on the Kingside and center with 21 Rae1 and 22 f4, as the Bulgarian IM Minev suggested.

21 ...	Nh7!
22 Bg2	

A correct retreat. Of practical value is the ability to recognize one's own errors quickly; there is then often still enough time to minimize potential damage. That's quite true here.

22 ...	Ng5
23 f4!?	

A brave, double-edged advance, especially in time pressure. Even so Smejkal feels that the positional 23 Rfd1! is sounder.

23 ...	exf4!

Black is also quite brave, for this capture opens the position and increases White's central strength. Black counts on having sufficient play against White's somewhat loose position. This evaluation is correct but his coming play insufficiently energetic. Safe, sound, and

good enough for equality is 23 ...Ne6! and after 24 f5 Nd4.

24 gxf4	Ne6
25 e5!	Nd4
26 Rae1	Kh8
27 a4	b6
28 Kh1	f6!
29 e6	Rfe8?

This move costs valuable time, which White can use to consolidate his position. Moreover, the Rook will be chased back with additional loss of time. The attack against the e-pawn turns out to be a sham. The moment is ripe here for 29 ...g5!, especially because White has no time for 30 f5?? in view of 30 ...Qd6. After 29 ...g5! Smejkal considers 30 Bc1 the only correct move and rates the chances as dynamically equal.

30 Rf2!	

But now Black is in trouble. It's too late for 30 ...g5? because with h2 protected White has 31 f5 Qd6 32 Be4. White now threatens 31 f5 transforming the e-pawn into a protected passed pawn. Black feels constrained to prevent this but incurs the disadvantage of weakening his Kingside and of increasing the potential of White's Queen Bishop.

30 ...	f5
31 Bc6!!	

An elegant way to take advantage of Black's last move. After 31 ...Nxc6 32 bxc6 White doubles Rooks on the g-file and Black's g-pawn is indefensible. However, the alternative-allowing White's King Bishop to reach d7-results in Black's being tied in knots.

31 ...	Rf8
32 Rg1!	

The careless 32 Bd7?? allows 32 ...Rxd7.

32 ...	Kh7
33 Bd7	Rf6
34 Bxd4!	

An attractive, practical time-pressure move; Black is now completely without counterchances, and White runs no risk of time pressure errors. The key advantages of space and passed e-pawn remain.

34 ...	cxd4
35 Qd5!	

Of course not 35 Qxd4? Rxe6! and an even endgame after 36 Rxg7+ Qxg7 37 Qxg7+ Kxg7 38 Bxe6

Rxd3, etc. White will take off the d-pawn when it is safe to do so!

35 ...	Bd6
36 Rfg2	

And here 36 Qxd4? allows 36 ...Bc5.

36 ...	g6
37 Rf2	Kg7
38 Rc1!	Bc5
39 a5!	

White pays attention to both sides of the board; Queenside, center Kingside. Such an approach makes it almost impossible for a cramped defender to parry all threats.

39 ...	Kh7
40 Re2	Bd6?!

Allows White a risk-free win. There is nothing better than 40 ...Kg7, even though 41 Rxc5! bxc5 42 b6 does lead to a winning breakthrough.

41 axb6	Bxf4

Allowing White a passed pawn on b7 is equivalent to suicide. However, Black's days are also numbered after 41 ...axb6 42 Qxd4.

42 Rf1	Bb8
43 b7!	

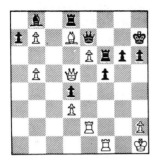

White now infiltrates with heavy artillery along the c-file, and then something must break in Black's position. White's Kingside does look semi-barren, but he is quite safe because Black has no attacking power to swing over there.

43 ...	h5
44 Rc1	f4
45 Qf3	Kh6
46 Rc8	Rff8
47 Rec2!	g5
48 Rxd8	Rxd8
49 Rc8	

White's infiltration route is clear and potent. As soon as the Queen joins in, the end will be near.

49 ...	Bd6
50 Qc6	Rf8
51 b8=Q	

"In won positions there is more than one way to skin the *King*." Equally winning is 51 Rxf8 Qxf8 b8=Q! Qxb8 (52 ...Bxb8 53 e7+) 53 e7.

| 51 ... | Bxb8 |
| 52 Rxf8 | g4 |

If 52 ...Qxf8 53 e7+, Black could resign.

53 Rf7	Qb4
54 e7+	Bd6
55 Qc1	

Or 55 Qxd6+ Qxd6 56 e8=Q.

55 ...	Bxe7
56 Qxf4+	Bg5
57 Rf6+	Kh7
58 Qf5+	
Black resigns	

GAME 15

**White: R. Holmov
(U.S.S.R.)**

**Black: V. Jansa
(Czechoslovakia)**

Played at Luhacovice (Czechoslovakia) International Tournament, May 1973.

English Opening

Using an interesting Queen maneuver, Black brings about an early endgame, in which he has virtual equality. In the ensuing play, Black consistently prepares and executes his thematic pawn advance on the Queenside and obtains full equality. At the critical moment White undertakes an unmotivated, reckless central pawn push and quickly begins to suffer from it. Black's pieces spring to life, and White has all he can do to protect the resulting weak spots. Although little material remains, Black's Rook and two Bishops accomplish a mating attack, and White is done in on move 37.

1 Nf3

A Reti or King's Indian Reversed?

1 ...　　　　c5

Offering a Sicilian after 2 e4.

2 c4

White prefers an English Opening.

2 ...	Nc6
3 Nc3	Nf6
4 d4	cxd4
5 Nxd4	g6
6 g3	

Sticking to the English. With 6 e4 he could establish the Accelerated Dragon Variation of the Sicilian Defense.

6 ...	Bg7
7 Bg2	0-0
8 Nc2	

White has a slight central superiority and feels that the best way to keep Black cramped is to prevent the exchange of Knights. This seems logical, but the Knight is not usefully placed on c2 and the text move has little theoretical import. It's O.K., but that's all. The normal way to handle this English / Kings's Indian position is 8 0-0 Nxd4 9 Qxd4 d6, as we'll see in Tal-Torre, Leningrad 1973, Game 52.

| 8 ... | d6 |
| 9 0-0 | Qa5! |

A creative idea. Black, taking advantage of the passively placed White King Knight, shifts his Queen to the Kingside for action there.

10 Bd2	Qh5
11 e4	

Black was planning 11 ...Bh3 to exchange Bishops and thus weaken White's King position. White therefore sees nothing better than to allow an endgame in which his advantage, if any, is minimal.

11 ...	Qxd1
12 Raxd1	

The Queen Rook inhibits the meaningful development of the King Rook, and White must soon lose a move to make its useful development possible. Therefore, 12 Rfxd1! is better, and White's greater central influence could amount to an infinitesimal plus.

| 12 ... | Bg4!? |

To shorten the White King Bishop's diagonal.

13 f3	Be6
14 b3	Rfc8

Black's thematic counterplay is against White's c pawn, so this is the right method. The Queen Rook should be used on either the a- or b-file.

| 15 f4 | Rab8 |

Here 15 ...a6? is faulty in view of 16 Na4! since Black can't guard b6 with 16 ...Nd7 because 17 f5 traps the Queen Bishop.

16 Rc1

Clearly indicating that White's 12th move lost a tempo. Still there is nothing better since White must prepare to contest the c-file.

16 ...	a6
17 Rfe1	b5!

Black has successfully realized his thematic advance against White's c-pawn. Chances are dynamically balanced. With reasonable play the result should be a draw since the absence of Queens minimizes each side's winning chances. However, careless or unstrategic play by either side could well be punished.

18 e5??

According to Jansa, White thought for about five minutes before pushing the e-pawn confidently forward. The move is reckless, pointless, horrible, stupid, or a combination of all of these, and there is no explanation for a grandmaster's making it. It accomplishes absolutely nothing and ensures the death of his e-pawn. Given Black's threat to exchange on c4, saddling White with a weak isloated c-pawn, the only move worth considering is 18 cxb5. After 18 ...axb5 White has 19 Nd5!?. Jansa suggests 19 ...Nxd5!? 20 exd5 Nd4 as a reply and rates the positions after 21 dxe6 Nxc2 22 exf7+ Kxf7 23 Bd5+ Kf8 and 21 Nb4 Rxc1 22 Bxc1 Bg4 as even.

| 18 ... | dxe5 |
| 19 fxe5 | Ng4 |

White's e-pawn is now attacked three times and defended only once. To protect it White has to part with his King Bishop, thereby weakening his King position and giving Black the two Bishops in an open position. The future course of the game will show both factors to be decisive.

20 Bxc6	Rxc6
21 Nb4	Rcc8
22 Ncd5?!	

White will now have no chances for active play. Theoretically no better is 22 Nxa6 Ra8 23 cxb5 Nxe5, but White's passed Queenside pawns afford at least some practical chances if Black misplays the position. As played White must simply await the execu-

tioner.

| 22 ... | Rb7! |
| 23 Bf4 | |

A piece is lost after 23 cxb5 Rxc1 24 Rxc1 a5.

| 23 ... | bxc4 |

White will now have a weak isolated c-pawn and e-pawn and a weakened Kingside, whereas Black has two powerful Bishops and active Rooks. Against a capable master like Black, such a situation is hopeless for White.

24 bxc4

Equivalent is 24 Rxc4 Rxc4 25 bxc4 g5! 26 Bxg5 Nxe5 with play similar to the game.

| 24 ... | g5!! |

A strategically correct decision, which hastens White's demise. By winning White's e-pawn for the currently unimportant g-pawn, Black can pump all his pieces into White's camp.

25 Bxg5	Nxe5
26 Nxe7+	Rxe7
27 Bxe7	Nf3+
28 Kf2	Nxe1
29 Kxe1?!	

Allows Black's Rook to enter White's position via the e-file with decisive effect. A shade better is 29 Rxe1, though Black's attack must soon be decisive after 29 ...Rxc4!

29 ...	a5!
30 Nd3	

If 30 Nd5? Bxd5.

30 ...	Re8!
31 Bg5	Bg4+!
32 Kf2	Bd4+
33 Kg2	Re2+

The Rook + two Bishop combination waylays White's King.

34 Kf1	Rxa2

With the primary threat of 35 ...Be2+, and 35 Re1 allows 35 ...Bh3 mate.

35 Nf4	h6!

With the help of tactics, Black chases the Bishop away from its defense of the King. 36 Bxh6 is met by 36 ...Rxh2 with the double threats of 37 ... Rxh6 and 37 ... Rh1+.

36 Bd8	Rxh2
37 Ke1	Be3!
White resigns	

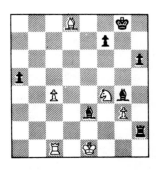

Forget the Rook- there is no defense to the mate threat of 38 ...Rh1.

GAME 16

White: G. Estevez
(Cuba)

Black: R. Holmov
(U.S.S.R.)

Played at Luhacovice (Czechoslovakia) International Tournament,
May 1973.

English Opening

Using a sophisticated strategic
opening, Black obtains solid equality. White's play is sufficiently
careful and sound to keep the
chances approximately balanced.
However, Black is not satisfied to
draw against the tournament tailender. He opens the position on the
Kingside, mainly to the benefit of
White's Bishop. After some unsatisfactory Queen and Knight maneuvers, Black is clearly in trouble, and
White has the realistic attacking
chances. When Black neglects to
prevent a simple Knight shot, it is
suddenly mate in two!

1 Nf3	Nf6
2 c4	e6
3 Nc3	Bb4

A sophisticated strategic idea,
whereby Black tries to apply pressure against the e4 square. This is
similar to the Nimzo-Indian Defense
(see Game 25); but with White's d-

pawn still back home, the strategy is
not quite so firmly based on proven
positional principles. The two most
common moves for Black are 3...d5
and 3...c5.

4 Qc2!

The best response. White prevents the doubling of his pawns and
gives the Queen a useful central location.

4 ...	0-0

If Black wants to keep the
Bishop he must play 4...c5 so that the
Bishop can retreat in safety to a5.

5 a3

Forcing the Bishop off makes
the point of White's 4th clear.

5 ...	Bxc3
6 Qxc3	b6!?

Black usually aims for direct
central influence with 6...d6. Even
so, White's two Bishops and flexible
central pawn formation give him the
typical first-move advantage. One
recent example is Portisch-Larsen,
Las Palmas 1976: 7 b4 e5 8 Bb2 Nc6
9 e3 Ne4 10 Qc2 f5 11 Be2 a5 12 d3.
White's a shade better and went on
to win in 37.

7 b4

Black's Queen Bishop now

gets too much scope on the center diagonal. More logical is 7 g3! Bb7 8
Bg2 d5 9 d4 dxc4 10 Qxc4 Be4 11
0-0 with some advantage for White
in Vaganian-Korchnoi, Moscow
1975.

7	...	Bb7
8	Bb2	d6
9	e3	e5!

Holmov tried 6 ...b6 in Sha-
mkovich-Holmov, 1972 U.S.S.R.
Championship, and in this position
continued 9 ...Nbd7 10 Be2 c5 11 d4
Qe7 12 0-0 Ne4. The text is an
improvement which makes it harder
for White to challenge Black's center.

10	Be2	Nbd7
11	0-0	Re8
12	d3	c5

The opening phase has ended
with both sides having a good position. White has the two Bishops and
no weaknesses; Black's Queen
Bishop has a good diagonal and
Black has greater center influence.
The position is in balance.

13 Nd2

With the idea of exchanging the
light-square Bishops. This is a defensive idea rather than a way of
playing to win. But Black's central
influence makes it difficult for White
to develop an active plan.

13	...	Re6
14	Bf3	Bxf3
15	Nxf3	h6
16	b5	

With the long -range idea of a
Queenside pawn roller by means of
17 a4, 18 a5, etc, but Black can put an
effective stop to that. More promising is the central advance 16 d4!?.

16	...	a5!
17	bxa6 e.p.	

The opening of the Queenside
in this situation is more to Black's
advantage than to White's. It is difficult to recommend something attractive, however, since White's 16th
move gave up the contest for the c5
square, thus making a potential d4
much less attractive.

17	...	Rxa6
18	Qb3	Qa8
19	Rfd1	d5!

This advance leads to the liquidation of white's c-pawn and thus
leaves Black in slight, though undisputed, control of the center.

| 20 cxd5 | Qxd5 |
| 21 Qc2 | |

The exchange of Queens gives Black a comfortable endgame, especially in view of White's isolated a-pawn. Keeping the Queens on is unquestionably the correct practical approach.

| 21 ... | Qc6 |

Intending 22...Ra4 or 22 ...Qa4, but White can prevent that. The immediate 21 ...b5! is in order. Black then threatens the positional 22 ...Ra4 and because of his central superiority has a small but comfortable plus.

| 22 a4! | e4 |

This impatient advance leads to nothing but the opening of the White Bishop's diagonal. A more useful way to play for the win is 22...Ra8!, followed by using the Rook in the center. Objectively the position is essentially in balance, but the balance is dynamic, and so the better player - obviously Black here - has chances for the full point.

| 23 dxe4 | Qxe4 |
| 24 Qc3! | |

With White's first threat - thanks to the just opened diagonal - 25 Rxd7!.

| 24 ... | Qc6 |

O.K. but 24 ...Ra7 seems more efficient. The Queen is well placed in the center.

| 25 Qc4 | Qa8 |

Here too 25 ...Ra7 seems more efficient.

| 26 Qc3!? | |

In effect, an interesting way to offer a draw. White is satisfied with such a result against his famous adversary.

| 26 ... | Nf8?! |

But Holmov is not interested in drawing against the tournament tailender. 26 ...Qc6 instead repeats the position. The Knight move is a step in the wrong direction, however. 26 ...Ra7 is again more efficient.

| 27 Qb3 | Ng6?! |

And this is clearly wrong since it allows White's Rook to penetrate to d7. Holmov seriously underrates his opponent. The Cuban IM can be a creative tactician; at Leningrad Interzonal 1973 he defeated both Hubner and Tal (see Game 53) in fine games. In any case, to win requires good moves, and Holmov's misplacement of his pieces invites disaster.

| 28 Bxf6 | |

A fresh and open mind is behind this capture. To get his Rook to d7, White is willing to exchange off his "beautiful" Bishop.

| 28 ... | Rxf6 |
| 29 Rd7 | Qc6? |

Giving White the eighth rank is unforgivable. It is high time to reverse gears and play 29 ...Nf8!.

| 30 Rd8+ | Kh7 |
| 31 Qd1! | |

The Queen move contains a simple, though pretty, threat, which Black overlooks. Black's position is, nevertheless already very unpleasant. A Knight move loses the Queen Rook to 32 Qd3+. The only defense is 31...Rf5! since then 32 Qd3? attacking both Rooks can be met by 32 ...Rxa4!! 33 Rxa4 Qxa4 because 34 Qxf5?? allows 34 ...Qa1+ followed by mate. After 31 ...Rf5! White's sharpest is 32 h4! which threatens both 33 Qd3 and 33 Ng5+. White's advantage is indisputable, anyway. But what happens now is "a bit" worse.

31 ...	Re6??
32 Ng5+!	
Black resigns	

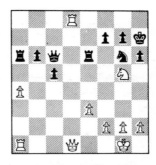

The forced 32 ...hxg5 allows 33 Qh5 mate!

GAME 17

White: R. Holmov
(U.S.S.R.)

Black: N. Spiridonov
(Bulgaria)

Played at Sochi (U.S.S.R.) International Tournament, September 1973, Round 13.

English Opening

Black employs an interesting strategic concept as early as move 4 and forces White to do some independent thinking that soon in the game. White's response is too eccentric, thus showing Black's opening strategy to be quite successful. Soon Black achieves a slight positional plus by controlling the dark squares on the Kingside. White decides to castle Queenside but subsequently does not maneuver successfully. In due course Black is able to open lines and generate strong pressure against White's King. Finally Black's Queen infiltrates White's camp, and some pretty tactics spell the end of the road for White's King. Overall a meaningful demonstration of how to defeat a superior opponent: a strategically noteworthy opening innovation, positionally logical maneuvering, thorough preparation for the potential attack, and energy and tactical sharpness in executing it.

1 c4	g6
2 Nf3	Bg7
3 e4	d6
4 d4	

If Black plays 4...Nf6, one of the standard variations of the King's Indian Defense will arise. Black's move order does, however, give some flexibility in what to do next.

4 ...	Bg4!?

An interesting, strategically creative way to apply pressure against White's d-pawn. Objectively no better than the standard 4...Nf6, it does force White to solve new problems. This is always a good practical approach against a theoretically well-prepared opponent.

5 Be2	Nc6

With the obvious threat of 6 ...Bxf3 followed by 7 ...Nxd4. If 6 Be3 Black continues the pressure on the d-pawn with 6 ...e5. How should White proceed?

6 Ng1?!	

With the idea of 6...Bxe2?! 7 Nxe2, when White's d-pawn is comfortably protected and White has a nice central superiority. Such abject retreats are, however, rarely sound. Spiridonov recommends indirect protection with 6 Nbd2! as White's best and gives the following variation: 6 ...e5 (6 ...Nxd4?? 7 Nxd4 and

White wins a piece) 7 d5 Bxf3 8 Nxf3
Nd4 9 Nxd4 exd4 10 Qb3 Qc8 11 c5!
with a slight edge to White.

6 ...	Bd7!

Making White's KN look
rather silly back home.

7 Be3	e5!
8 d5	Nd4
9 Nf3	Nxf3+

Black decides to play on the
dark squares on the Kingside. An
equally good approach is to undermine White's center with 9...Nxe2
10 Qxe2 f5!.

10 Bxf3	Bh6!

The point of Black's moves 7
through 9. With the center diagonal
now closed, Black gladly exchanges
his bad Bishop for White's good one.
The net result will leave Black
comfortable on the dark squares, his
remaining Bishop having more
scope than White's.

11 Nc3?!

Leads to new and serious weaknesses. The safe move is 11 Qd2.
Double-edged but playable is 11
0-0!? since after Bxe3 fxe3 White
may have some counterplay along
the f-file.

| 11 ... | Bxe3 |
| 12 fxe3 | Qh4+! |

13 g3	Qg5

Black's Queen is actively
placed, and White's advanced g-
pawn will be attackable in just a
moment. Overall Black is already
clearly superior. He has the better
Bishop and active Queen; White
has only weaknesses.

| 14 Qe2 | h5! |
| 15 0-0-0 | |

Obviously the Queenside is the
only place where the King will feel
at least half safe.

| 15 ... | h4 |
| 16 g4 | |

Opening lines will only help
Black get at White's weaknesses.

| 16 ... | Nf6 |
| 17 Rhg1?! | |

Why use a Rook to protect a
pawn when 17 h3 will do the job?

17 ...   Ke7

Black wants to connect Rooks and start working on White's Queenside, so he doesn't want to castle there himself. However, for the moment he also isn't sure whether he wants to castle on the Kingside. The text seeks middle-ground. Hindsight tells us, however, that 17...0-0! is quite safe and would save Black a move or two over the game.

18 Kb1   Rhd8
19 Qd2   Be8
20 Rc1   a5!

Black's 19th move freed d7 for the Knight so that it can get to a more useful location on c5, where it will also be able to watch White's King. The text move ensures that the Knight won't be bothered by White's b4.

21 h3   Nd7
22 b3   Nc5
23 Kb2?

The King is less safe here than on b1. A better defensive formation is 23 Rc2!.

23 ...   c6!

The beginning of the undermining of White's King position.

24 Rc2   Kf8!

A good precautionary move. Black ensures that White's Knight will never get to d5 with *check*.

25 Be2   Ra6!
26 Kb1

White admits his error on move 23 but at the cost of two tempi. This has given Black enough time to get his attack going.

26 ...   Rb6
27 Rb2   a4!
28 Bd1?!

Too defensive. Even worse is 28 b4? because of 28 ...a3. White has to try 28 Nxa4!?. Black is much better after 28 ... Nxe4! 29 Qd3 (29 Qc2? Qxe3!) Nc5 30 Nxc5 dxc5 31 e4 cxd5! 32 exd5 Rf6!, but White at least has a protected passed d-pawn and some chances. As played he has none.

28 ...   cxd5!
29 exd5

After 29 Nxd5 Black moves away the Rook and then threatens Nxe4. In addition, after 29 Nxd5 White is stuck with isolated, doubled e-pawns. With the text White improves his pawn formation but ...

29 ...   Ra8!

...Black starts on the final phase of his attack. White can't prevent the opening of the a-file and the doubling of Black's Rooks thereon.

30	Rf1	axb3
31	axb3	Rba6
32	Ra2	

The Rooks must be opposed, but the resulting lack of control of b5 by White allows Black to further denude White's King.

32	...	Rxa2
33	Nxa2	b5!
34	b4	

From now on there is no chance for successful defense.

34	...	Ne4
35	Qd3	Ng3
36	Re1	Qf6!
37	Bb3	Qf2
38	Rc1	bxc4
39	Bxc4	Bb5!

With the help of tactics, Black finishes the job nicely. The threat is 40...Rxa2! and 40 Bxb5 allows 40...Qxa2 mate so...

40	Rc2	Bxc4
41	Qxc4	Qe1+
42	Kb2	Qxe3

Not only is Black a pawn up, but the Queen has decisively penetrated White's position. The end is near.

| 43 | Nc3 | Qa7! |

Threatening 44...Qa1+ 45 Kb3 Ra3 mate. If now 44 Nb1, Spiridonov gives 44...Rb8 45 b5 Ne4! 46 Qxe4 Rxb5+ 47 Kc1 Qg1+ as winning for Black. White decides to shorten the agony with ...

| 44 | Kc1?! | Qg1+ |
| 45 | Kd2 | |

Obviously 45 Nd1 allows 45 ...Ra1+, and 45 Kb2 leads to 45 ...Qa1+ 46 Kb3 Ra3 mate.

| 45 | ... | Nf1+ |
| | **White resigns** | |

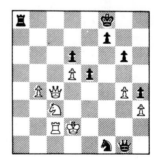

The forced end is 46 Ke2 Qe3+ 47 Kxf1 Ra1+ 48 Kg2 Qg3 mate.

GAME 18

White: P. Keres
(U.S.S.R.)

Black: L. Popov
(Bulgaria)

Played at Dortmund (West Germany) International Tournament, May 1973, Round 6.

Sicilian Defense
(New Taimanov Variation)

Popov uses a dynamic variation, and when White does not play energetically enough, Black gains dynamic equality. Early in the middlegame, Keres could draw by repeating moves, but, as White against a less famous opponent, he feels that he must try to win. Such hopes are forlorn, however, and Popov plays a perfect game. He gains some advantage by virtue of his chances for a Kingside attack. When Keres' defense is not the best, a beautiful combination decides the day.

1 e4	c5
2 Nf3	e6
3 Nc3	

Played often. Even so, the normal 3 d4 seems more flexible and better to me.

3 ...	a6
4 d4	cxd4

5 Nxd4	Qc7

The New Taimanov Variation. The Bulgarian IM has made it his specialty and feels quite comfortable in it. For maximum sucess - especially when playing someone who is better - it is important to select a variation which "feels comfortable".

6 g3	

White's next step is usually to develop the KB and then castle. The fianchetto is quite popular but without the development of Black's QN not quite as efficient as otherwise. For 6 Be2, see Tal-Hubner, Leningrad 1973, Game 54.

6 ...	Nf6

O.K., but more effective is 6... Bb4!, pretty much forcing 7 Nde2, and then 7 ...Nf6. White's formation is then a bit passive.

7 Bg2	d6
8 0-0	Bd7

Black goes about trying to develop his Queenside first. 8 ...Nc6?! is not accurate since after 9 Re1 Be7 White opens the a8-h1 diagonal and gains the advantage with 10 Nxc6 bxc6 11 e5! dxe5 12 Rxe5!. 9 ...Bd7?! is even worse since White has 10 Nd5!.

9 Re1	Be7

Black's move order takes away any chances White may have for tactics. Again 9...Nc6?! allows 10 Nd5! exd5 11 exd5+ Ne5 12 f4, with clear advantage to White.

| 10 a4 | Nc6 |
| 11 Nxc6 | Bxc6 |

Unquestionably the solid way to recapture and therefore to be played against a Keres. However, 11 ...bxc6!? may also be playable. Subsequently, in Round 13 against the West German master Suss, that is how Popov played, and after 12 Qe2 e5 13 b3 0-0 14 Bb2 Rfe8 15 Rad1 Bg4 16 Bf3 Bh3 17 Bg2 Bg4 the players agreed to split the point.

12 b3

This and the following are too passive to give Black any trouble. Only with 12 a5! b5 (otherwise 13 Be3) 13 axb6 e.p. Qxb6 14 Ra3!, as in Korsunski-Sideif-Zade, Baku 1975, can White hope for some advantage.

12 ...	0-0
13 Bb2	b6
14 Qd4	Rfd8
15 Rad1	Qb7

The opening phase has ended satisfactorily for Black. He has some pressure against White's e-pawn and will get in ...b5, thereby gaining some play on the Queenside. Even though Black has nothing beyond

the third rank, everything is harmoniously placed, and there are no weak spots in Black's camp. Black has full dynamic equality.

16 Rd2

Not a meaningful location for the Rook, but it is difficult for White to come up with concrete plans.

16 ...	b5!
17 axb5	axb5
18 b4	

Not a pretty move since it weakens the c4 square and the pawn itself is weak here. Nevertheless, Black's 18...b4 had to be prevented.

18 ...	Rac8
19 Ra1	Ra8
20 Rdd1?!	

As the better player *and White*, Keres feels honor-bound to play for the win. But the position is, if anything, considerably more comfortable for Black than for White.

White's best practical approach is to play 20 Re1!? and hope that Black will be satisfied to repeat the position after 20 ...Rac8 21 Ra1 Ra8, etc. Chances are good that he would do so.

	20 ...	Ne8!
	21 Qe3	Bf6
	22 h4	h6
	23 Re1	

White is still suffering from an inability to do anything.

	23 ...	Nc7!

Not so for Black, who is ready for 24 ...Na6 winning the b-pawn. White must exchange Rooks.

24 Rxa8	Nxa8!

Now the Knight is ready for ...Nb6 and ...Nc4. Thus White again, must rush to simplify.

25 Nd1	Bxb2
26 Nxb2	Nb6
27 Ra1	d5!

Black has gotten in this thematic central advance and stands at least equal. White must search for ways to hold the balance.

28 Qd4!

White gains by closing the center, and now threatens 29 e5! with advantage since Black's Bishop

would be very passive. Inferior are both 28 exd5?! Bxd5 29 Bxd5 Nxd5 30 Qd4 Qc6 with White having weaknesses both on the Queenside and Kingside and 28 e5?! d4! 29 Bxc6 Qxc6 30 Qe2 Nd5 31 Nd3 Qc4 with serious weaknesses in White's Queenside.

28 ...	e5!

A fine way to keep the position open. This reactivates Black's Bishop and underscores White's weaknesses on the Kingside.

29 Qxe5	dxe4
30 Rd1!	Re8!

But not 30 ...Rxd1+? 31 Nxd1 and in the endgame Black's weaknesses are more exploitable than White's, and White's Queen has a commanding central location.

31 Qc5?!

Up to here White has defended quite well, but from now on, apparently tired and frustrated by Black's perfect play, he quickly goes under. White does threaten 32 Rd6 but actually allows Black's Knight to head where it wants to with a gain of tempo. 31 Qd6 is better.

31 ...	Nd7
32 Qe3	Ne5
33 Rd6?!	

Starting to leave his King without protection.. 33 Ra1 is safer.

33 ...   Qa8!
34 Qb6?

Allowing the following combination which leads to a forced loss. Defensive resources are still offered by moves such as 34 Rd1, 34 Qc3, and 34 Qc5.

34 ...   Qa1+
35 Nd1   e3!!

Suddenly White has no defense. Thus if 36 Qxe3 Nf3+ or if 36 Bxc6 e2. And after 36 Bf1 Popov gives as simplest 36 ...Nf3+ 37 Kg2 Nd4+ 38 Rxc6 Qxd1!. The text is equally hopeless.

36 fxe3   Bxg2
37 Kxg2

The tactical 37 Rd8 is foiled by 37 ... Bc6 38 Rxe8+ Bxe8 39 Qd8 Kh7!.

37 ...   Qa8+!
38 Kg1   Nc4
White resigns

White's Queen, Rook, and Knight stand so awkwardly that he loses a whole Rook: 39 Qd4 Nxd6 40 Qxd6 Rd8, etc.

GAME 19

White: L. Portisch
(Hungary)

Black: P. Keres
(U.S.S.R.)

Played at Petropolis (Brazil) Interzonal Tournament, July 24, 1973, Round 1.

Queen's Gambit Declined (Semi-Tarrasch Variation)

For a repeat performance against the same opponent, Portisch prepares a strategic novelty in the early opening. Keres is not able to solve the requirements of the position, and when he ventures on a dubious Queen sortie, his position nearly becomes critical. Portisch sacrifices a pawn for strong initiative, regains it soon, and forces a vastly superior endgame. It is doubtful whether the endgame can be held even with perfect defense, but Keres is too demoralized to put up any reasonable effort, whereas Portisch is sharp all the way through. Portisch demonstrates very well how to defeat a superior opponent: a strategically meaningful opening idea, clear and incisive middlegame, transposition into a superior endgame, and energetic play there.

1 c4	Nf6

2 Nc3	e6
3 Nf3	c5

With this move Keres shows his interest in Tarrasch or Semi-Tarrasch formations. Instead, 3 ...d5 brings about the Orthodox Queen's Gambit Declined, and 3 ...Bb4 gives us Game 16.

4 g3	d5

Continuing with his plan. In the middle 1970's 4 ...b6 followed by 5 ...Bb7 became popular.

5 cxd5	Nxd5

Leading to the Semi-Tarrasch. The capture by the Knight prevents, at least for the moment, the imposition of an isolated d-pawn. However, Black has less central influence than after the "pure" Tarrasch, which would result after 5 ...exd5 6 d4.

6 Bg2	Be7
7 0-0	0-0
8 d4	Nc6
9 Nxd5	

Thus far both sides have developed simply and normally. Here, however, White had to make his first decision. The text leads to an exchange of Knights and a strengthening of Black's center and gives Black an isolated d-pawn. This strategically simple approach is part of Portisch's prepared plan and is fully playable. However, theoretically better chances for an advantage are offered by the more active and potentially sharper 9 e4!?, whether Black captures White's Knight or retreats to b6 or forward to b4.

9 ...   exd5

The only reasonable recapture. After 9 ...Qxd5? 10 Be3! White has a sizable lead in development and great potential for his KB to rake Black's Queenside.

10 Be3!?

The novelty Portisch prepared especially for this game. White applies additional pressure against Black's c-pawn, thus in effect forcing it to declare its intentions. White also overprotects the d4 square. Less than a year earlier at San Antonio 1972 against the same opponent, Portisch played 10 dxc5 Bxc5 11 Bg5 f6 12 Rc1 Bb6 13 Bd2, gained a minute advantage, and won when Keres didn't defend the middlegame accurately. The text move is quite successful in its maiden appearance. Current theory, however, contends that 10 dxc5! is White's best chance for a slight advantage.

10 ...   Bf6?!

Finding himself in an unfamiliar situation, Keres goes for counterplay. The future proves him wrong to do so. Equally unsatisfactory is 10

Qb6?! 11 dxc5 Bxc5 12 Bxc5 Qxc5 13 a3 and Black's isolated d-pawn was a permanent weakness in Petrosian- K.Grigorian, 1973 U.S.S.R. Championship, even though Black did squeeze out a draw on move 49. The blockading 10 ...c4! is correct. Then after the intended 11 Ne5?! (11 b3 with equality is better), 11 ...Bf5!, Black's coming play on the Queenside already gives him a slight edge, as in Tal-Alburt, 1975 U.S.S.R. Championship (draw in 31).

11 dxc5!   Bxb2
12 Rb1

As a consequence of the last two moves White's Rook now exerts significant pressure against Black's Queenside and will in due course penetrate there.

12 ...   Bf6
13 Ne1

In effect forces the d-pawn forward and thus increases the scope of White's KB. However, Black does gain some time and space. Therefore, 13 Nd4!? seems stronger as in Ornstein-Schneider, 1975 Swedish Championship. After 13 ...Qa5? (13 ...Re8 is better) 14 Bxd5 Rd8 White can gain a decisive advantage with 15 Bxc6!.

13 ...   d4
14 Bf4   Qa5?

A Queen sortie difficult to understand and explain. Keres is too fine a player not to realize that such a move- development is incomplete- is not positionally justified. Perhaps he felt adventurous in Round 1 or felt too dissatisfied with his position to consider playing normal moves. In any case, it is imperative to complete development. In order, therefore, is 14 ...Re8 15 Nd3 and now either 15 ...Bg4 or ...Na5 followed by 16 ...Bd7 and 17...Bc6. In either case, Black's disadvantage is small.

15 Nd3!

Be my guest! White gets a very strong initiative for the pawn. Moreover, it is hard to see how Black can develop his Queenside without giving a pawn back.

15 ...	Qxa2
16 Bd6	Re8

Keres criticizes this and sug-

gests instead 16 ...Rd8 17 Nf4 Be5. White clearly achieves a substantial advantage with 18 Bd5!, however.

17 Nf4

Planning Nd5 or Bd5, depending on circumstances. Black lacks a fruitful continuation, so his willingness to return the pawn and complete the development of the Queenside is understandable.

17 ...	Bf5
18 Rxb7	Be4
19 Bxe4	Rxe4
20 Qb1	

Excellent practical play and also no doubt the theoretically strongest move. The middlegame looks fairly unclear, but in the endgame White's control of the seventh rank and the passed c-pawn give him a significant advantage. Black must exchange Queens since 20 ... Qa6? is worse: 21 Qxe4 Qxb7 22 Nd5!.

20 ...	Qxb1
21 Rfxb1	Ree8

Keres does not like this either and recommends 21 ...Rc8. But then 22 Rd7! followed by doubling Rooks on the seventh also leaves Black in quite a precarious situation. If White plays perfectly - and Portisch does- there just seems to be no satisfactory defense.

22 Rc7	Rec8
23 Rbb7	Rxc7
24 Rxc7	

Black's Knight must now give way, and White's c-pawn can then move forward. Black originally planned to play 24...Nb4 but then decided that 25 Nd3! was too strong: 25...Nxd3 26 exd3, followed by pushing the c-pawn, or after 25 ...Nd5, 26 Rb7!, and again the c-pawn advances. The retreat 24... Nd8 is met by 25 Nd5 h5 26 Rd7, planning both 27 Nxf6+ gxf6 28 Be7 and 27 Nc7 followed by 28 Na6. Keres' actual move loses at least as quickly and surely.

24 ...	Na5
25 Nd5	Bd8
26 Ne7+	

Getting rid of Black's Bishop is the simplest way to win. If now 26 ...Kf8 27 Nc6+ Ke8 28 Nxd8 Kxd8 29 Rxf7, or if 26...Kh8 27 Rd7 h6 28 Nd5 Kg8 29 Nb4, followed by 30 c6.

26 ...	Bxe7
27 Bxe7	h6
28 c6!	

Passed pawns must be pushed.

28 ...	Rb8
29 Bd6	Kh7

Black has no way to prevent the loss of material. Two other choices are 29...Rb1+ 30 Kg2 Rc1 31

Rc8+ Kh7 32 c7, and the pawn soon queens, and 29 ... Rb6 30 Rc8+ Kh7 31 c7 Rxd6 32 Rh8+ Kxh8 33 c8=Q+ Kh7 34 Qf5+, winning the Knight.

30 Rxf7!

The mark of master technique: giving up one advantage (the passed c-pawn) for an even greater one (decisive material and positional superiority).

30 ...	Rb1+
31 Kg2	Nxc6
32 Rc7!	Nd8

The winner after 32...Rb6 is 33 Bf8, and after 32...Rc1, 33 Be5!.

33 Rxa7

The position Portisch had in mind. White is a pawn up and has eliminated Black's passed pawn. Black's d-pawn is very weak and White's Rook and Bishop combination has good chances to get at Black's g-pawn. Black is ultimately lost, though Keres manages to do it with extra speed.

33 ...	Rb5?!

Somewhat better is 33...Kg6 34 Be5 Ne6, though 35 g4! followed by 36 f4 is decisive.

34 f4	Nb7
35 Be5	Rb4
36 Bxd4!	g5

37 Kf3	Kg6
38 Ra6+	Kf7
39 e3	
Black resigns	

Black is two pawns down already and about to lose a third.

GAME 20

White: J. Rukavina
(Yugoslavia)

Black: V. Korchnoi
(U.S.S.R.)

Played at Leningrad (U.S.S.R.)
Interzonal Tournament, June 18,
1973, Round 12.

Queen's Gambit Declined (Meran Variation)

The most dramatic attacking game of the Leningrad Interzonal. After an unbalanced and fighting opening, Black achieves approximate equality. However, he indulges in time-wasting maneuvers, and White builds up a strong attacking formation. As the decisive action approaches, both contestants have exhausted almost all their time and have only seconds left for the remaining complications. Here Rukavina shows that he has nerves of steel. He sacrifices a Rook, follows it up accurately, and wins convincingly when Korchnoi misses the right defense. Later analysis showed the sacrifice not to be fully sound, but in a practical game, with seconds left on the clock, genius-level defenses are not to be found. For this game Rukavina received, deservedly, the prize for the most creative achievement.

1 Nf3	d5
2 d4	Nf6
3 c4	e6
4 Nc3	c6
5 e3	

Black's move order discourages the routine 5 Bg5 and thus White satisfies himself with allowing the Meran Variation. It is not that 5 Bg5 is not playable, but that with 5 ... dxc4!? 6 e4 b5 7 e5 h6 8 Bh4 g5 Black can force hair-raising complications. Modern players do not have anything per se against complications - witness the popularity of so many obscure variations in the Sicilian Najdorf - so the lack of popularity of this so-called "Botvinnik Variation" is simply a question of fashion. In the many years to come it may reappear in modern tournament practice.

(In the 1980's, mostly because of Garry Kasparov's exploits, 5 Bg5 has become very popular in grandmaster play.)

5 ...	Nbd7
6 Bd3	dxc4

Black's 6th and 7th moves form the idea behind the Meran. Black allows White to establish a strong central presence with an early e4, while he gets ready to challenge White's center from the flank with a ...c5.

7 Bxc4	b5
8 Bd3	Bb7

The early lines went 8 ... a6, followed by 9 ... c5. Modern tournament practice has preferred the developmental text.

9 e4

White logically and consistently establishes a strong central presence. Nevertheless the quiet 9 0-0 is at least equally good. For this see Game 34, Portisch-Polugaevsky, Portoroz 1973.

9 ...	b4
10 Na4	c5

Doubly attacking White's center: d4 from the flank and e4 by Bishop and Knight. Thus White's next is forced.

11 e5	Nd5
12 dxc5	

White has two fundamental choices here: either to capture Black's c-pawn with the Knight or pawn or to ignore it with, for example, 12 0-0. After the latter Black usually continues 12 ...cxd4, and White 13 Re1. This is a good flexible way to handle the position for White and perhaps he retains a slight edge. The capture with 12 Nxc5 gives Black excellent chances for equality after 12 ...Nxc5! 13 dxc5 Bxc5 since 14 Bb5+ leads to nothing after 14 ...Ke7, when Black has excellent control of the central squares to compensate for his King location.

The text move is White's third possibility. It is probably the most innocuous one because White's QN has nothing to do on the edge of the board.

12 ...	Qa5!
13 0-0	Bxc5
14 Re1	

Because of the active location of Black's pieces, White has little opportunity for an initiative. 14 Nxc5 Nxc5 just further develops Black, and 14 a3 Be7! 15 Bd2 0-0 16 Re1 Rfd8 17 Qb3 Rab8 18 Be4 Bc6 19 axb4 Bxb4 gives Black sound equality, as in Uhlmann-Larsen, Monte Carlo 1968.

14 ...	N5b6
15 Nxb6	Qxb6

The chances here are approximately in balance. Black has excellent development and central presence. His one slight drawback is that he is short of potential defenders on the Kingside and so to castle there immediately is fraught with clear dangers; e.g., after White's Ng5.

16 Qe2   Rc8
17 a3!?

Immediately challenging Black
to a sharp fight. The developmental
17 Bd2 is safer.

17 ...   Bxf3!?

Black in turn responds with a
fighting move. There are two advantages to the text: White's potentially
useful attacking Knight is exchanged
and White's   pawn structure is
weakened. But the demerit is also
clear: by exchanging his marvelous
QB, Black allows White's Queen
and KB strong pressure against
Black's Kingside. All in all, it's a
move to play in going for a risky
win. The balancing, safe move is
17...a5.

18 gxf3!

Forced, since 18 Qxf3? allows
18...Bd4 19 Qg3 bxa3! with advantage to Black: 20 Rxa3 Bxe5!, etc.

18 ...   b3?!

Sealing of the Queenside is
fine with White since it allows him
to concentrate   on his attacking
chances against Black's Kingside.
Here   18...Bd4 is harmless since
White can protect his e-pawn easily
with f4. Black has no particular way
to strengthen his pressure, so here is
a good time for 18...0-0!. The unbalanced position then offers dynami-

cally even chances.

19 Rd1   Rc7

Protecting the Knight so that
castling   doesn't   allow White
Bxh7+ followed by Rxd7.

20 Bf4   0-0
21 Rd2   Nb8?

The consequence of 18 ...b3?! is
that Black has difficulties finding
active play. But the Knight retreat is
pointless, time wasting, and wrong.
21... Rfc8! is correct followed by 22
...Nf8!. Then Black's King gets
needed protection and the doubled
Rooks can get some play along the c-
file.

22 Rad1   Nc6
23 Qe4   g6
24 Bg5!

White is efficiently fashioning
strong play against Black's King,
particularly on the dark squares.

24 ...   Rd7?!

Rukavina questions this move
since Black chases the Queen pretty
much where it wants to go. The
immediate 24...Be7 saves a tempo.

25 Qf4!   Be7

25...Rd4?! is a further waste of
time because of 26 Be4!.

26	Bf6	Bxf6
27	exf6	

White's triple isolated f-pawns are a horrible strategic weakness *but* the f-pawn on the sixth is potentially a mortal enemy of the Black King. Rukavina has quite consistently aimed at reaching this type of position, correctly believing that his attacking power will prevent Black from getting at his pawn weaknesses. At this point White has a significant advantage, and Black must find the only moves to prevent being mated.

27	...	Kh8!

27 ...Qd8? is refuted by 28 Bxg6!.

28 Be4!

Excellent central play. White positions his Bishop actively and invites an exchange of Rooks, which would increase White's dominance because Black's remaining Rook would be tied to protecting his King.

28	...	Nd4
29	Kg2	

The King will not be particularly well placed here. Therefore, 29 Kh1!? is possibly better.

29	...	Rg8
30	h4	

Played to prevent a potential ...g5 but has the disadvantage of loosening White's King position. The centralizing 30 Qe5! is strongest. If then 30 ...Nc6 31 Bxc6 Rxd2 32 Rxd2 Qxc6 33 Rd6 Qc8 34 Qd4 and White has complete control of the board. Therefore, 30 ...Rgd8 is necessary, but after 31 h4! White is a couple of tempos ahead of the game. Starting here both sides were about out of time, and so their failure to play perfect chess is understandable.

30	...	Qc5
31	Qg5	e5!?

To allow the endgame bind after 31 ...Qxg5?! 32 hxg5 Rgd8 33 f4 is plain suicide.

32	f4!	Ne6
33	Qxe5!	

White may have been able to sacrifice the Queen with 33 Rxd7 Nxg5 34 fxg5, but the situation is not clear after 34 ...Qc4!. And why should White give up his Queen when he has a won position by retaining it?

33 ...	Rxd2
34 Rxd2	Qc1
35 Bd5!?	

With seconds remaining on his clock White is brave enough to sacrifice a whole Rook, and Caissa rewards such bravery. Objectively, though, the active, logical 35 Rd7! is correct. Black then lacks a satisfactory continuation: if 35...Nxf4+ 36 Kh2 Ne2 37 Rxf7! Qg1+ 38 Kh3 Qf1+ (38...h5 allows 39 Qxh5+!! gxh5 40 Rh7 mate) 39 Kg4 h5+ (if 39 ...Qxf2 40 Rxh7+ Kxh7 41 Qh5 mate!) 40 Kg5!.

35 ...	Qxd2

There is no objective basis for criticizing this natural move, especially since it keeps the draw in hand. Subsequently, however, it was discovered that with 35...g5!! Black could win; e.g., 36 hxg5 Nxg5! 37 fxg5 Qxd2 and Black's attack would come first. But how is it possible to notice something as exotic as 35 ...g5!! when there is no time to think?

36 Bxe6	Qd8??

This blunder, however, is inexcusable. Obviously 36...fxe6? allows 37 f7+ Rg7 38 f8=Q mate, and not so obviously 36...Re8? loses to 37 Qc7!! Qe2 38 Qxf7! Qe4+ 38 Kg3

and Black will be mated on g7. 36 ...Qd1! is fairly logical and obvious though, and after 37 Bxf7 Qg4+ 38 Kf1 Qd1+, Black has a clear perpetual check.

37 Bxf7	Rf8
38 Qe7!	

Winning by force, and obviously overlooked by Black. There is no defense to the coming 39 Bxg6!.

38 ...	h5
39 Bxg6	Qd5+
Black resigns	

There is little question that after 40 Kh2 Qg8 Black is lost: 41 f7 Qg7 42 Qg5, etc. Even so, the circumstances surrounding the resignation are interesting and illustrative of the tremendous nervous energy a master expends in tough games in tough tournaments. After Korchnoi played 39...Qd5+ (by far the only reasonable move), he decided he didn't like it after all, moved the Queen back to d8, and from there to b6 (a horrible move which allows three mate-in ones!). This both perplexed and shocked Rukavina, who was in terrible time pressure also. What Rukavina did was repunch Korchnoi's clock and gesture to indicate that the completed move (39...Qd5+) must stand. At this point the controlling arbiter was about to interfere, but Korchnoi simplified matters by quickly resigning. Eye-witnesses report that this episode so unnerved Korchnoi, that he spent the next several hours walking it off on the streets of Leningrad. This must have been excellent medicine, for Korchnoi quickly recovered his form and nerves, won a number of games, and finished in a tie for first place with Karpov.

GAME 21

**White: V. Korchnoi
(U.S.S.R.)**

**Black: T. Ghitescu
(Rumania)**

Played in European Team Championship at Bath (England), July 7, 1973, Round 2.

King's Indian Defense (Normal Variation)

Ghitescu adopts a variation which is a specialty of Rumanian masters, and after very exact and careful play he gains clear equality. White seems to have little else but to acquiesce to wholesale exchanges and a dead-drawn endgame. However, Korchnoi cannot get himself to do so. Instead, in order to play for the win he starts retreating his pieces. Suddenly, Black is better. A further error allows a devastating pin which leads to the loss of a pawn. But Korchnoi "prefers" to lose a piece and must resign on move 33. From complete equality to a painful loss in just nine moves - White's harsh penalty for refusing to look for the truth on the chess board.

	1	d4	Nf6
	2	c4	g6
	3	Nc3	Bg7
	4	e4	d6
	5	Nf3	0-0

6 Be2

White's development carries the plain name "Normal Variation." The name is apt for two reasons: (1) White's development is simple, unassuming, and center-oriented. He will bring out his minor pieces first and then look at the subsequent plan for action. (2) When the King's Indian had its resurgence after World War II, this variation was the most common.

6 ...   e5

Having castled, Black initiates thematic pressure against White's center. The initial target is invariably d4.

7 0-0

By far the most flexible response. White can, however, obtain a slight endgame advantage with 7 dxe5 dxe5 8 Qxd8. Closing the center immediately with 7 d5 is called the Petrosian Variation and was quite fashionable in the late 1950's.

7 ...   exd4!?

The thematic move to apply pressure to the center is 7 ...Nc6, which is also the usual move here. Fairly common also is 7 ...Nbd7. The text is a specialty of Rumanian Masters. Generally it is not advantageous to give up the fight for a central square-such as the d4 square here- without gaining something in return. Here Black hopes to get quick pressure against e4.

8 Nxd4   Re8
9 f3

There is no other satisfactory way to protect the e-pawn. Obviously awkward is 9 Bf3, and 9 Qc2 is also without problems for Black. Denker-Gheorghiu, 1971 U.S. Open continued 9...Nbd7 10 Be3 c6 11 Rfe1 Nc5 12 f3 a5 with a fine game for Black.

9 ...   c6!

Planning to annihilate White's center, starting with 10...d5. White has two logical responses.

10 Kh1

This is one of them. By removing the King from the a7-g1 diagonal, White eliminates many of the tactical possibilities which would result after Black's ...Qb6. The alternative is 10 Nc2, which directly aims at preventing Black's 10...d5. Nevertheless, Black still must proceed thus; otherwise White's central superiority will quickly become overpowering. After 10...d5! 11 cxd5 cxd5 12 exd5 Bf5, Black had good play for the pawn in Botez-Gheorghiu, 1966 Rumanian Championship: 13 Bc4 Qb6+ 14 Kh1 Na6 15 g4?! Rac8.

10 ...   d5

10...Nbd7 is possible, but the text is unquestionably the most consistent approach.

(Currently 10...Nbd7 is the most common move for Black.)

11 cxd5   cxd5
12 Bb5

By forcing Black to interpose on d7, White wins Black's d-pawn. This turns out to be only temporary, however. Instead of the text move, Yugoslav GM Bukic recommends 12 Bg5. It seems to me that Black retains equality after 12...dxe4.

12 ...   Nbd7!?

Black must interpose something since 12...Rf8?! allows 13 e5, and after 12...Re7?!, too strong is 13 Bg5!. But what should Black interpose? Theory considers only 12...Bd7, but then 13 exd5! leads to a slight plus because Black has difficulties in recovering his pawn. The text is an interesting attempt at strengthening Black's play. He refrains from any overt action to immediately recover material and develops his Queenside with gain of time by pushing back White's KB. Black expects that in due course White's advanced d-pawn will be unsupportable.

13 exd5   a6
14 Ba4   b5

15 Nc6	Qb6
16 Bb3	Bb7

This is basically the critical position for judging Black's opening idea. He has completed his development, his pieces stand harmoniously, and with an imminent ...Bxc6 he can recover the sacrificed pawn. Clearly White must give back the material, but can he transform the material advantage into a positional one?

17 a4

Leads to nothing but a general exchange of Queenside material. The only worthwhile idea is 17 Bg5!, as GM Gheorghiu suggested, with the idea of 17 ...Bxc6?! 18 dxc6 Qxc6 19 Nd5! with some advantage to White because of his active piece placement. (The immediate threat is 20 Rc1 followed by 21 Nc7.) Instead of 17 ...Bxc6?! Black should instead continue with 17 ...Nc5 or 17 ...a5!?. His chances for equality then are excellent.

17 ...	Nc5!

18 Bg5	Nxb3
19 Qxb3	Bxc6
20 dxc6	Qxc6
21 axb5	axb5
22 Rxa8	

The position is rather equal and symmetrical and a draw here would be a consistent result. Neither side has any realistic winning chances. If instead 22 Qxb5 Black's simplest response is 22...Rxa1! 23 Rxa1 Qxb5 24 Nxb5 Rb8, and Black will soon recover the b-pawn for dead equality: 25 Nc3 h6!, etc.

22 ...	Rxa8
23 Rc1	

With this move White shows his determination to play for a win. Again complete equality results after 23 Qxb5 Qxb5 24 Nxb5 Rb8, etc.

23 ...	h6!
24 Be3	

A blunder is 24 Nxb5?? hxg5! and Black's Queen is safe because of the back-rank mate after 25 Rxc6?! Ra1+, etc. The first rank weakness will plague White throughout the game.

24 ...	Qc4!
25 Qd1?	

Black has played excellently all the way through, and White has to concede the honorable draw after 25 Qxb5 Qxb5 26 Nxb5 Rb8. But

Korchnoi cannot face such a prospect. However, playing for a win by retreating one's pieces invariably leads to the opposite.

> **25 ...   b4!**

Of course. Black now gains space on the Queenside and across the board. Black is already better.

26 Na4

Equivalent is 26 Ne4.

> **26 ...   Qe6!**
> **27 Nb6   Re8**
> **28 Nc4?**

Walks into a deadly pin. The safe 28 Bg1! is required. Obviously Black has some advantage, but White should be able to protect his weak spots.

> **28 ...   Rc8!**
> **29 Qd3**

29 b3 allows 29 ...Rxc4! 30 Rxc4 Qxe3.

> **29 ...   Nd5!**
> **30 Bd2**

About equivalent to 30 Re1 Nxe3 31 Nxe3 Bxb2.

> **30 ...   Bxb2!**

A pretty move based on back-rank mate motifs: 31 Nxb2? Rxc1+

32 Bxc1 Qe1+ 33 Qf1 Qxf1 mate.

> **31 Re1?**

After 31 Rb1 or 31 Rf1 White has a miserable position a pawn down. But what happens now is worse.

> **31 ...   Nf4!**

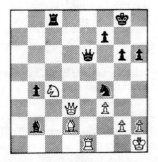

Another back-rank combination leads to a decisive win of material. 32 Rxe6 Nxd3 leads to a hopeless endgame, and 32 Bxf4? obviously leads to mate. Only marginally better than the text is 32 Qd6 Qxc4! 33 Bxf4 Bg7 and the passed b-pawn leads to a sure win.

> **32 Qc2?!   Qxc4**
> **33 Re8+**

If 33 Qxb2, 33...Nd3 is decisive.

> **33 ...   Kh7**
> **White Resigns**

After 34 Rxc8 Black mates with 34...Qf1.

GAME 22

White: R. Hubner
(West Germany

Black: V. Korchnoi
(U.S.S.R.)

Played in Public Training Match at Solingen (West Germany), December 1973, Match Game 3.

Ruy Lopez
(Open Variation)

Korchnoi plays into a variation that Hubner has had success with in the past. The result here too is that Black does not gain full equality out of the opening. White has control of the dark squares, the superior Bishop, pressure against Black's d-pawn, and attacking chances on the Kingside. With careful maneuvering Black's position should be defensible, but Korchnoi does not feel comfortable in the position and puts up very weak resistance. Hubner first wins a pawn, then gains two pieces for a Rook, and also obtains a killing attack against Black's Kingside. Soon Black's situation is so hopeless that he resigns even as he makes a desperate Rook sacrifice. Overall the game is an easy task for Hubner, and his clever opening selection deserves much credit.

1 e4	e5
2 Nf3	Nc6
3 Bb5	a6
4 Ba4	Nf6
5 0-0	Nxe4

This Open Variation was briefly discussed in Game 13. It has never-been as popular as the closed variation. Its leading practicioner was ex-World Champion Dr. Max Euwe. Of the present leading grandmasters, only Korchnoi uses it- and secondarily at that. As a matter of fact, Korchnoi is the author of the section on the Open Variation in the *Encyclopedia of Chess Openings* published in 1974. *(The Open Variation of the Ruy Lopez has become Korchnoi's main defense to 1 e4 and he also is the author of the section on the Open Variation in the Second Edition of the Encyclopedia of Chess Openings, published in 1981.)*

6 d4!

To hope for any advantage, White must hurriedly open lines against Black's King. 6 Re1 Nc5 leads to nothing.

6 ...   b5

The normal way of handling the Open. There is no brutal refutation of the Riga Variation: 6...exd4 7 Re1 d5 8 Nxd4 Bd6!?; nonetheless White is demonstrably better after the following complications: 9 Nxc6 Bxh2+ 10 Kh1 Qh4 11 Rxe4+dxe4 12 Qd8+ Qxd8 13 Nxd8+ Kxd8 14 Kxh2.

7 Bb3	d5
8 dxe5	Be6

We now have the normal position in this variation. Black's disadvantage stems from an inherent looseness in his position: Queenside, d-pawn, Knight on e4, possibly an insufficiently protected Kingside. As partial compensation Black does have fairly smooth development, but White's position is without noticeable weaknesses, so there is little that Black can hope to accomplish against it. White has the choice of two main approaches. The older, solid move is 9 c3, which strengthens d4 and allows the KB to retreat to c2. The alternative is the game continuation.

9 Qe2

This variation became fashionable after its successful use in the 1948 Match Tournament for the World Championship. It prepares dynamic undermining of Black's d-pawn by means of 10 Rd1 and 11 c4.

9 ...	Be7
10 Rd1	0-0?!

After the debacle here, Korchnoi never ventured this subvariation again. In Match Game 5 here and in Match Game 4 against Mecking in the 1974 Candidates Matches, he switched to 10...Nc5, eventually equalizing. Both games were drawn.

11 c4	bxc4
12 Bxc4	

The first important position in our subvariation. The pressure against Black's d-pawn is quite real, and there are no smooth ways to minimize it. Therefore considerable theoretical work has been done on the Queen sacrifice 12...dxc4 13 Rxd8 Rfxd8, but after 14 Nc3!, White's chances are indisputably superior. Black's most common defensive method is 12...Qd7 13 Nc3 Nxc3 14 bxc3 f6 15 exf6 Bxf6. In E.C.O., Korchnoi's analysis concludes that this variation gives Black eventual equality. But since he himself doesn't follow his recommendations, his confidence in them must not be total.

12 ...   Bc5

Another reasonable continuation that Korchnoi had previously played with success. The exchange of the dark-square Bishops gives Black some defensive time but weakens considerably the dark squares in his position. This idea is playable but does not lead to full equality.

13 Be3	**Bxe3**
14 Qxe3	**Qb8**

The double attack on the KB and b-pawn forces White's reply.

15 Bb3	**Qb6**

In Matanovic- Korchnoi, Yugoslavia-U.S.S.R. 1966, Korchnoi played 15 ...Na5, and after 16 Nbd2 Qa7! 17 Qxa7 Rxa7 18 Rac1 c5 19 Nxe4 Nxb3 Black had equality. Subsequently in Hubner-Demarre, World Student Championship, Dresden 1969, White improved with 16 Ne1! (threat 17 f3) Nxb3 17 axb3 Qb6 18 Qxb6 cxb6 19 b4! f6 20 f3 Ng5 21 exf6 gxf6 22 Nc3 and gained a clear endgame advantage. Thus Hubner was looking forward to a repeat performance. However, Korchnoi used the move in the 1973 U.S.S.R. Championship, which concluded shortly before this match, and thus is the first one to vary. Hubner does demonstrate that in his hands it is White for choice, anyway. *(In the 1981 edition of ECO, Korchnoi considers 15 ...Na5 as Black's correct move and after 16 Ne1 Nxb3 17 axb3 gives 17 ...f5! as the improvement for eventual equality.)*

16 Qe2!

Tukmakov-Korchnoi, 1973 U.S.S.R. Championship, went 16 Qxb6 cxb6 17 Na3 (17 Bxd5?? Rad8 18 Bb3 Bxb3 and Black wins) 17 ...Rfd8 18 Nc2 Na5 19 Nb4 (19 Ncd4!? with a small plus is better) 19 ... Nc4! 20 Bxc4 dxc4 21 Nxa6 Rxd1+ 22 Rxd1 h6! 23 Nb4 Ra4 and Black had equality (24 a3 c3!). However, having lost the first two match games, Hubner wants more than a minute endgame advantage.

16 ...	**Rad8**

An alternate approach, suggested by Petrosian, is 16 ...Ne7 with ...c5 as a follow up.

17 Nc3!	**Nxc3**
18 bxc3	**Qc5**

Korchnoi's attempted improvement on the 18 ...Ne7 of Tal-Geller, Budva 1967, in which White was clearly better after 19 Rab1 Qa5 20 c4 Rfe8?! 21 Ng5. With the text Black further protects the d-pawn and thus threatens 19 ...Bg4 with counterplay, while he prevents White's c4. Even so Black's position is without many prospects, and the a-pawn will soon need protection.

19 h3!	**Bc8**

Thereby planning some play against White's e-pawn after a ...Rfe8. Equivalent to the text is 19 ...a5.

20 Qd3!

Aiming at h7 after a Bc2 or Ng5. Black's Kingside is now clearly short of defenders.

20 ...   Rfe8
21 Re1

With White's e-pawn protected, the potential Ng5 becomes a stronger threat.

21 ...   g6

There is no way to avoid this weakening.

22 Rad1!

White has a lovely harmonious position with all his pieces actively placed. White has potential against Black's Kingside, Queenside, d-pawn, and dark squares. All that Black can do is laboriously try to protect his weak spots.

22 ...   a5?

And this just creates a new one on b5. The defensive 22 ...Ne7 is in order.

23 Ba4!

With the simple but devastating threat of 24 Qb5! which would win at least a pawn.

23 ...   Bd7??

Even so there is no reason to panic. Unpinning the Knight is in order; i.e., either 23 ...Re7 or the safer 23..Rf8. Black's position is quite unpleasant, but at least he has a position.

24 Qxd5

Wins a pawn and the game. Black's house of cards collapses completely.

24 ...   Qb6
25 Ng5!

Making hay while the sun shines is the surest way to riches. The weaknesses of Black's Kingside are irreparable.

25 ...   Rf8
26 Qc4!

Threatening 27 Rxd7 and 27 Qh4, among others.

26 ...   Nb8

Black has *sacrificed* a pawn to
get this position?

27 Rb1	Qa6
28 Qh4	h5
29 Rxb8!	

Adding a decisive material
superiority to his positional one.
Only *Black's* time pressure makes
him play on: he has no time to recognize the hopelessness of his situation!

29 ...	Rxb8
30 Bxd7	Qd3
31 Ne4!	Rb6
32 e6!	fxe6

33 Qe7	Qd5
34 Ng5	Rxf2
Black resigns	

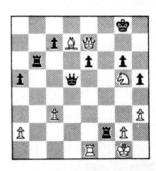

White had a multitude of wins,
among them 35 Bxe6+ Rxe6 36
Qh7+ Kf8 37 Nxe6+ Ke8 38 Nxc7+.

GAME 23

White: E. Cobo
(Cuba)

Black: G. Kuzmin
(U.S.S.R.)

Played at Capablanca Memorial Tournament, Cienfuegos (Cuba) February- March, 1973.

King's Indian Defense (Normal Variation)

Black decides to surprise his opponent with an opening novelty. But the "novelty" is so antipositional that Black is significantly worse almost immediately. A further error makes it impossible for him to develop his Queenside smoothly. On the other hand, White systematically obtains the advantage along the d-file and on the Queenside. Black's premature attempt at counterplay is quashed efficiently, and then all of Black's weaknesses come home to roost. Kuzmin had a successful tournament at Cienfuegos; Cobo did not. In this game, however, White shows that poor chess moves will be punished quite severely. Starting with move 7 Black is never in the game.

1	c4	Nf6
2	Nc3	g6
3	e4	d6
4	d4	Bg7
5	Nf3	0-0

6 Be2

With some transposition of moves the normal variation of the King's Indian has been reached. We already saw this variation in Game 21, in which Black continued with the usual 6 ...e5.

6 ...　　　　c6

Less common but playable. Black still plans ...e5 but first establishes control of d5.

7 0-0　　　　Qb6?

Officially this is an opening innovation, but it is so bad that it must be called an opening error. The Queen has no chance of leading the attack on White's d-pawn and will be driven back with loss of time. As mentioned above, 7 ...e5 is correct. If Black is in the mood to experiment, then 7 ...a6 intending ...b5 is a reasonable try.

8 Qc2!

Protects the e-pawn and b-pawn and frees d1 for the KR. White gains the advantage with simple good moves.

**8 ...　　　　Re8
9 h3!**

To play Be3 without being bothered by ...Ng4.

9	....	e5
10	dxe5!	dxe5
11	Be3	Qc7
12	Rfd1	

The resolution of the center tension is theoretically on Black's terms. But here White gains a clear advantage in development and control of the d-file. His advantage is considerable.

12 ...   Nbd7?

Black will now have extreme difficulty developing his Queenside. 12 ...Be6 is imperative.

13 b4!

To establish a grip on d6.

13	...	Nf8
14	Bc5	N6d7

Clumsy, but otherwise the e-pawn can't be protected.

15	Bd6	Qd8
16	c5	

A dream position for White out of a closed opening. He has a bind on the Queenside and control of the d-file, whereas Black's forces are completely passive.

16 ...   Qf6
17 Bc4!

Excellent nonroutine play. White prepares to exchange, as soon as it appears, Black's only potentially active piece.

17	...	Ne6
18	Bxe6	Qxe6
19	Na4	

On the way to c4 where it will control d6 and attack the e-pawn. Other good ideas are 19 a4 and 20 b5 and even the immediate 19 b5!?.

19	...	Nf8
20	Nb2	f6
21	Nc4	Qf7
22	a4	Be6
23	Nfd2	Rac8

Black has laboriously managed to bring out his Queenside pieces, but overall he is very cramped, his prospects bleak.

24 a5

Clearly planning a6. The immediate 24 f4! is also very strong.

24 ...   Bxc4

Hoping to develop his Knight to the vacated e6 square. After 24 ...a6 White can play 25 f4!.

25 Nxc4   Ne6

To allow White's next is quite undesirable, but so is 25 ...a6 26 f4!.

26 a6!   Nd4?

Black's first and last attacking move in this game. It makes matters worse by giving up control of f4, but human nature wants at least to threaten something.

**27 Qd3   Red8
28 f4!**

With Black's Queenside in ruins, White turns to the center, where he establishes a new Black weakness - the e-pawn. White's play is a model of logic and simplicity.

**28 ...   Ne6
29 fxe5   fxe5
30 Qf1!**

This quiet retreat wins material by force, since the e-pawn can't be protected.

**30 ...   Qxf1+
31 Kxf1   Rd7
32 Bxe5**

The well-deserved first fruit.

**32 ...   Bxe5
33 Nxe5   Rxd1+
34 Rxd1   bxa6
35 Rd6!**

Forcing the Knight back.

**35 ...   Nd8
36 Rd7**

With the penetration of the Rook, the game is over. Black's best now is 36...a5 37 bxa5 Ne6. But after 38 Nd3!, White is a clear pawn ahead and has the vastly superior position.

**36 ...   Rb8?!
37 Rxa7
Black resigns**

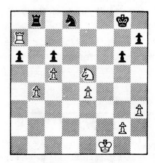

37...Rxb5 loses to 38 Ra8, and Black has no reasonable move to counter White's threatened 38 Rxa6.

GAME 24

White: G. Kuzmin
(U.S.S.R.)

Black: B. Larsen
(Denmark)

Played at Leningrad (U.S.S.R.) Interzonal Tournament, June 17, 1973, Round 11.

Sicilian Defense

Larsen reacts to an unusual variation with an even less common subvariation and quickly succeeds in throwing White off course. As a result, White remains a pawn down with nothing to show for it. A momentary lapse by Black does allow White to gain good drawing chances. But after White muffs his chance, Black scores a convincing endgame win. An effective fighting win very much in Larsen's style, with psychological overtones throughout.

1	e4	c5
2	Nf3	Nc6
3	Bb5	

A continuation significantly less common than 3 d4. It has two major points: to weaken Black's pawn formation with a timely Bxc6 and to quickly complete Kingside development by castling.

3	...	Nf6!?

The most popular defenses are 3...e6 and 3...g6. We'll see an example of the latter in Game 44, Hecht-Spassky, Dortmund 1973. But the text is very much in the Larsen tradition: he selects a move which, though playable, is not currently popular, and thus forces the opponent to start solving practical problems at a very early stage.

4	e5

Something must, of course, be done about the attacked e-pawn, and this is one response. The protecting 4 Nc3 allows 4...Nd4! with equality, since after 5 Nxd4 cxd4 Black gains time because of the attack on the QN. White's most flexible and perhaps best plan is Bronstein's 4 Qe2!?

4	...	Nd5!

At first glance, 4...Ng4!? to attack the e-pawn seems attractive. However, after 5 Bxc6! dxc6 6 h3! Nh6 7 0-0 g6 8 d3 Bg7 9 Nc3, Black's KN remains out of action, and this yields White the better chances, in Seret-Puhm, 1975 French Championship.

5	0-0

This quiet move leads to nothing, but even after the more active 5 Nc3, Black keeps a steady equality with 5...Nc7! 6 a4 g6 7 0-0 Bg7 8 Re1 0-0 9 d3 Nd4 10 Bc4 d5 11 exd6 e.p. Qxd6, as in Haag-Padevsky 1958.

| 5 ... | Qc7 |

Here too there is nothing wrong with 5 ...Nc7!, but Larsen characteristically selects a more unbalancing plan.

| 6 Re1 | e6 |
| 7 b3?! | |

Rather too slow. Larsen's fighting approach is starting to bear fruit. White should himself play actively with 7 Nc3! but has allowed Black to preempt the fight plan.

| 7 ... | b6 |

To get the QB onto a useful central diagonal.

8 Bf1?!

Again very passive. Both 8 Bc4 with the plan 9 Bxd5 and 10 Nc3 and 8 Bd3 with the idea 9 Be4 are better.

8	Bb7
9 Bb2	a6
10 Na3	Be7
11 Nc4	0-0

A psychologically interesting moment. Black has completed his development healthily and now plans to liquidate White's center outpost with 12 ...f6. Black can then expect to have a slight plus. Such an outcome is logical because White has consistently refrained from meeting the challenge to his move-one initiative.

12 Nd6?

After running from a fight for his first eleven moves White finds that he doesn't like his position. So he makes a complete about face and sacrifices a pawn - a valuable central pawn at that - to open the position. However, since he has fullfilled none of the prerequisites for such an opening to be effective, his chances for success are minute, and the text move must be rated as the losing moment.

12	Bxd6
13 exd6	Qxd6
14 d4	cxd4
15 Nxd4	Nf4!
16 Nxc6	

(Instead of the text, Kuzmin, in the Russian language tournament book, gives as better 16 c4! and feels that White has a nice position as compensation for the pawn. I believe that this evaluation is over optimistic.)

| 16 ... | Qxc6 |

So Black has a sound extra pawn and his QB has a marvelous diagonal. None of White's tactics have a chance of success: 17 Bxg7? is refuted by 17...Nh3+, and 17 Qd4 leads to nothing after 17 ...Nh3+ 18 Kh1 f6 19 Qh4 Ng5.

17 Qg4	Ng6
18 c4	d6
19 Rad1	e5
20 Re3	f5!

With his extra central pawn, it is actually Black who should have the superior attacking chances.

21 Qg5	Rf6
22 Rg3	f4
23 Rgd3	

White's situation is critical. 23 Rg4? loses to 23...Bc8, and 23 Rh3 is rather pointless. So White hopes for some miracle along the d-file.

| 23 ... | Ne7? |

By moving too quickly, Black throws away almost all of his advantage. As Larsen tells it, he saw the following sacrifice but overlooked something. After the accurate 23 ...Nh8!, planning the attacking ...Rg6 and the defensive ...Nf7, White's game would be in the last moments. But after the text move, the fight is renewed.

| 24 Rxd6! | Rxd6 |

25 Rxd6	Qxd6
26 Bxe5	

The mate threat on g7 allows White to win Black's Knight, thus leaving White with only the small material disadvantage of B and pawn for R. Also very important is that White's Q and QB are very active and several of Black's pawns are weak. White's chances for a draw are excellent here.

26 ...	Qg6
27 Qxe7	Be4

After 27...Re8 28 Qxb7 Rxe5 29 Qxa6, White has two pawns for the Exchange and Black has no decisive continuation. A serious alternative is 27...Bxg2 28 Bxg2 f3 29 Qxg7+ Qxg7 30 Bxg7, but, as both Larsen and Tseitlin note, White can hold after either 30 ...fxg2 31 Bd4! b5 32 cxb5 axb5 33 a4!, and after the disappearance of the Queenside pawns Black has no winning chances, or after 30...Kxg7 31 Bxf3

Rd8 32 Bd5 and White has two
pawns for the Exchange and can
keep out Black's Rook.

28 c5!

Superior to 28 Bxf4?! Re8 29
Qg5 Qxg5 30 Bxg5 Bb1, when
Black has excellent winning chances
since he either wins the a-pawn or
gets his Rook to the eighth rank.

| 28 ... | bxc5 |

A way to lose is 28...Re8?? 29
Bc4+ Kh8 30 Bxg7+.

29 Bxf4

Spoiling the fruits of his previous ingenious play. Correct is the
obvious 29 Bc4+ Kh8 and then 30
Bxg7+ Qxg7 31 Qxe4. Larsen feels
that White's drawing chances are excellent because all Black's pawns
are so weak.

| 29 ... | Re8 |
| 30 Qd6 | |

30 Qxc5? loses to 30 ...Bxg2.

30 ...	Qxd6
31 Bxd6	Rd8
32 Bc4+	

32 Bxc5? loses a piece after 32
...Rd1 and 33...Bd3.

| 32 ... | Bd5!! |

Gets rid of a pair of Bishops and
leads to a winnable R vs. B endgame
in which White has only one pawn
for the exchange. Instead, after 32
...Kh8 33 f3, White has some drawing chances since Black's King is
far from the e-pawn after 33 ...Rxd6
34 fxe4.

| 33 Bxd5+ | Kh8 |
| 34 g3 | |

Unfortunately for White, 34
Bxc5? Rxd5 wins a piece since
White must part with his Bishop to
save his King.

| 34 ... | Rxd6 |
| 35 Bc4 | g5! |

In general, with pawns on both
sides of the board, one pawn for the
exchange is insufficient to hold the
game. Invariably the stronger side is
able to penetrate somewhere. So
too here. There is no way to set up a
satisfactory defensive formation.
White's 37th and 38th moves do
lose time, but in the larger picture
that is inconsequential. White is
theoretically quite lost, and his *practical* chances also are scant.

36 Kg2	Kg7
37 a4	a5
38 Kf3	Rh6
39 Kg2	Kf6
40 h3	Ke5

Black's King cannot be stopped
from reaching a useful location. The

position is simple enough that
Larsen did not even bother to adjourn
the game.

41	Bg8	Kd4
42	Bc4	Rf6
43	Bg8	Kc3
44	Bc4	Kd2

On the way to e1. White can
prevent this only for a short while.

45	Kf1	h5
46	Be2	h4
47	gxh4	gxh4
48	Bc4	Rf3!
49	Kg2	Rc3
50	f4?!	

Speeds up the loss, but there is
no long-term defense, anyway.

50	...	Ke1
51	f5	Rg3+

52	Kh2	Rf3
White resigns		

White's in zugzwang after 53
Be6 Kf2, and must decide whether to
lose the f-pawn or the b-pawn (giving up the h-pawn means giving up
the King!). Either way, the resulting
position is completely hopeless.

GAME 25

White: S. Gligoric
(Yugoslavia)

Black: G. Kuzmin
(U.S.S.R.)

Played at Leningrad (U.S.S.R.) Interzonal Tournament, June 22, 1973, Round 14.

Nimzo-Indian Defense (Normal Variation)

This is a strategic effort all the way through. After the opening White has an isolated d-pawn, but the active placement of his pieces gives him a slight edge overall. At an appropriate moment, White dissolves his isolated pawn and should still retain the advantage of the somewhat freer position. But a moment of carelessness by Black allows White to transpose into a Q + P endgame in which White wins a pawn by force. Theoretically the position is an ultimate win for White, but the road is long. Apparently dejected however, Kuzmin resigns after adjournment and thus deprives us of seeing Gligoric's technique and himself any chances for a half point.

1	d4	Nf6
2	c4	e6
3	Nc3	Bb4

The Nimzo-Indian Defense, first brought into tournament practice by Latvian-born Danish grandmaster Aron Nimzovich. Introduced over fifty years ago, it has stood the test of time and is today an even more popular opening than in its early years. The basic point of the Bishop move is to exert indirect pressure on the key e4 central square. Black is quite prepared to exchange his KB for White's QN in order to retain this pressure. If this saddles White with doubled c-pawns, then Black can try to attack them. White, on the other hand, has the Bishop pair and greater central influence. All in all, an interesting, dynamic fight is assured- thus its continual popularity.

4 e3

Rubinstein's move is by far the most popular modern approach. In effect, White says, "I'm not going for any drastic refutation of 3 ...Bb4 but will first complete my development and then decide what to do next."

4 ...   c5

This immediate challenge to White's center is currently the most popular move. Somewhat more in the original Nimzovichian manner is 4 ...b6 and 5 ...Bb7. The flexible 4 ... 0-0 is also playable.

5	Bd3	0-0
6	Nf3	d5

7 0-0

White has completed his basic development, and it is now Black's turn to make decisions. The two reasonable approaches are to develop the QN and to start to clear center tension. Thus 7 ...Nc6, 7 ...Nbd7, 7...cxd4, and 7 ...dxc4 seem logical. And in fact at various times all of these have been popular. In this game Black chooses a line which became common in the middle 1970's.

7 ...   dxc4
8 Bxc4   a6

With the logical plan of 9 ...b5 and 10 ...Bb7. However, this cannot really be executed, and the move can easily turn out to slightly weaken the Queenside and lose time. More effective is the straightforward 8 ...cxd4 9 exd4 b6.

9 Bd3

Good also is the preventive 9 a4!. In Spassky-Petrosian, 1975 U.S.S.R. Spartakiad, White obtained a clear advantage after 9 ... cxd4 10 exd4 Qa5?! 11 Bg5 Nd5 12 Ne4! Nd7 13 Qe2 Re8 14 Rfc1 Nf8 15 Nc5! and won in 41 moves.

9 ...   Nbd7

Black's problem is that the immediate 9 ...b5?! is met by 10 Ne4!, when there is no good way to complete Queenside development without losing the c-pawn.

10 a4   cxd4

10 ...b6?! misplaces the KB after 11 Na2! Ba5 12 e4!.

11 exd4   b6

To fianchetto the QB seems logical, but this leads to a very passive location for the QN. Perhaps better, therefore, is 11 ...Nb6 12 Qe2 Nbd5 13 Bg5 Be7 14 Rfe1 Re8, as in Portisch-Panno, 1968 Lugano Olympiad, where White's attacking chances were fewer than in this game.

12 Qe2   Bb7
13 Rd1   Re8
14 Bf4   Nf8
15 Ne5

This type of position, with White having an isolated d-pawn but with some space advantage, is well known in chess literature. Here two special factors tilt the   position clearly in White's favor: the weakness of Black's a-pawn prevents active play by the QR, and Black's QN (now at f8) has no active prospects. If now 15 ...Ng6 16 Nxg6 hxg6 17 Be5! and Black has just weakened his Kingside.

| 15 ... | Nd5 |
| 16 Bd2! | f6 |

If Black exchanges White's QN, then after 17 bxc3 White's center is strengthened. The text does lead to a slight weakening of the Kingside and e-pawn, but White's Knight cannot be tolerated too long on the active e5 square.

| 17 Nc4 | Be7 |
| 18 Nxd5! | |

Black was planning 18 ...Nb4, which would bother both White's KB and d-pawn quite unpleasantly. Therefore it is in White's interest to exchange the Knight. Compared to the position after Black's 15th, Black's Kingside has been weakened.

| 18 ... | Qxd5 |
| 19 Qg4 | f5 |

With this and the following moves, Black is able to gain some space for his KB and N, but again at the cost of further weakening his Kingside and the important e5 square. None of these factors by itself is large, but Black is forced to accumulate more and more weaknesses. White is clearly, though not decisively, better.

20 Qg3	Bh4
21 Qh3	Rad8
22 Bc3	Ng6
23 Ne3!	

Black, of course, threatened 23 ...Nf4, and 23 Nxb6?? is a blunder because of 23...Qc6 followed by 24 ...Nf4. Therefore White liquidates his isolated d-pawn, thereby opening the position so that several of Black's weaknesses can be exposed to direct action. This is a well-known technique to handle isolated d-pawn positions.

| 23 ... | Qd6 |
| 24 d5! | Qe7 |

Renewing the threat of ...Nf4.

25 Bc4	Nf4
26 Qf3	Nxd5
27 Bxd5	Bxd5
28 Nxd5	

Obviously Black will recapture, but how? The answer will be critical to the result of the game.

28 ...   Rxd5?

The losing moment. Generally speaking, the defending side should exchange pieces in order to lessen the pressure; thus Black's move seems strategically in order. However, the tactical possibilities in moves 30 to 33 are of overriding importance here.   Correct is 28 ...exd5!, since then 29 g3 leads to nothing after 29...Bf6, and 29 Qxf5? is downright bad because of 29 ...Rf8. Therefore the best that White has is 29 Rxd5 Rxd5 30 Qxd5+ Qf7 31 Qd4, and after 31...Bd8!, Gligoric rates White's position as only slightly better. The usual strategic factors   lead to the plus: Black's Queenside has been weakened, there is looseness on the Kingside too, and White's Q and B are actively placed. Black's potentially saving factor is that little attacking material is left with which White can realize his advantages.

29 Rxd5   exd5

Now after 30 Qxd5+, we would be back into the previous note. But White has something better: he can now chase Black's pieces back.

30 g3!   Bf6
31 Re1   Qd7
32 Rxe8+   Qxe8

33 Qxd5+   Kh8

Worse is 33...Qf7 34 Qa8+, and White will obtain a passed pawn on the Queenside.

34 Bxf6   gxf6
35 Qxf5

And so o e of Black's weaknesses- the f-pawn- has fallen, and White is a sound pawn up. Theoretically this should be a win, but because the extra pawn is on the same side as the King, the technical problems involved are considerable. The "defending" Queen is such a strong attacking piece that the stronger side always has to worry about allowing perpetual check. In the moves to come before the time   control at move 40, White is essentially satisfied to keep the status quo.

35 ...   Qc6
36 b3   Kg7
37 h4   a5
38 Kh2   Qd6
39 Qe4   Qc5
40 Kg2   Qd6
41 Qg4+   Kh6
42 Qf5
Black resigns

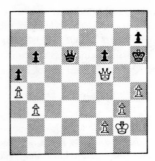

White sealed his 42nd move and Black decided to resign without resuming play. There were two main factors involved in his decision: respect for Gligoric's technique and disgust at himself for the error on move 28. Gligoric indicates that his winning method would have consisted of placing his g-pawn on g4, h-pawn on h5, and his f-pawn on f3 and then playing his King to h3 and his Queen to e3 via e4. Presumably then he would be ready to advance his f-pawn and possibly the g-pawn. All of this is good, but even so a slight misstep is often all that is required for perpetual check to rear its ugly head. Black would certainly have not been criticized if he had decided to play on.

GAME 26

White: G. Kuzmin
(U.S.S.R.)

Black: G. Forintos
(Hungary)

Played in European Team Championship at Bath (England), July 13, 1973, Round 7.

Queen's Gambit Declined (Orthodox/Tartakower Variation)

In the opening White tries to employ a modern strategic approach, but a premature central break allows Black to equalize. When White becomes careless in an approximately even middlegame position, Black uses relatively simple tactics to win two pieces for a Rook. Black consolidates his material advantage well, first in the middlegame and subsequently in the endgame. White resigns when he must lose a valuable Queenside pawn. A rather easy win against a Soviet grandmaster. Black played normally and well; White did not.

1	d4	Nf6
2	c4	e6
3	Nf3	d5

Turning down the opportunity

for the Queen's Indian with 3...b6 in preference to the Orthodox Defense to the QGD.

4	Nc3	Be7
5	Bg5	0-0
6	e3	h6

This move with the 7th move follow up has been a modern day mainstay for a long time. There is, however, some resurgence of the "ancient" 6...Nbd7. For one example see Game 33, Polugaevsky-Portisch, Portoroz Play-off 1973.

7	Bh4	b6

In the position after White's 7th move Black stands satisfactorily from the standpoint of King safety and center influence. In fact Black's only serious developmental problem is what to do with his QB. Over fifty years ago, Tartakower hit on the idea of the QB fianchetto, and this has been Black's most popular approach ever since.

8 Be2!

Apparently innocuous, but in combination with the text a creative strategic idea of Korchnoi's. The move order employed here is the most accurate, since after 8 Bxf6 Bxf6 9 cxd5 exd5 10 Be2 Black can place his QB more actively with 10 ... Be6. For a long time the mainline was 8 cxd5 Nxd5 9 Bxe7 Qxe7 10 Nxd5 exd5 11 Rc1 Be6 12 Qa4 c5 13

Qa3 Rc8, and with 14 Bb5!?, White scored a dramatic and convincing win in Fischer-Spassky, Match Game 6, 1972. However, improvements were subsequently discovered for Black, and it has become easier for Black to equalize after 8 cxd5 Nxd5 than after Korchnoi's plan.

8 ...	Bb7
9 Bxf6!	Bxf6
10 cxd5	exd5

Instead 10 ... Bxd5?! gives White too much influence in the center. What is the strategic basis of White's play? The clearing of the central tension has fixed White's pawn formation so that Black's Bishop pair is pretty much biting on granite. On the other hand, White's Knights are very flexible, and the KN can, for instance, be brought to f4 to pressure Black's d-pawn. As a result of 7 ...b6 Black has a slight structural weakness on the Queenside, and if Black plays ...c6, then the Queenside weakness will be accentuated. White can then choose a Queenside pawn advance or a central break with e4, after due preparation, of course. Overall, in the hands of a fine strategic maneuverer, White's position offers many more chances for meaningful progress than Black's.

11 Qb3

O.K., but more flexible is 11 0-0 first to see what setup Black will

choose.

(The Karpov-Kasparov World Championship Matches of the 1980's have brought 11 b4!, which tries to contain the Black Queenside, to the fore as White's most popular plan.)

11 ...   c6

Permanently protecting the d-pawn at the cost of weakening the Queenside and deadening the QB. An alternate approach is 11 ...Re8 followed by ...Qd6.

12 0-0   Nd7

In an earlier round, Pytel (Poland) - Szabo (Hungary) went 12 ...Re8 13 Rac1 Nd7 14 Rfe1 Nf8 draw! The conclusion makes some practical sense: White's position is somewhat better, but Black is the better player! .

13 e4?!

Without the development of the Rook's, this central break lacks punch and Black can easily equalize. 13 Rad1 or 13 Rac1 is indicated.

| 13 ... | dxe4 |
| 14 Nxe4 | c5! |

Opening the a8-h1 diagonal gives Black even chances. White's most fighting response is 15 d5, with the advanced passed d-pawn being partly weak and partly strong. The text move is rather toothless.

15 Nd6	Qb8!
16 Nxb7	Qxb7
17 Bc4	

White is in no shape for a sharp sortie such as 17 Ne5?!. Forintos gives the following refutation: 17 ...Bxe5! 18 Bf3 Qc7 19 Bxa8 Bxh2+ 20 Kh1 Rxa8 21 g3 Bxg3 22 fxg3 Qc6+, and Black has two pawns for the exchange and the better position.

| 17 ... | Rad8 |
| 18 Bd5 | Qa6! |

There is no reason for Black to acquiesce to the passive 18...Qb8.

19 Rad1?

This automatic developing move suffers from tactical deficiencies. 19 Bc4! is correct and required. Black then has the choice of "playing the game" after 19...Qa5 20 d5 or satisfying himself with a draw after 19...Qb7 20 Bd5, etc.

| 19 ... | cxd4! |
| 20 Nxd4?! | |

Not completely satisfactory, but somewhat better, is 20 Bc4 Qa5 21 Nxd4 Nc5 22 Qe3, though Black's advantage is clear after 22 ...Rfe8. White, however, is still ignorant of Black's coming combination.

20 ...	Nc5
21 Qf3	Rxd5!
22 Qxd5	Rd8

Strange as it may seem, White's Queen has no square to retreat to from which it can protect the Knight. Thus Black gains the clear material advantage of two minor pieces for a Rook. Black has no fundamental weaknesses, so with normal, careful play, his material advantage must tell.

| 23 Qc6 | Bxd4 |

Usually it is better for the stronger side to keep a Rook to go with the minor pieces, since this way the potential activity of the weaker side's "extra" Rook is minimized.

Here 23 ... Rxd4? is clearly inferior, since after 24 Rxd4 Bxd4 25 Qe8+ Kh7 26 b4 Ne6 27 Qxf7, White is already better: 27 ...Qc4? 28 Re1!,etc.

24	b4	Ne6
25	Rd2	Qa3!
26	Rb1	Bf6!

Here it's difficult for Black to make any progress without liquidating the pin along the d-file. Black has seen that his position is quite safe after the Rook exchange.

27	Rxd8+	Nxd8
28	Qc4	

28 Qe8+Kh7 also leads to nothing for White. Every one of Black's pawns and minor pieces is protected thus White will have no chances for successful counterplay. With his next move Black makes his Queen more mobile.

28	...	Qa4!
29	h4	Ne6

Black could prevent White's next with 29 ...h5. But getting in h5 is without real significance for White, since he has no good way to bother Black's King.

30	h5	Nd4!
31	Re1	Qd7!
32	Qd3	Qc6
33	Qe4?!	

Entering an endgame here ensures that White will have no practical chances for survival. Keeping the Queens on is an absolute must. Theoretically White is lost, of course, but the presence of Queens always affords some practical chances.

33	...	Qxe4
34	Rxe4	Kf8
35	a4	a6!

Preventing White from fixing Black's Queenside pawns after 36 b5.

36	b5	a5!

And not 36 ...axb5?! 37 axb5 Nxb5?! because of 38 Rb4, and after the liquidation of the Queenside, White's chances for a draw are excellent. After the text, Black's Queenside pawns are safe from exchanges, and he can start working on White's potentially attackable a-pawn.

37	Kf1	Ne6!
38	Ke2	Nc5
39	Rg4	Ke7
40	Ke3	Ke6
41	Ke2	

White can do nothing and must await the executioner.

41	...	Kd5
42	Rf4	Ne6

White resigns

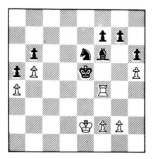

White's a-pawn cannot be saved: 43 Rg4 Bd4! followed by 44 ...Nc5.

GAME 27

**White: W. Uhlmann
(East Germany)**

**Black: A. Lutikov
(U.S.S.R.)**

Played at Leipzig (East Germany) International Tournament, October 1973.

English Opening

Right out of a strategic opening, White delivers a masterful demonstration of the value of the initiative. The initiative is transformed into an extra pawn, and the extra pawn, by means of an instructive R+P endgame, into the win. Of course, Black's opening play is questionable; nevertheless, White's refutation is outstanding in every way.

1 c4   d6

Quite an unusual response but perfectly playable. The game will generally enter, by transposition, one of the more standard openings.

2 Nc3   e5

The English has been reached. By transposition, we have reached Game 6, Smejkal-Balashov, Sochi 1973. 2 ...g6 instead leads to King's Indian formations.

3 Nf3

Undoubtedly more active than the 3 g3 of Game 6. The usual approaches for Black now are 3...g6, 3 ...f5, 3...Nc6, and 3...Nf6. But Lutikov often has original tastes in the opening.

3 ...   Bg4

Most likely not the best move, but considerably more logical here than in Game 6. Here, at least, the Bishop is attacking something.

4 d4!

Starting active central play as quickly as possible. Logical for Black now is 4...Nd7, which develops as it defends. White can then choose between 5 e3 and 5 g3.

4 ...   Bxf3?!

Black is intent on immediately justifying his 3rd move, but the exchange is not strategically well-motivated. Black achieves an unbalanced position all right, but it is unbalanced in White's favor!

5 exf3!?

With this recapture White gives his first priority to rapidly completing his development. There is also nothing wrong with 5 gxf3, the capture toward the center.

5 ...   exd4?

Black only thinks of strategy and forgets about everything else. With this move Black ensures himself a sound 4-pawn vs. 3 pawn Queenside majority, and his three Kingside pawns will readily hold White's four. Unfortunately for Black, White now gains a devastating advantage in development; this will be of infinitely greater importance than the respective pawn formations. Correct for Black is one of the normal Knight developing moves.

6 Qxd4   Nc6
7 Qe4+   Nge7

It doesn't matter what Black interposes, White always has the same response: e.g., 7...Qe7 8 Nd5! or 7...Be7 8 Nd5!.

8 Nd5!   Qd7

Since Black is not able to complete his development of his Kingside (8...g6?? 9 Nf6 mate), he must rush to get his King to safety on the Queenside.

9 Bd2   0-0-0
10 0-0-0   Kb8?!

No benefit derives from placing the King here. Therefore Black should save the tempo with something like 10...Re8 or 10...Qe6.

11 Bc3   Nxd5
12 Qxd5!

White wants to keep as many lines open as possible so that the Bishops can develop maximum scope. Therefore 12 cxd5 is less accurate.

12 ...   Rg8?!

With the logical plan 13...g6 and 14...Bg7, but White convincingly demonstrates that there is no time for it. The best is to accept a lifeless but materially equal endgame after 12 ...Qe6 13 Re1! Qxd5 14 cxd5.

13 c5!

Opening lines for the primary threat of 14 Bc4. Black has no satisfactory response.

13 ...   Be7
14 Bc4   Bf6

Rather than defend further with 14...Rdf8, Black tries to buy some breathing room at the cost of a pawn. Neither alternative is attractive.

15	Qxf7	Qxf7
16	Bxf7	Rgf8
17	Bxf6	gxf6
18	Bd5!	

Making it very unattractive for Black to recover the sacrificed material with 18...dxc5?! 19 Bxc6 bxc6, since Black's Queenside majority has been devalued by the triple isolated c-pawns, and White's 4-to-2 Kingside pawn majority offers good potential for creating a passed pawn (s).

18	...	Nb4
19	a3!	Nxd5
20	Rxd5	dxc5
21	Rhd1!	

Of all the pieces, the Rooks especially need open spaces and active prospects to demonstrate their inherent value. White prefers to keep his Rook (s) as active as possible, even though he may not be ahead any material. 21 Rxc5 is unquestionably playable since after 21 ... Rfe8 White has the parry 22 Rd1!, but White is confident that the active text offers more.

| 21 | ... | Rxd5 |
| 22 | Rxd5 | Kc8? |

Playing an inferior ending a

pawn down is hopeless. Black has to hold on to his material with 22 ...b6. Uhlmann then gives this variation: 23 Rd7! h5 24 Rh7 Rg8 25 g3 Rg5 26 f4 Rf5 27 Kc2 with White considerably better. This is quite true, but Black's 4-to-2 Queenside pawn majority definitely confers some practical chances for successful resistance.

23 Rxc5

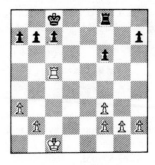

So White has transformed his initiative into an extra pawn. Even though White has a doubled pawn on the Kingside, the fact that he has a 4-to-2 majority there gives him an excellent chance of creating two passed pawns. On the other hand, Black is too passive to hope for a viable passed pawn on the Queenside. Even so the win is not routine, but Uhlmann clearly and impressively demonstrates the use of an active Rook.

| 23 | ... | Kd7 |
| 24 | Kd2 | Rf7?! |

Black could establish a more

easily protectable Queenside pawn formation if he played 24...b6! here.

25 Ra5!   a6
26 g4!

White's Rook is actively placed, and White's King has a flexible location in the center where it can head in the direction that offers the most realistic chance for results. Therefore White should start using his strength: the Kingside pawn majority.

26 ...	Ke8
27 f4!	Rd7+
28 Ke3	Kf7
29 h4!	Rd1
30 h5!	h6
31 Rc5	c6
32 Rc3!	

With the dual plans 33 Rb3 and 33 Rd3.

32 ...   Rg1

Black tries to keep his Rook active. This is perfectly logical and sound. The passive 32...Rd7 might allow him to hold out longer, but no bonus points are given for length of a game; of importance to the practical player is the creation of chances for his opponent to go wrong. For instance, if now 33 Kf3?, Black has 33...f5! when White's Kingside pawn formation is ruined and Black should draw without too much difficulty: 34 gxf5 Rh1! 35 Kg4 Kf6 36

Rb3 Rg1+ etc.

33 Rb3!

White also correctly gives preference to his Rook's activity.

33 ...   b5

This weakening is practically forced since the attempt to bring the Rook back with 33...Re1+ 34 Kd4 Re7 leads to a position in which White's King easily penetrates the Queenside, starting with 35 Kc5!.

34 Rc3   Re1+

Allowing White's pawns to remain whole robs Black of all hope for anything. Absolutely necessary is 34...Rxg4 35 Rxc6 Rh4!. After 36 Rc5, Black still is in great difficulties; e.g., 36...Rh3+ 37 Ke4! Rb3?! 38 Kf5! followed by 39 Rc7+. Even so, he's much better off than in the game.

35 Kf3   Rb1

After 35...Re6, Uhlmann gives this convincing variation: 36 f5 Rd6 37 Ke3! Ke7 38 b4!! (to immobilize Black's Queenside pawn majority) followed by 39 Rd3 and a won K+P endgame.

36 b4   Ra1
37 Ke4
Black resigns

White threatens 38 Kf5 followed by 39 Rxc6. After the only reasonable defense, 37 ...Re1+ 38 Kf5 Re6, White has a choice of wins. *(Probably simplest is 39 Rd3 Ke7 (White was threatening 40 Rd7+) 40 Re3 with a won K+P endgame: 40 Rxe3 41 fxe3 c5 42 bxc5 a5 43 Ke4 etc.)*

GAME 28

White: D. Marovic
(Yugoslavia)

Black: T. Petrosian
(U.S.S.R.)

Played at Amsterdam (Netherlands) IBM International Tournament, July 1973, Round 8.

King's Indian Defense
(Kavalek-Soltis Variation)

A tough, rough, gutsy win. The course of this game does not demonstrate the most effective way to score against a typical superior opponent. On the other hand, former World Champion Petrosian can hardly be called "typical", and to try to defeat him, more than "usual" chess is required. Be that as it may, Marovic doesn't mind having his King position opened up or allowing Black two powerful center pawns. He has seen that Black's shaky King position gives White good practical chances. This is what happens. In mutual time pressure, Black allows White to sacrifice a Knight for Black's center pawns, and this opens Black's position for the remaining White pieces. When Black defends inaccurately, he is quickly swept overboard by White's sharp, resolute play.

1 c4   g6

2 Nf3   Bg7
3 d4   d6

By placing his d-pawn here immediately, Black indicates his interest in a King's Indian-like pawn formation. The flexible 3...Nf6 leaves the way open for ...d5 and a Grunfeld formation.

4 Nc3   Nf6
5 g3

Instead, with 5 e4 White can transpose into the Normal Variation seen in Games 21 and 23. The text move, preparing the KB fianchetto, is another good, positional approach.

5 ...   0-0
6 Bg2   c6

As is often true in the King's Indian, Black has the choice of going for either ...c5 or ...e5. For instance, the immediate 6...c5 leading to the Yugoslav Variation is quite playable. We'll see this later in Game 51, Taimanov-Smejkal, Leningrad 1973, and Game 52, Tal-Torre, Leningrad 1973. The most straightforward way to go for ...e5 is 6...Nbd7 followed by 7...e5. 6...Nc6 is also quite possible and popular. After 7 0-0 a6 we have the Panno Variation, to be seen in Game 60, Quinteros-Tukmakov, Leningrad 1973. The text move is a rare guest in modern tournament practice. Black can still be planning ...Nbd7 and ...e5, but probably has something else in mind.

7 0-0   Qa5

A move which was first brought into modern tournament practice by GM Lubomir Kavalek in the 1960's and which has been steadily and successfully employed by American IM Andrew Soltis in the 1970's *(GM since 1980)*. In recognition of both of their contributions, the name Kavalek-Soltis Variation is appropriate. The idea behind the move is to swing the Queen over to the Kingside (to h5) and to support the advance ...e5. Depending on White's response, Black will choose one of the two.

8 h3

White's best move according to the most modern theory. It contains the nasty tactical point that after 8 ...Qh5? 9 Ng5! Black is helpless against the coming 10 Bf3!. In other variations, too, the move serves the useful purpose of taking away g4 from Black's minor pieces.

8 ...   Bf5?!

Unusual, not to say extravagant. Black plans the exchanging 9 ...Ne4, and if now 9 Bd2 Qa6 10 b3 Ne4 and Black stands well. However, to play ...Bf5 there is no reason to move the Queen to a5 first. In this context, 7 ...Bf5!? is more logical. In the game position, the centrally indi-

cated move is 8 ...e5. That's what Kavalek and Soltis play.

9 Nd2!   e5
10 d5

An early blockade of the center is often perfectly satisfactory for Black. Here, however, because of the awkward location of his Queen and QB, Black will be forced to lose a couple of tempos. Therefore White will be able to retain his first-move advantage.

10 ...   c5
11 a3   Na6
12 e4   Bd7
13 Nb3   Qd8
14 Bg5

The opening phase is over. White has a clear space advantage in the center and on the Queenside. White is potentially able to start play in the center and Kingside with f4 or on the Queenside with b4. Black's only hope lies on the Kingside, but he must be careful that any lines that he opens do not rebound to White's advantage. Overall, White has the theoretically and practically superior chances, but Black is still fully in the game.

| 14 ... | Qe8 |
| 15 Kh2 | h5 |

An attempt at Kingside play. The h7 square is freed for the Knight's retreat, and the h-pawn can be pushed forward to h4.

16 Re1	Nh7
17 Be3	Qd8
18 Nd2!	

The Knight is needed on the Kingside. At first glance 18 Nc1 with the idea 19 Nd3 looks attractive since from d3 the Knight can be used both for the Queenside (b4) and Kingside (f4). However, Black has 18 ...h4! 19 g4 Bf6! followed by 20 ...Bg5 and Black has a meaningful control of the dark squares on the Kingside. After the text move, 18 ...h4 can be met by 19 g4! Bf6 20 Nf3! and Black will be stymied on the Kingside, while White will start his Queenside action with an early b4.

| 18 ... | b6 |
| 19 f4! | |

Having a choice, White prefers the more active plan of going for Petrosian's King. Against Petrosian that seems to be the best approach.

Only a Fischer can hope to defeat him in positional maneuvering. The move, however, is double-edged, since after Black's response, the position gets opened a lot.

| 19 ... | h4! |
| 20 gxh4! | |

20 g4?! exf4! again gives Black control of the dark squares.

20 ...	Qxh4
21 Nf3	Qe7
22 Qd2!	

Puts the Queen on a useful square and allows the QR to join the fray. To exchange the center pawns is not in Black's interest since after 22 ...exf4?! 23 Bxf4 White threatens very strongly 24 e5, and the preventive 23 ...f6 weakens Black's Kingside and locks in the KB. Therefore with his next move Black prepares for and anticipates White's fxe5.

22 ...	Rad8
23 fxe5	dxe5
24 Re2	Bc8

Planning to maneuver the QN to c7, e8, and then to the excellent blockading post d6. With his next White prevents that plan since 25 ...Nc7? will lose to 26 d6.

| 25 Nb5! | f5!? |

A very double-edged break. Black sees that White has a protected passed d-pawn and the initiative on the Queenside, and thus he wants to create counterchances on the Kingside. It is not really clear who will benefit from the coming line opening. A quieter alternative is 25 ...Nb8. With hindsight we know that the QN never enters the game, and this is an obvious handicap to Black. With 25 ...Nb8 the Knight can be brought closer to the action.

26 exf5   gxf5
27 d6!?

With only about ten minutes left, Marovic decides on this risky advance. The d-pawn is less safe here than on d5, and Black also gets control of the e6 square. 27 Bf2! e4 28 Rg1! seems positionally more justified, with White having the more realistic attacking chances.

27 ...   Qf6
28 Bf2   e4
29 Bh4   Qg6?!

The Queen will not be well placed here since White's QR will go to g1. After the game, Petrosian recommended 29 ...Qh6! as better. The extremely complicated position then seems to yield dynamically even chances. In practice, the player in better command of his nerves is usually successful. In this game, it will be White.

30 Ng5   Nf6
31 Rg1

White now has the superior attacking chances ; however, with both sides in time pressure, the result is most uncertain.

31 ...   Kh8
32 Qe1   Nh5?

As Petrosian tells it, he was so transfixed by the thought of getting his KB to check on e5, that he paid no attention to White's possibilities. Reasonable defensive moves are 32 ...Rde8 and 32 ...Qe8.

33 Nxe4!!

Although nearly out of time, White keeps his cool. Annihilation of the center pawns allows White a decisive opening of lines. In time pressure Black puts up weak resistance, and White is quickly rewarded for his bravery.

33 ...   fxe4
34 Bxe4   Qe6
35 Re3!

The mate threat on h3 must be dealt with.

35 ...   Rde8

If 35...Bd4 White wins after 36 Bxd8 Bxe3 37 Qxe3 Rxd8 38 Rg6! Qe5+ 39 Kg1.

36 Be7!   Rf5?!

The threat was 37 Bg6, but a better defensive try is 36 ...Qe5+ 37 Kh1 Rxe7! 38 dxe7 Qxe7 since now 39 Bg6 can be met by 39 ...Qb7+.

37	Bxf5	Qxf5
38	Rg5	Qf7
39	Qh4	Kg8?

Giving up a piece for nothing. Better is 39 ...Qf4+ 40 Qxf4 Nxf4 41 Re4 Ne6 42 Rg6 Nf8! though the endgame after 43 Bxf8! Rxf8 44 Re7 will be lost in due course.

40 Rxh5

And White is up an exchange and two pawns and has a winning attack. Even so, Black's next can only be understood as a nervous reaction to the recent happenings.

40 ...   Bxh3?

Without even the slightest hope for a trap since White can take the Bishop with complete safety in any one of three ways.

**41 Kxh3
Black resigns**

GAME 29

White: G. Sax
(Hungary)

Black: L. Polugaevsky
(U.S.S.R.)

Played at Hilversum (Netherlands) International Tournament, June 12, 1973, Round 1.

Sicilian Defense (Najdorf Variation)

Polugaevsky plays the opening creatively and quickly reaches an excellent position. By move 20 he is ahead a pawn and has what must be called a clearly won game. However, at that moment the worm turns. Sax repeatedly finds the best practical chances, and the position begins to drift away from an exceedingly easy win. As Sax continues to do his best and Polugaevsky keeps blundering, a position in which Black must play correctly to keep the balance arises. Finally White is better and after adjournment, White brings home the point with effective Queen and Knight maneuvers. A good practical fighting effort by Sax. For Polugaevsky, a clear indication of poor sporting form-something the further course of the tournament repeatedly confirmed.

1 e4	c5
2 Nf3	d6
3 d4	cxd4
4 Nxd4	Nf6
5 Nc3	a6

Polugaevsky is one of the world's leading experts on the Black side of the Najdorf. The Najdorf is unquestionably his primary weapon against the e-pawn.

6 f4

The move to choose if White wants active play, but it has a clear positional basis. The positional 6 Be2 is quieter. The most popular, complicated move is 6 Bg5; it arises in the next game. The clear strategic point of 6 f4 is to get in e5, which chases away Black's KN and possibly allows further advance to e6. Black has two general approaches to this strategic threat.

6 ...   Qc7

One approach is obvious enough: Black plays ...e5 himself either here or later. However, that move's disadvantages are clear: the d5 square is permanently weakened and the scope of the KB decreased. More popular now is to prevent White's e5 by applying pressure against that square, as in this game.

7 Bd3	g6
8 0-0	Bg7
9 Nf3	Nbd7
10 Qe1!	

Again aiming for e5, and in case of ...e5, the Queen will have good Kingside prospects on h4. What should Black's response be?.

10 ...   Nc5!?

An original and creative idea, first employed in this game. Rather than prevent White's e5, Black, by effectively regrouping his Knights, tries to take the sting out of that advance. Safer, however, is 10...0-0.

11 Kh1?!

It is desirable to move the King out of a possible check, but the time loss here is not justifiable. In a later game, Sax-Minic, Zagreb 1975, Sax improved with the immediate 11 e5! dxe5 12 fxe5 Nfd7! 13 Bf4 Ne6 14 Bg3, and obtained a clear advantage after 14...Nb6? (the double-edged 14...Qb6+ is better) 15 a4!.

11 ...	b5!
12 e5	dxe5
13 fxe5	Nfd7
14 Bf4	Bb7!

Black has achieved active and harmonious development and can look to the future with confidence. Experts have suggested two reasonable moves here for White. GM Szabo recommends 15 Qe3. IM Minic prefers 15 Qg3, with the probable continuation being 15 ...Ne6 16 Rae1 0-0 17 Be4 Bxe4 18 Rxe4 Qc6. In both cases the complicated position offers equal chances.

15 Ng5?

Sax selects this premature attacking sortie instead, and the punishment is swift.

15 ...   Qc6!
16 Rf3?!

The mate threat prevents defenses like 16 Qg3?: 16 ...Nxe5! 17 Bxe5 Bxe5. The minor evil is still the retreat Nf3!.

16 ...	h6!
17 Nge4	Nxd3
18 cxd3	Nxe5
19 Bxe5	Bxe5
20 Rc1	

The net result of White's ambitious 15th and 16th moves is that he has lost his valuable e-pawn for nothing. Moreover, Black has the Bishop pair and a generally lovely position. White's position is theoretically so bad that it could easily be called hopeless. When I discussed the course of this game

with Sax in the summer of 1976, he
said that at this moment he had only
one minute left to complete his next
twenty moves, whereas Polugaevsky
had loads of time. When I ques-
tioned him further by asking,
"Didn't you actually have two
minutes or so?", he thought a while
and replied, "No, I think only one
minute, because all I wanted to do
was to make the time limit (as a
matter of chessmaster's honor) and
then resign." Thus the game here
starts an interesting psychological
turning point. Sax feels 100 percent
certain of an imminent loss, and,
with nothing to lose, starts playing
freely. Polugaevsky, sure of a win,
tries not to take the slightest chance.
Objectively, White is quite lost for
many moves to come, but he has the
important factor of momentum. On
the other hand, Black becomes less
and less certain of the position, and
his nerves finally go completely to
pieces.

| 20 ... | Qb6 |
| 21 a4 | Rc8 |

O.K., but why not 21...b4! to
shunt the QN to some inactive
square?

| 22 axb5 | axb5 |
| 23 Rd1 | b4 |

O.K., but Black can win additional significant material - with no
meaningful danger- by 23...f5!.

| 24 Na4 | Qd4 |
| 25 Re3 | 0-0 |

The unprotected KB gives
White a shade of active play. More
accurate is 25...Bf4! first and after 26
Re2 0-0 since then 27 Qh4 is harmless because of 27...Bg5!

| 26 Nec5 | Bf4 |
| 27 Rxe7 | Bd5 |

White has his pawn back, but
Black's active Bishops control the
board. Even so, the position is
sufficiently open that White has
some practical hope, and he's become tactically sharp so that he
doesn't miss a chance.

28 Ne4!

The Black QB's diagonal must
be closed. After 28 Nd7, decisive is
28...Rc2!.

| 28 ... | Bb3 |

Looks like the last straw for
White, since 29 Ra1? loses to 29
...Bxa4 30 Rxa4 Rc1. But with no
time on his clock, White "sees" a
momentary respite with ...

| 29 Rd7! | Qe5?! |

Obviously not 29...Qxd7??
because of 30 Nf6+, but the Queen
now gets kicked around and winds
up in poor location. The active 29
...Qe3! is correct, when White is at

the end of his tricks. Then material loss is unavoidable and White retains a miserable position.

30 d4   Qg7?!

That's a hell of a place to put a Queen. Black has clearly lost his bearings around here. There seems to be nothing wrong with 30 ... Qf5, and if 31 g4 Qb5.

31 Nac5   Bxd1
32 Qxd1

Not 32 Ne6? fxe6 33 Rxg7+ Kxg7 and Black has a significant material advantage, since 34 Qxd1? loses to 34...Rc1. After the text move White must still be lost because it is not clear what he has for the Exchange. Even so, with Black's Queen misplaced on g7, White has some hope. And hope is what is needed in theoretically lost positions.

32 ...   Rcd8??
Walking into a triple fork is awful. It clearly indicates the condition of Black's nerves and is the best possible explanation for the things that happen. 32 ...Rfe8! is correct to prevent the potential Ne6 and threaten an immediate win with 33 ...Rxe4! 34 Nxe4 Rc1.

33 g3!

A useful zwischenzug which prevents back-rank mates later on.

33 ...   Be3
34 Ne6   fxe6?

The weakening of the e6 square gives White's remaining Knight forking chances there. Safe, sound,and correct is the obvious 34 ...Rxd7 35 Nxg7 Kxg7. After 36 d5 f5! Black's two Rooks are somewhat superior to White's Queen, though White should draw.

35 Rxg7+   Kxg7
36 Nc5!   Rde8
37 Qb3   Rf1+?

Black is too materialistic here and pays no attention to the strategic consequences. Correct is 37 ...Bxd4 38 Nxe6+ Rxe6 39 Qxe6 Bxb2 40 Qe7+ Rf7 41 Qxb4 Bf6. White has a slight material advantage, but there is so little material and the pawn formations are so similar that White has no real chances to win.

38 Kg2	Re1
39 Nxe6+	Kh7
40 d5	

A position won for White. The passed d-pawn is a terror, the Q and N combination paralyzes Black's Rooks, and Black's b-pawn is unprotectable. White wins smoothly and safely.

40 ...	Bg5
41 Qxb4	Re2+
42 Kh3	Re5
43 Qd6	Bf6
44 b4!	

Passed pawns must be pushed! Black has no hope of coping with both passed pawns and can just as well resign.

44 ...	Kg8
45 b5	h5
46 Nc5	Rf5
47 Nd7	Kf7
48 Qc7	Bd8

48 ...Rxd5? loses to 49 Qc4 among others.

49 Qc4	g5
50 Qd3	g4+
51 Kg2	Kg6

51 ...Rf3 allows 52 Qh7 mate!

52 b6	Kg5
53 d6	

If Black won't resign, White will make two Queens! The move also prevents Black's ...Bc7.

53 ...	Rf3
54 Qd2+	Kg6
55 b7	
Black resigns	

GAME 30

White: J. Timman
(Netherlands)

Black: L. Polugaevsky
(U.S.S.R.)

Played at Hilversum (Netherlands) International Tournament, June 1973, Round 5.

Sicilian Defense (Najdorf Variation)

In a complicated, active, modern variation, a sharp fight is to be expected. Timman tries a new idea on move 12, but there is no upcoming fight. Three moves later Black has lost his Queen! A rare but perfect example of chess blindness, by a very fine grandmaster.

	1 e4	c5
	2 Nf3	d6
	3 d4	cxd4
	4 Nxd4	Nf6
	5 Nc3	a6
	6 Bg5	

Throughout the 1960's and 1970's this has been by far the most popular weapon against the Najdorf. *(This has continued to be so during the 1980's also.)* It is sharp and active. White clears the back rank on the Queenside for quick castling there. This will get the King to reasonable safety and allow

the QR to participate in a potential attack against Black's center, an area where Black's King will most likely be. In addition the QB gets ready to pin the Knight; after the logical followup 6 ...e6 7 f4, the threat of e5 is in the air.

	6 ...	e6
	7 f4	Nbd7

Black has a wide choice here. Also good and playable are 7 ...Be7, the supersharp 7 ...Qb6 (Fischer's b-pawn Variation), and the sharp 7 ...b5 (Polugaevsky Variation), something he only plays part of the time.

8 Qf3

The most common and probably best move. White is ready to castle, and the Queen prevents an immediate 8 ...b5? because of 9 e5. However, periodically White chooses 8 Qe2. We'll see two examples of this: Game 37, Savon - Mecking, Petropolis 1973, and Game 64, Tukmakov-Browne, Madrid 1973.

	8 ...	Qc7
	9 0-0-0	b5
	10 Bd3	

(The text is White's most solid continuation, whereby he first tries to complete his development before starting his attack. According to the theory of the 1980's White can also

expect a slight opening advantage with the sharp 10 e5 or with the supersharp 10 Bxb5.)

10	**...**	**Bb7**
11 Rhe1		

All White's pieces are harmoniously developed centrally or toward the Black King. If now 11 ...b4?! White gets an overpowering attack after 12 Nd5!; therefore Black must choose a more modest plan.

11	**...**	**h6?!**

(With 11 ...Be7 Black could transpose into Spassky-Fischer, Match Game 15, 1972. Spassky continued with 12 Qg3 and after Fischer's 12 ...0-0-0?! Spassky obtained the advantage with 13 Bxf6 (even stronger is 13 Bxb5!) 13 ...Nxf6 14 Qxg7. According to current (1988!) opening theory Black must play the immediate 12 ...b4! with unclear consequences after 13 Nd5!?.) The text is Polugaevsky's novelty, which already had given him a full point in Geller-Polugaevsky, Kislovodsk 1972. *(However, Timman's response pretty much refutes it; Black's correct move was subsequently determined to be 11 ...Qb6.)*

12 Qh3!

And this is Timman's novelty, prepared in conjunction with fellow Dutch grandmaster Donner just the night before. This was an excellent guess as to what Polugaevsky would play. The reward for such excellent foresight is quite often a good score. Geller had played the obvious 12 Bh4 but after 12 ...Be7 13 Nd5?! Nxd5 14 exd5 Bxh4 White's attack was insufficient and Black, with an excellent defense, repulsed it.

12	**...**	**0-0-0**

The King must speed to safety, since White was threatening 13 e5! dxe5 14 Nxe6!.

13 Bxf6

All part of the previous night's plan. A subsequent game (our No. 45), Spassky-Donner, Amsterdam (IBM) 1973, went 13 f5?! e5 14 Ne6??.

13	**...**	**Nxf6**
14 Nd5!		

Still the previous night's work. Of course the e-pawn is pinned: 14 ...Bxd5? 15 exd5 Nxd5 allows 16 Nxe6! and 14 ...Nxd5 15 exd5 Bxd5 16 a4! gives White excellent compensation for the pawn in a sharp position. Even so this last line is the way to go. But Polugaevsky, flustered by the unexpected turn of opening events, tries something else.

14	**...**	**Qa5??**

15 Nb3!
Black resigns

Black's Queen is trapped and lost! He can choose 15 ...Qa4 16 Nb6+ or 15 ...Qxa2 16 Nc3, but either way he gets only one minor piece for it. Getting a Rook for the Queen with 15 ...Qxe1 is also obviously inadequate.

GAME 31

**White: L. Polugaevsky
(U.S.S.R.)**

**Black: L. Szabo
(Hungary)**

Played at Hilversum (Netherlands) International Tournament, June, 1973 Round 10.

King's Indian Defense (Samisch Variation)

Black tries a dubious opening idea, and as early as move 10 White establishes a significant advantage. But his strategy over the next ten moves is so uncertain that White loses a pawn, fails to get any compensation for it, and then leaves an Exchange en prise. Szabo takes full advantage of offered chances and wins convincingly. But Polugaevsky is not to be recognized-his nightmarish tournament continues.

	1 c4	g6
	2 e4	Bg7
	3 d4	d6
	4 Nc3	Nf6
	5 f3	

As so often happens in modern master practice, a "normal" position is reached via an unusual order of moves. The Samisch has been Polugaevsky's primary weapon against the King's Indian, so Szabo

should be well prepared. Now Black almost invariably plays 5 ...0-0 and after 6 Be3 has to decide what to do next. But Polugaevsky knows all the normal variations quite well, and so Szabo plans a little surprise. He reasons that White is so out of form in this tournament that he may not find the right responses.

5 ...   b6!?

With the strategic plan ...c5. After the preliminary 5 ...0-0 6 Be3, the plan with 6 ...b6 is a well known, popular way to defend against the Samisch. Is it even better a move earlier?

6 Bd3!

An accurate response. Now 6 ...c5! is refuted by 7 e5! when White's KB will get to e4 with decisive effect. Since White himself now threatens e5, Black's choices consist of 6 ... e5?! (a change of plans), 6 ...Bb7, and the text.

6 ...   a6

Giving the Rook a flight square on a7.

7 Nge2   c5?!

With 7 ...0-0 8 Be3 c5 Black can transpose into known channels, but he is determined to be original and to challenge White's ingenuity.

8 e5!   dxe5

The effect of not interpolating 5
...0-0 6 Be3 is now very apparent. In
the usual lines, Black's Knight can
retreat in comfort to e8, but here that
square is not vacant!

9 dxe5   Ng8

A sad necessity, since after 9
...Nfd7?! 10 Be4 Ra7 11 f4! Black's
Queenside is tied up in knots. After
the text, 10 Be4 is harmless because
Black has the freeing Queen ex-
change.

10 Bf4?!

Starting here White loses the
thread of the game and goes
downhill move by move. Protecting
the e-pawn thusly is both awkward
and antipositional. The obvious 10
f4! is strong. White then has a
significant advantage: he is well
ahead in development and has clear
central superiority.

10 ...   Bb7
11 0-0

Now the e-pawn will be unprotectable. 11 Qd2!? Nd7 12 Qe3 is
worth consideration. This threatens
13 e6, and after 12 ...e6 13 Be4! Bxe4
14 Qxe4, White will have time for
15 Bg3 and 16 f4.

11 ...   Nd7

Obviously White's e-pawn
cannot be protected; therefore, it is
logical to devalue Black's Kingside
pawn formation with 12 e6! fxe6,
and then continue with 13 Ne4!?.
After 13 ...Bxb2 14 Rb1 the situation
is unclear, but White has undeniable
compensation for his missing
pawns. Instead White tries to protect
the e-pawn indirectly but overlooks
some elementary tactics.

12 Qa4?!   b5!
13 Qc2

A sad necessity. After 13 cxb5
axb5 14 Qxb5? Black wins a Bishop
with 14 ...Ba6.

13 ...   b4
14 Be4!   Bxe4
15 Nxe4   Bxe5
16 Rad1

At the moment Black has won
the valuable e-pawn, and White
must strain hard to get some compensation in his superior develop-

ment. 16 Bxe5 Nxe5 is fruitless since 17 Nxc5? allows 17 ...Qb6, winning the pinned Knight.

16 ...	Bxf4
17 Nxf4	Kf8!

An excellent dual-purpose defensive move. Black ensures that a White Qa4 doesn't pin Black's Knight and allows an eventual castling by hand. White now has two reasonable plans. With 18 Nxc5 Qb6 19 Rxd7 Qxc5+ 20 Kh1 Nf6 he can accept an approximately even middlegame, or he can play 18 Rd2 with the idea of 19 Rfd1, getting fair compensation for the pawn.

18 Qa4?!

The Queen is only superficially well placed here; in fact it's quite uncomfortable.

18 ...	Ra7
19 Rd5?!	

A truly clumsy move. The Rook takes this useful square away from the Knight and sets itself up for a fork. 19 Rd2 is correct, and after 19 ...Qc7! 20 Nd5!. Then White still has some practical compensation for the pawn.

19 ...	Qc7

Attacking the Knight and threatening 20 ...Nb6. White is clearly in trouble.

20 Nd3?

Leaving the exchange en prise is plain stupid. The only correct move is 20 Rfd1!. Then 20 ...Nb6? is refuted by 21 Rd8+ Kg7 22 Qe8. Black's only correct move is 20 ...Ngf6!. After 21 Nxf6 Nxf6 22 Rd8+ Kg7 White has no compensation for the missing pawn. But it is better to be down a pawn than a pawn *and* Exchange.

20 ...	Nb6
21 Qc2	Nxd5
22 cxd5	Kg7!

Up enough material Black correctly consolidates his King position and brings the extra Rook into the game.

23 Ndxc5	Nf6
24 Qc4	Qe5!

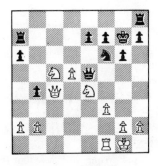

Black is even willing to give up a pawn to get his Rooks active play. Once Szabo got his chance, he started to exploit his superiority with fine accuracy and energy.

25	Nxf6	Qxf6
26	Qxb4	Rc8
27	Rd1	Rac7
28	Ne4	Qe5
29	Nc3	Qe3+
30	Kf1	

The King isn't safe here, but neither is it safe on h1; e.g., 30 Kh1 Rc4 31 Qb7 Rd4! 32 Rg1 Rcc4! 33 Qxa6 Rh4!.

30	...	Rc4
31	Qb7	Qe5!

Threatening the h-pawn and 32 ...Rb8 followed by 33...Rxb2. Something has to give.

32	Re1	Qxh2!
33	Qxe7	Rb8
34	Re2	Qg3!

Materially White is only a shade worse, but positionally he is in a severe bind. He can hardly move a thing; e.g., 35 Kg1 Rxc3! 36 bxc3 Rb1+, or 35 Rd2? Rxc3! 36 bxc3 Rb1+ 37 Ke2 Re1+. Black is meanwhile threatening to push his h-pawn and rip open White's King position. White's best chance for prolonging his hopes is 35 Qe3!.

35 d6?

Passed pawns must be pushed; *except* when they will be lost, as here.

35	...	Rd4!
36	d7	Qc7

The end of the d-pawn and the game. Everything White does from now on can be dispensed with.

37	Re6	Rxd7
38	Qf6+	Kg8
39	Rc6	

Equally hopeless is 39 Rxa6 Rd2!.

39	...	Qd8
40	Ne4	Rd1+
41	Ke2	Qd3+
42	Kf2	Qd4+

A mark of sensible practical play. Why try to mate White when the endgame is "kid's stuff?"

43	Qxd4	Rxd4
44	b3	f5
44	Ng5	

After 45 Nf6+ Kg7 46 Rxa6 Rf8 White's Knight is trapped.

45	...	Rd2+
46	Kg3	Rxa2
47	Rc7	Rxb3
48	Nxh7	

White is down an exchange and a passed pawn. His chances for a successful attack are less than one in a million.

48	...	Rb6
49	Ra7	a5
50	Ng5	a4!
51	Nh3	a3
52	Nf4	g5
53	Nd5	Rbb2
54	Nf6+	Kf8
55	Nh7+	Ke8
56	Nxg5	Rxg2+

57	Kf4	Ra1
58	Kxf5	a2
59	Ne6	Re1
60	Ra8+	Kd7
White resigns		

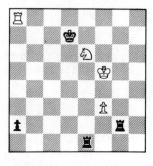

GAME 32 ✓

White: O. Panno
(Argentina)

Black: L. Polugaevsky
(U.S.S.R.)

Played at Petropolis (Brazil) Interzonal Tournament, August 12,
1973, Round 14.

Reti Opening

At the start of this game,
Polugaevsky was one of the tournament leaders, and to draw with Black
would satisfy him completely. It is
rather surprising, therefore, that he
chooses a double-edged variation.
But once in it, he must soon acquiesce to an inferior, unpleasant
endgame. Panno takes full advantage of the risk-free, superior position and brings home the win with a
technically flawless performance.
All the way through, White has a
lovely position.

1	Nf3	d5
2	c4	d4

This double-edged response
clearly defines the Reti. Black's
move is playable according to theory; even so, under the circumstances, 2 ...c6 or 2 ...e6 is safer and
more practical.

3 e3

White immediately challenges
the intruder. A sound alternative is
3 g3 c5 4 Bg2 in order to complete
the development of the Kingside
first. Instead of 4 Bg2, White played
4 e3!? Nc6 5 exd4 Nxd4 6 Nxd4
Qxd4 7 d3 Bg4 8 f3!? in the decisive
Round 17 Game, Polugaevsky-
Portisch. This position is quite unclear, but White won in good style
in 39 moves.

3	...	Nc6
4	exd4	Nxd4
5	Nxd4	Qxd4
6	d3	

Preparing to chase the Queen
away with 7 Nc3 and 8 Be3. 6 Nc3 is
usually equivalent. In Game 68,
L.Espig-Vasiukov, Dubna 1973,
Black continued with 6 ...Bg4?! and
White with 7 Qa4+.

6	...	e5
7	Nc3	Nf6?

This sound-looking, normal
Knight-developing move is a serious
opening error. The key question here
is whether White can gain control
over the important d5 square. Since
the text does nothing to prevent this,
the answer is "yes" with a significant advantage to White. The
correct way was demonstrated later
in Andersson-Portisch, Madrid
1973: 7 ...c6 8 Be3 Qd6 9 Be2 Ne7!
(on the way to f5!) 10 Ne4 Qc7 11 0-
0 Nf5 12 Bd2 Be7 with full equality.

8	Be2	c6
9	Be3	Qd8
10	d4!	exd4
11	Qxd4	

White now is master of the board. His Queen is powerfully placed, and if the Queen is exchanged, his QB will be equally powerfully located. The greater central influence (pawn on c4), edge in development, and more active pieces will lead to a marvelous situation for White. Black's Knight, though apparently on a good central square, has nothing to do there. If the Knight could get to f5, Black would have equality, but his faulty 7th move robbed Black of this chance.

| 11 | ... | Qxd4?! |

The resulting endgame will be depressingly lifeless for Black. A considerably better practical alternative is 11 ...Qa5!.

| 12 | Bxd4 | Be7 |
| 13 | 0-0-0 | 0-0 |

14 h3!

Not only preventing a ...Bg4 or ...Ng4 by Black but also planning a Kingside pawn advance consisting of g4, f4, f5. This would tend to completely suppress the activity of Black's pieces.

14	...	Be6
15	Rhe1	a6
16	f4!	

All of White's pieces are usefully developed, and the pawn advance starts.

| 16 | ... | Bb4?! |

This does not work out well, but it is difficult to suggest something good. 16 ...b5?! is also inadequate because of 17 Bf3 with the dual threats of 18 f5 and 18 Bxc6. The minor evil is 16... Rfe8, protecting the KB.

17	g4!	b5
18	f5!	Bxc4
19	Bxc4	bxc4
20	Bxf6!	gxf6
21	Re4!	Bxc3
22	bxc3	

White has played the previous exchanges like a real trooper and has a significant advantage because of the better pawn formation, more active Rook (s), and potentially the more active King. Any one of these factors is insufficient to win, but the combination is deadly. In realizing his superiority, Panno demonstrates the finest technique possible. Black doesn't have a chance.

22 ...	Rfd8
23 Rxc4	Rxd1+
24 Kxd1	Rc8

Black must start defending his weaknesses. Grossly insufficient is the "active" 24 ...Rd8+ 25 Kc2 Re8 because of 26 Rxc6 Re3 27 Rxf6 Rxh3 28 Rxa6, etc.

| 25 Ra4 | Ra8 |
| 26 Rd4 | |

Attempting to get to d6. 26 Rb4 or 26 Kc2 is equally good.

26 ...	Rb8
27 Kc2	Rb5
28 Rc4!	

But here 28 Rd6?! is inaccurate since Black gets ample counterplay by attacking the a-pawn as follows: 28 ...Ra5! 29 Kb3 Rb5+ 30 Kc4 Ra5! 31 Kb3 Rb5+ 32 Kc2 Ra5 33 Kb1 Rb5+, and if 34 Ka1, than 34 ...Rc5! is adequate.

| 28 ... | Ra5 |

After 28...c5? 29 a4 Ra5?! Black's Rook is stalemated, and White wins by penetrating with his King, starting with 30 Kd3.

| 29 a4 | h5 |

The c-pawn cannot be saved; thus Black correctly looks for counterchances on the Kingside.

| 30 Kb3! | h4!? |

By protecting his a-pawn White wins a pawn, whereas Black hopes to get an advanced passed h-pawn by eventually penetrating with his King or Rook and winning White's h-pawn.

| 31 Rxc6 | Kg7 |
| 32 Rd6 | |

Black is in zugzwang and so must lose another pawn. A simpler and more effective way to accomplish the same result is 32 Kb4! since this places the White King one square farther forward for the coming Queenside pawn advances.

| 32 ... | Re5 |
| 33 Rxa6! | |

33 Rd1 Re3 34 Rh1 is very passive, and 33 Rd3 is ineffective because after 33 ...Re1 Black's Rook is very active and can threaten ...Rg1 and ...Rg3. Thus White correctly

gets himself another passed pawn and then returns his Rook to stop Black's pawn.

33 ...	Re3
34 Rd6!	Rxh3
35 Rd1!	Kh6

Or 35 ...Re3 36 a5 h3 37 a6 Re7 38 Ra1 h2 39 Kb4! (Panno) when White's King will assist his pawn to queen.

36 a5	Re3
37 a6	Re8
38 Ra1	h3
39 Kb4!	

White's King must help the pawns. Premature is 39 a7? Ra8 40 Kb4 h2, and White can't prevent the coming 41 ...Rxa7!.

39 ...	Kg5
40 a7	h2
41 Kb5!	Kxg4

Now after 41 ...Ra8 White has 42 Kb6.

| 42 c4 | Kxf5 |

42 ...Kg3 43 c5 Kg2 is thematic, but after 44 c6 h1=Q 45 Rxh1 Kxh1 46 Kb6, etc., White will wind up a Queen ahead.

43 Rh1
Black resigns

White will win the h-pawn (43 ..Rh8 44 Rxh2 anyway) and then Queen his pawns.

GAME 33

White: L. Polugaevsky
(U.S.S.R.)

Black: L. Portisch
(Hungary)

Played at Portoroz (Yugoslavia) Play-Off Match Tournament for selection of qualifiers for Candidates Matches, September 7, 1973, Round 3.

Queen's Gambit Declined (Orthodox Variation)

Portisch has especially prepared an old variation with which to surprise his opponent, who is known for his fine knowledge of all modern openings. This surprise is effective, and Black achieves virtual equality out of the opening and into the early middlegame. In a dynamically even position, Polugaevsky tries an interesting sacrifice. The sacrifice is good enough for equality, but White, who is short of time, does not continue accurately, and soon it is Black who gains the superior chances. Pressed for time, White defends very poorly. At adjournment, Black has a won endgame. A fine fighting game by Portisch, who shows himself off to advantage in the opening, middlegame, and endgame.

1 d4	Nf6
2 c4	e6
3 Nf3	d5
4 Nc3	Be7
5 Bg5	0-0
6 e3	Nbd7

Around the turn of the century, when the QGD first became a popular opening, this was the way Black defended. It is a solid approach whose disadvantage is that Black's QB remains locked in.

7 Rc1	a6!

This is the ancient subvariation Portisch prepared especially for this play-off. Black plans to play ...dxc4 and then ...b5, bringing the QB into action on b7. More common is 7 ...c6 with the probable followup 8 Bd3 dxc4 Bxc4 Nd5 10 Bxe7 Qxe7 11 Ne4 b6 12 0-0 and a slight plus for White, as in Portisch-Ljubojevic, Milan 1975.

8 a3	

Caught by surprise, Polugaevsky reacts cautiously. The move has little point, however. One logical alternative is to enter the Exchange Variation with 8 cxd5, making Black's 7th move something of a waste of time. The next time Polugaevsky had White against Portisch - in Round 9 - that is what he chose and after 8 ...exd5 9 Bd3 c6 10 Qc2 Re8 11 0-0 Nf8 12 Rce1 had a slight edge. For more complicated play, 8 c5!?, as in Hort-Portisch, Madrid 1973, is reasonable.

8 ...	c6
9 Bd3	h6
10 Bh4	dxc4
11 Bxc4	b5
12 Ba2	

On d3 the Bishop gets in the way, and 12 Be2 is passive. The text move has no disadvantage.

12 ...	c5
13 0-0	Bb7
14 dxc5	Nxc5
15 Nd4	Rc8
16 f3	

The pawn formation is rather symmetrical and both sides have sound development and no weaknesses. White may have a minute advantage since he can get a slight center superiority after e4. However, having no weaknesses, Black shouldn't have much trouble holding the balance.

| 16 ... | Qb6 |
| 17 b4 | |

Preventing 17 ...b4.

| 17 ... | Ncd7 |
| 18 Bf2 | Bd6! |

Black locates his KB more aggressively, pointing it at h2.

19 e4	Qc7
20 g3	Qb8
21 Qe2	Ne5!?

The Knight impudently challenges White to do something about it. The text is enterprising and psychologically effective. Objectively somewhat stronger is the flexible 21 ...Rfd8! and only after 22 Rfd1, 22 ...Ne5.

22 Rfd1

The sharp 22 f4? fails to 22 ...Neg4 23 e5 Nxf2 24 Rxf2 Rxc3! 25 Rxc3 Ne4 with advantage to Black. GM Gufeld has, however, correctly pointed out that White could exploit the absence of Black's QN from the Queenside by playing 22 Nb3!, and after 22 ...Nc4 23 Nc5! or after 22 ...Ned7 23 Na5!, in either case with some advantage to White who then controls more space.

| 22 ... | Rfd8 |

Now 23 f4? is again faulty after 23...Neg4!, etc, but with 23 Nb3! White can keep the game in strategic balance: 23...Nc4 24 Nc5, etc. Instead, White commits a tactical and psychological error. Up to the playoff, Polugaevsky had been quite successful against Portisch; therefore, despite his shortage of time, he decides on the following sacrifice. Clearly he's confident that he can sweep Black off the board. But Portisch defends and maneuvers perfectly; it is White who, affected by time pressure, goes to pieces quickly.

23 Nxe6!?   fxe6
24 Bxe6+   Kh8
25 f4

If White wants to get this in he must do so immediately since after 25 Bxc8 Bxc8!, 26 f4? is impossible because of 26 ...Bg4.

25 ...   Rxc3!

This countersacrifice eliminates White's central pawn advance and keeps the position in balance.

26 Rxc3   Nxe4
27 Re3   Nxf2
28 Kxf2

The material balance shows that White has a Rook and pawn to balance Black's two minor pieces, and materially this is slightly insufficient. However, White's Rooks have nice open files; thus White has sufficient compensation. If Black's Knight now retreats, to 28...Nc6, White plays 29 Bf7! followed by 30 Re8+ and after exchanging Queens and one set of Rooks,White, with a Rook remaining has good prospects

against Black's Queenside. Therefore Portisch prefers a sharper plan, particularly in view of White's time shortage.

28 ...   Nc4!?
29 Bxc4   bxc4
30 Qxc4   Rf8

With the pawn that he just won, White now has a slight material advantage. However, all of Black's pieces are very active, and the immediate threat is 31 ...Bxf4!. The game hangs in balance. But with only 5 minutes left, White has the more difficult practical problems to solve.

31 Rd4?

This direct defense finds an elementary refutation. Correct is 31 Ke1! with complicated, dynamically equal play. After 31 ...Bc8!? White keeps the balance with 32 Qc6!? (Gufeld)

31 ...   Be5!

Attacks the Rook, which dares

not move off the fourth rank because of 32 ...Bxf4!.

32	Rde4	Bxe4
33	Rxe4	Qb6+
34	Kg2	Bf6

Of course, Black now has a clear material advantage. But White, paradoxically enough, has no more weaknesses, and so Black's task in winning this position is quite difficult.

35	Re6	Qb5
36	Qxb5?!	

Exchanging under these terms is not attractive since Black will gain both of White's Queenside pawns in exchange for his own. A better approach is 36 Qc6!.

36	...	axb5
37	Rb6	Ra8
38	Rxb5	Rxa3
39	h4??	

White goes completely to pieces here. By weakening his g-pawn, he gives Black a ready-made attacking object. The correct pawn move is 39 g4! with the idea of exchanging one set of pawns with 40 g5. Also reasonable is 39 Rd5 followed by b5.

39	...	Bc3
40	Rb6	Be1
41	Rg6	

What a stupid location from which to protect a pawn. The game is adjourned here and upon resumption Black wins quite easily. White only has one pawn for the piece, and the awkward location of his pieces gives him no hope for any kind of resistance.

41	...	Bxb4
42	h5	Be1
43	Kh3	Kg8
44	Kg2	Kf7
45	Kh3	Re3
46	Kg2	Re6!
47	Rg4	Ra6!
48	Rh4	

Another stupid spot for the Rook, but Black was threatening to go after the h-pawn with 48 ...Ra5.

48	...	Ra2+
49	Kh3	Bf2
50	Rg4	Ra5
51	Kg2	Bd4
52	Rh4	Bf6
53	Rh1	Ra1!
54	Rh3	
White resigns		

At long last White decides to give up the ghost, without even bothering to await Black's reply. Black has several winning methods, one of which (given by Szabo) is 54 ...Ke6 55 Kf3 Kf5 56 g4+ Ke6 57 Rh2 Ra3+ 58 Ke4 Ra4+ 59 Kf3 Rxf4+! 60 Kxf4 Be5+ and 61 ...Bxh2.

GAME 34

White: L. Portisch
(Hungary)

Black: L. Polugaevsky
(U.S.S.R.)

Played at Portoroz (Yugoslavia) Play-off Match Tournament for selection of qualifiers for Candidates Matches, September 11, 1973, Round 6.

Queen's Gambit Declined (Meran Variation)

A perfect example of how to defeat a superior opponent. White selects a strategically sound opening in which he has prepared a significant improvement and obtains a slight but risk-free advantage. An erroneous freeing attempt by Black is refuted by a sharp combination, with the result that White enters an endgame up a pawn. This minimal material advantage is realized in a technically faultless manner.

1	c4	Nf6
2	Nc3	e6
3	Nf3	d5
4	d4	c6
5	e3	Nbd7
6	Bd3	dxc4
7	Bxc4	b5
8	Bd3	Bb7
9	0-0!?	

Except for transpositions, this game has followed our Game 20, Rukavina-Korchnoi, Leningrad Interzonal 1973, in which White continued with the centrally active 9 e4. Portisch prefers a less commital approach, especially since he has an opening novelty in mind.

9	...	b4
10	Ne4	Nxe4

Before this game this was thought to be a routine equalizing method. It is O.K. but only as long as Black continues accurately. A good equivalent is 10 ...Be7 11 Nxf6+ Nxf6 12 e4 0-0 13 Qc2 h6 14 Rd1 and now 14 ...c5! with approximate equality.

11	Bxe4	Be7?!

To first chase the Bishop back with 11 ...Nf6! is imperative and only after 12 Bd3 to play 12 ...Be7. This transposes into the equalizing line given in the previous note.

12 Nd2!

Portisch's key novelty! The primary point is to allow the KB to remain on the a8-h1 diagonal since this makes it difficult for Black to achieve the freeing ...c5. Moreover, the Knight can find very good placement on either c4 or e4. Formerly the routine 12 b3 0-0 13 Bb2 was played and Black had no difficulty equalizing after 13 ...Nf6 14 Bd3 c5!; e.g., 15 dxc5 Bxc5 16 Rc1 Be7 17 Ne5 Qd5, as in Panno-Olafsson, Portoroz 1958.

| 12 ... | 0-0 |
| 13 b3 | Rc8?! |

The Rook placement here is more awkward than good. After the game, 13 ...Nf6 14 Bf3 Nd5 was recommended as Black's best, and this appeared soon thereafter in Polugaevsky-Sveshnikov, 1973 U.S.S.R. Championship. Black equalized after 15 Bb2 c5! 16 dxc5 Bxc5 17 Nc4 Qe7 18 Rc1 Rac8, etc., and drew in 36. However, the immediate 15 Ne4!, preventing Black's ...c5, does retain an edge for White.

14 Nc4	Nf6
15 Bf3	Nd5
16 a3!	

Out of this apparently quiet strategic opening. White has gained the following advantages: a clear superiority of central space, superior

pawn formation, and pressure along the a-file. Since these have been obtained for "free," White is significantly better.

| 16 ... | a5 |

The a-pawn will be weak here, but 16 ...bxa3 is equally unattractive. The sharp 16 ...c5?! is met by the simple 17 dxc5!.

| 17 Bd2 | c5? |

Black is too weak to afford this active advance. White now wins material by force with an effective combination. Black's best is the defensive 17 ...Ra8.

| 18 dxc5 | Bxc5 |
| 19 Nxa5!! | Ba6 |

Worse is 19 ...Qxa5 20 axb4 followed by 21 bxc5, and White has a strong Bishop pair to go with his extra pawn.

| 20 axb4! | Bxb4 |

There is little pleasure in 20 ...Bxf1 since after 21 bxc5 White has two terrific passed pawns for the exchange.

21 Bxb4	Nxb4
22 Qxd8	Rfxd8
23 Rfd1	Rxd1+
24 Rxd1	

The combination has brought

the clear advantage of a passed b-pawn. Interestingly, the forces at work are the same as in Game 13, Geller-Portisch, Portoroz 1973. But whereas Geller couldn't do anything with his extra b-pawn, Portisch realizes his advantage with fine technique.

24 ...	Kf8
25 h3	Rc5
26 Rd8+	Ke7
27 Rb8	

Should Black now exchange Rooks, Knights, or nothing? The answer is not easy, but in as much as the exchange of pieces generally favors the stronger side, Black's offer to exchange Rooks cannot be right. 27...Nd3!? seems like the most practical continuation.

27 ...	Rb5?!
28 Rxb5	Bxb5
29 g3!	Kd6
30 Nb7+	Kc7
31 Nc5	

At the moment Black may appear to have a defensible position, but that is only a mirage. White's b-pawn is quite safe, and so Black has no counterplay, whereas by offering exchanges White will force Black's defenders to give way.

| 31 ... | h6 |

Necessary to prevent White's Knight from getting to g5.

32 Bg2!	Na2
33 Bf1	Kc6
34 Bxb5+	Kxc5

Equally dismal is 34...Kxb5 35 Nd3 Nb4 36 Ne5 f6 37 Nf3!, and if 37...e5 then 38 Nh4! and the Knight will go after Black's Kingside pawns. The value of the text move is that White's Bishop will not be able to directly menace Black's pawns. But even so, the passed b-pawn will be decisive, since the Bishop will be able to protect it, and then White's King will be available for various active forays.

35 Be8	f6
36 Bd7!	e5
37 h4	e4

This does prevent the White King from reaching f3, but at the cost of a weak pawn on e4. The pluses and minuses are about in balance. A move to keep the status quo is 37...Nc3.

| 38 Kg2 | Nc1 |
| 39 Be6 | Nd3? |

39 ...Kb4 is more logical since the various K+P endgames after 40 h5 Nxb3 41 Bxb3 Kxb3 seem drawn; e.g., 42 f3! f5! 43 g4! Kc4!! 44 gxf5 Kd5!, etc. An immediate 40 Kh3 is foiled by 40 ...Nd3. Thus White must be satisfied with 40 Bd5 Nxb3 41 Bxe4. Black is very weak on the light squares, and so White's King has good chances of penetrating Black's Kingside. Even so, Black keeps reasonable practical defensive chances. As played, Black allows White to start up a bind on the Kingside, and Black is totally defenseless.

| 40 h5! | Ne1+ |
| 41 Kh3 | Kd6 |

White's King has to head toward the center anyway; thus 41 ...Nd3 42 Kg2 Ne1+ 43 Kf1, etc, simply forces White to execute the correct maneuver.

| 42 Bf5 | Ke5 |
| 43 g4! | |

Keeping the bind. 43 Bh7?! f5! is inferior.

| 43 ... | Nc2 |

The "active" 43 ...Nd3 can be met by both 44 Kg2 and 44 f4+.

44 Kg2	Kd5
45 Bh7	Nb4
46 Kf1!	Nc6
47 Ke2	Nb4
48 Kd2	Na2
49 Bf5	
Black resigns	

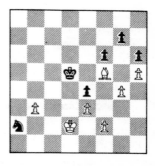

Here the lights went out in the tournament room; so the game was adjourned; however, Black resigned without continuing. With Black's pieces forced to watch his weak e-pawn, White's King can assist in the advance of the b-pawn; for instance, 49 ...Nb4 50 Kc3 Na2+ (50 ..Nd3 51 f3!) 51 Kb2 Nb4 52 Ka3, etc.

GAME 35

White : W. Uhlmann
(East Germany)

Black: V. Savon
(U.S.S.R.)

Played at Capablanca Memorial Tournament, Cienfuegos (Cuba) February-March 1973.

English Opening

Savon tries an esoteric approach against the English Opening but comes out with a clear central inferiority and nothing to show for it. Uhlmann applies additional pressure with some fine maneuvering, and Savon makes his situation worse by an unmotivated exchange of Bishop for Knight. Black's attempts at Queenside counterplay are parried with deft action in the center. Twice Uhlmann eschews winning endgames to keep the action in the middlegame and thus, he hopes, to take advantage of Black's time pressure. Objectively such an approach carries some dangers, but in this particular situation White is rewarded. Black volunteers a serious weakening of his Kingside and then oversteps the time limit in a rather helpless position.

1	c4	Nf6
2	Nc3	g6
3	e4	e5

A somewhat esoteric plan, though playable. The conventional 3 ...d6 4 d4 leads to the King's Indian Defense.

| 4 | Nf3 | Nc6?! |

But this is carrying originality too far. Correct is 4 ...d6 5 d4 Nbd7 with transposition into a King's Indian type of variation.

| 5 | d4! | exd4 |

Giving up the center so early is nothing but an admission of the bankruptcy of Black's strategic idea associated with 4 ...Nc6?!. But unfortunately 5 ...d6 is met by 6 dxe5!, and now 6 ...Nxe5 leads to the same type of position, and 6...dxe5 allows 7 Qxd8+! Kxd8 8 Bg5 and a most unpleasant pin (8 ...Bg7?? 9 Nd5 wins).

6	Nxd4	Bg7
7	Be3	0-0
8	Be2	Re8
9	f3	

White already has a significant central advantage as the result of Black's 4th and 5th moves. Most importantly, Black cannot hope to attack White's center, and Black's QN even gets in the way of his trying to generate Queenside counterplay.

| 9 | ... | d6 |
| 10 | 0-0 | Ne5?! |

Giving up pressure on the d4 square just allows White a freer hand to position his pieces for maximum effectiveness. 10...Bd7 is more logical.

11 Qd2!	a6
12 Rad1	Bd7

The opening phase has ended significantly in White's favor: he has a clearly superior and secure center and every one of his pieces is fully deployed, whereas Black is cramped and lifeless. The next step is to apply additional pressure by redeploying the pieces. With his next White sets up an annoying Bishop pin.

13 Bg5!	Nc6

Stamping his 10th as a waste of time. Black tries to reduce the pressure by attempting a Knight exchange.

14 Nb3	

White correctly wants to keep up the pressure and thus retains the Knight. A more useful retreat though is 14 Nc2!, an idea that White gets a couple of moves later.

14 ...	a5
15 Nd5!	

More pressure.

15 ...	a4
16 Na1!	Be6
17 Nc2	

So White's Knight has found the correct spot after all. On c2, the Knight guards the important d4 square and can go to e3, where it overprotects the d5 outpost. Black is still without counterplay.

17 ...	Bxd5?!

Black is anxious to remove the annoying Knight before White can play 18 Nce3 and recapture on d5 with the Knight. But after the text, White has even more central influence and the two Bishops in a position which will soon be rather open. Black's position is unpleasant in any case, but 17...Ne5 followed by 18...Ned7 seems likes a better defensive plan.

18 cxd5	Ne5
19 Kh1!	

Good practical precaution. Black's counterplay must come by

means of ...c6, and White ensures that Black can't play ...Qb6 with check.

| 19 ... | Qb8 |
| 20 Ne3 | c6 |

With White's Queen no longer controlling the h6 square, Black may seem to have a chance here for 20...h6, but that is not so. Uhlmann gives this refutation: 21 Bxf6! Bxf6 22 f4 Nd7 23 Bb5 Qd8 24 Ng4 Bg7 25 e5! h5 26 e6!! since 26...fxe6 27 dxe6 Rxe6?! loses to 28 Bc4, and little better is 26...hxg4 27 Bxd7 Re7 28 f5! and Black's weakened Kingside will soon crumble.

| 21 dxc6 | bxc6 |
| 22 Bxf6! | |

A little combination based on the strategic factor that Black's remaining Knight will be unprotected on d7. Instead, White gains nothing from 22 Qxd6 Qxb2 23 Rd2 Qb6 24 Bxf6 Qxe3!.

22 ...	Bxf6
23 f4	Nd7
24 e5!	Be7

After 24 ...Bg7 White has many good continuations, among them 25 Qxd6 Qxb2 26 Bf3. But the clumsy text can't be any better.

| 25 exd6 | Qxd6 |

The game is immediately over after 25 ...Bxd6 26 Ng4! h5 (or 26 ... Bf8 27 Bf3) 27 Nh6+ Kg7 28 Nxf7! Kxf7 29 Bc4+, etc.

26 Qc3

Counting on Black's time pressure, White wants more than the won endgame after 26 Qxd6! Bxd6 27 Rxd6 Rxe3 28 Bf3 Nf8 29 Rxc6 when White's a pawn ahead with the better position. The course of the game proves Uhlmann right, but objectively it isn't the smartest thing to do.

| 26 ... | Qf6!? |

The only defense. After 26 ...Qc5 Uhlmann gives this pretty line: 27 Bc4! Nb6 (27...Bf6?! 28 Bxf7+) 28 Ng4! h5 (28...Qh5 29 Ne5 is a positional crush) 29 Bxf7+ Kxf7 30 Nh6+ with mate to follow.

27 Qc2

Here, too, a larger advantage is to be gained by entering the endgame by means of 27 Bf3!.

| 27 ... | Bf8! |

The counter on White's Knight allows Black to save all material and reasonably consolidate his position. Now 28 Ng4 is parried by 28...Qf5 with an attack on White's Queen. White seems to have overlooked this in playing his 26th move.

28 Nc4	Ra7
29 Bf3	Rb8
30 g3	

Black stands well enough and after 30 ... Rb4, for example, his disadvantage is relatively minor. But he commits a characteristic time pressure error.

| 30 ... | h5 |

Unmotivated pawn pushes are a hallmark of serious time pressure. With no time to think, it is easy to push a pawn. But the damage often is great. Here Black's Kingside is decisively weakened, and White immediately exploits this circumstance.

31 f5!	Nc5
32 fxg6	Qxg6
33 Qf2!	

But here, with Black's Kingside in shreds, White correctly wants more than 33 Qxg6 fxg6 34 Bxc6.

33 ...	Rb4
34 Ne5	Qg7
35 Rde1	

Black overstepped the time limit and lost.

As Black was playing 35 ...Rab7, his flag fell and he was forfeited. Not that it mattered much, since after 36 Bxh5 Rxb2, for example, White can win an Exchange with 37 Bxf7+ or go for more with 37 Qf5.

GAME 36

White: V. Savon
(U.S.S.R.)

Black: G. Garcia
(Cuba)

Played at Capablanca Memorial Tournament, Cienfuegos (Cuba) February-March 1973.

Pirc/Modern Defense

Faced with an oblique counter against his strong center, White reacts correctly in the beginning, but soon completely forgets what the game of chess is about. He ignores the center, King location, King safety, and piece coordination. Black takes advantage of White's "purposeful" carelessness and walks all over his opponent. In fewer than forty moves it's all over.

1	e4	g6	
2	d4	Bg7	
3	Nc3	d6	
4	f4		

Postponing Black's ...Nf6 gives both Black and White some options to the normal Pirc (1 e4 d6 2 d4 Nf6 3 Nc3 g6). Here Black could enter the Pirc itself with 4 ...Nf6 or head toward less explored waters with 4 ... Nc6 or 4 ....c6 or ...

4 ...		a6?!	

With the plan of ...b5 and ...Bb7, leaving the c-pawn in reserve for other things. The text is played intermittently, but I'm somewhat skeptical about its theoretical value. It seems too passive, given White's strong center.

5	Nf3	b5	
6	Bd3	Bb7	
7	Qe2	c5	

7 ...Nd7 is more frequently played , after which White keeps the advantage with 8 e5.

8	dxc5	dxc5	
9	e5!		

A position favoring White: he has a strong secure center and harmonious development, whereas Black's expanded Queenside can very easily become a weakness instead of a strength. In Tal-Szabo, Sochi 1973, played after this game, Black continued 9 ...Nc6?! 10 Be3! Nd4 11 Nxd4 cxd4 and now 12 Rd1! leads to clear superiority, according to Tal. Garcia's move is better.

9 ...		Nh6!?	
10	a4!		

10 Be4 is good, but the text, by getting Black to weaken his Queenside, is even better.

10 ...		b4	
11	Ne4	Qc8	
12	c3		

Starting here White begins to lose the thread of the position. The text itself is playable, but the followup is not. 12 Be3?? is a gross error because of 12...c4. Correct are such obvious moves as 12 0-0 or 12 b3 and 13 Bb2. In either case White has more space and stands better.

| 12 ... | 0-0 |
| 13 cxb4?! | |

Weakens the d4 square and removes Black's pawn weakness on c5. Castling is infinitely better.

| 13 ... | cxb4 |
| 14 Bd2?! | |

A modest location for the Bishop. 14 Be3 or 14 0-0 is better.

| 14 ... | Nc6 |
| 15 Rc1 | |

Why not 15 0-0?

| 15 ... | Nf5! |

Black has been developing his pieces toward important central squares and stands excellently. If now 16 Bxb4, Black plays 16...Qd8! 17 Bc3 Ncd4! 18 Nxd4 Nxd4 19 Bxd4 Qxd4 and with the two Bishops and active Queen has more than sufficient compensation for the pawn. White's soundest continuation is still 16 0-0. With the unmotivated text he continues on a suicidal course.

| 16 g4?? | Nh6 |
| 17 h3 | f5! |

Obvious and strong. White already lacks a satisfactory continuation.

| 18 Nc5 | fxg4 |
| 19 hxg4 | Nxe5! |

The punishment, taking full advantage of the weakness-prone White position.

20 Nxe5	Bxh1
21 Bc4+	Kh8
22 Ne6	Qb7!
23 Nxf8	Rxf8
24 g5??	

Allowing Black's Knight on the edge a triumphal return to the center is part of White's strategy of self-destruction. The only reasonable move is 24 Bxa6, thereby reestablishing material equality. White's position is shaky, but he has some chances to weather the storm. After the text, he has none.

24	...	Nf5
25	Nf7+	Rxf7
26	Bxf7	Nd4
27	Qe3	b3

White has won the exchange and is immediately on the brink of defeat. There is no defense to the threat of 28 ...Nc2+.

28	Bxb3	Nxb3
29	Rc4	Nxd2
30	Qxd2	h5!

Black now has a decisive positional *and* material advantage. His last move is an effective way to take care of any potential difficulties on his first rank. White's resulting h-pawn is a toothless tiger.

31	gxh6 e.p.	Bf6!
32	Rb4	Qa7
33	Kd1	Qc5!
34	Rb8+	Kh7

35	Qd3	Be4!

Black's Queen and Bishops control the board, and with elementary though pretty tactics Black enlarges his material advantage. If now 36 Qxe4 Qd6+ wins the Rook. White can only postpone this plan for a move.

36	Qb3	Bc2+!

37	Qxc2	Qd6+
White resigns		

GAME 37

White: V. Savon
(U.S.S.R.)

Black: H. Mecking
(Brazil)

Played at Petropolis (Brazil) Interzonal Tournament, August 2, 1973, Round 7.

Sicilian Defense (Najdorf Variation)

White makes all kinds of errors in losing this game; psychological, strategic, and tactical. He chooses a sharp variation with which he is unfamiliar, then when speed is essential he plays slowly, and finally he overlooks some of his opponents tactical threats. The result is a hopeless endgame and assured loss. On the other hand Black's play is faultless throughout: active and consistent in executing the ideas behind the opening, sharp in carrying out combinations, and decisive in endgame technique.

1	e4	c5
2	Nf3	d6
3	d4	cxd4
4	Nxd4	Nf6
5	Nc3	a6
6	Bg5	

White's first error. Objectively the move is fine- it is White's most popular continuation-but it is not part of Savon's normal repertoire (he prefers 6 Be2 or 6 f4), and it quickly becomes apparent that he is not comfortable with it.

6	...	e6
7	f4	Nbd7
8	Qe2	

The usual move is 8 Qf3, as we discussed under Game 30. Spassky has recently recommended 8 Bc4!? with the dual points that after 8 ...b5 White can bring a promising piece sacrifice with 9 Bxe6! fxe6 10 Nxe6 and that 8 ...Qb6 is met by 9 Qd2! Qxb2 10 0-0 giving White excellent play for the pawn.

Savon spent 15 minutes on 8 Qe2, indicating that he hadn't expected Black's 7th move and already felt unprepared. The primary point of the text is to aim for an early e5. In addition the Queen is somewhat less exposed here than on f3. But there are also clear drawbacks: Black gets in ...b5 quickly, White's KB is blocked off, and if it is developed via g2, then the c4 square will be weakened. This latter point will become apparent in the game.

8	...	Qc7
9	g4	

Playable, but 9 0-0-0 is more flexible and useful. White must eventually castle on the Queenside, and doing it immediately gives him more options later. We'll see 9 0-0-0 in Game 64, Tukmakov-Browne, Madrid 1973.

| 9 ... | b5 |
| 10 a3 | |

Prevents a ...b4 but at the significant cost of a tempo. 10 0-0-0!? is worth considering and after 10 ...b4 11 Nd5!?. White gets a significant edge in development-and therefore a strong attack- for the sacrificed piece.

10 ...	Be7
11 Bg2	Bb7
12 0-0-0	Rc8!

To establish immediate pressure along the c-file and threaten counterplay with 13 ...Qc4 is imperative. Less exact is 12 ...Nb6, which led to an advantage for White after 13 Bh4 h6 14 Bg3 0-0-0 15 Bf3 g5 16 fxg5 hxg5 17 e5! in Kuzmin-Stean, Hastings 1973/74.

13 Bh4?!

Planning 14 g5 and/or 14 Bg3, but there is insufficient time. White spent more than than half an hour on it, without apparently appreciating the strength of Black's response. Instead, 13 Bxf6! is correct. (13 Rhe1 also seems playable.) Then after 13 ...Nxf6 14 g5 Nd7 15 Kb1! Qc4 16 Rd3! White has a slight advantage, as in Shamkovich-Quinteros, Lone Pine 1975.

| 13 ... | Qc4! |
| 14 Qxc4? | |

By allowing Black's Rook to reach an active location on c4, White starts going from bad to worse. Also unsatisfactory is 14 Qf3? because of 14 ...b4 15 axb4 Qxb4 16 g5 Rxc3!, and Black has more than sufficient compensation for the Exchange. As Vasiukov points out, White should continue with the consistent 14 g5. Then after 14 ... Qxe2 15 Ndxe2 Ng4 16 Bf3 Ne3 17 Rdg1 followed by 18 Bf2, White is just a shade worse.

| 14 ... | Rxc4 |
| 15 Bf3?! | |

Again the wrong move. Here is the last chance to protect his weaknesses with 15 Bxf6 Nxf6 16 h3! , as IM Kaplan recommended.

| 15 ... | Nc5! |

Attacking the e-pawn three times, and there is no satisfactory way to protect it. 16 Rhe1 allows 16 ...Nfxe4! 17 Bxe7 Nxc3, and 16 Bxf6 fails to the simple 16 ... Bxf6 17 Nde2 Nxe4.

16 Be2

Black's Rook only looks trapped, and Black has a pretty combination in store. The beginning of the combination is simple enough, but the main point is quite unusual.

16 ...   Nfxe4!
17 Nxe4?

Savon is already short of time and recaptures without much thought. The move would be O.K. *if* Black did not have the shot on move 18. Imperative is 17 Bxe7 Nxc3 18 bxc3 Kxe7 19 Bxc4 Bxh1 20 Bxb5, although Black's superior pawn formation guarantees him a clear advantage after 20...Bb7.

17 ...   Bxe4
18 Bxe7   Nb3+!!

Only so! After the routine 18 ...Kxe7?! 19 Bxc4 Bxh1 20 Bxb5 Black is only a shade better because White's pawn formation is normal, not, as is in the previous note, inferior.

As Mecking tells it, Savon had an unhappy facial expression during the last few moves and, after the last Black move, the expression changed to shock, from the clear realization that White now is completely busted. When he played his 14th move White apparently hadn't noticed this check.

19 Kb1

At least equally hopeless is 19 Nxb3 Rxc2+ 20 Kb1 Rxe2+ 21 Ka1 Bxh1, etc.

19 ...   Rxd4
20 Bxd6   Bxh1
21 cxb3   Rxd1+
22 Bxd1   Kd7

Black's combination yields the Exchange and the superior pawn formation. The win should be only a matter of normal technique, but Mecking's active way of realizing his advantage is impressive.

23 Be5   f6
24 Bc3   Be4+
25 Ka2?!

The King is not only unsafe here, but also misplaced, for it allows Black's Rook to penetrate White's position. The centralizing 25 Kc1 is correct.

25 ...   Kc6
26 a4   Rd8
27 Be2   e5!

Giving White the unenviable option either of allowing Black to create a passed e-pawn or of permitting Black's Rook the full use of the seventh and eighth ranks. It doesn't matter what White plays any more: his position is hopeless and already fully resignable.

28	fxe5	fxe5
29	Bxe5	Rd2
30	Bf1	Rd1
31	axb5+	

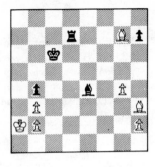

Opening the a-file allows immediate mate, though the end is also imminent after 31 Bh3 g5, etc.

31	...	axb5
32	Bh3	b4
33	Bxg7	Rd7!
White resigns		

Next comes 34 ...Ra7 mate!.

GAME 38

White: L. Ljubojevic
(Yugoslavia)

Black: V. Savon
(U.S.S.R.)

Played at Petropolis (Brazil) Interzonal Tournament, August 6, 1973, Round 10.

Caro-Kann Defense

A strange game. White employs something like a Kings's Indian Reversed formation and makes demonstrations on the Queenside. Chances are roughly in balance when White forces or allows a promising Exchange sacrifice by Black . But by now Black is short of time and does nothing with his opportunities. White consolidates his material advantage and wins rather effortlessly. White does not win as much as Black loses.

1 e4   c6

Late in the 19th century M.Kann from Vienna and H.Caro from Berlin recommended this defense, which soon thereafter received the name of the inventors. The defense has never achieved raging popularity but always has had a steady respectability. After the usual 2 d4 d5, Black's c-pawn supports the challenge to White's e-

pawn, and then after 3 Nc3 Black plays 3 ... dxe4. The resulting positions are fairly straightforward; White has a slight space advantage, Black a solid position free of fundamental weaknesses. Though Black's winning chances often are slight, his prospects for an honorable draw are excellent.

2 d3

The Yugoslav GM invariably prefers this modest move to the usual 2 d4. He likes Old Indian/ King's Indian Reversed formations with the extra move for White and the hope that Black's first move will not turn out to be particularly useful. In theory White's plan should be harmless, but in practice Ljubojevic has scored many successes.

2 ...   d5
3 Nd2   g6?!

By far the most common response, but I don't think that it is fully satisfactory because the fianchettoed KB has little meaningful scope. A steadier route to equality is the symmetrical 3 ...dxe4! 4 dxe4 e5 5 Ngf3 Qc7.

4 Ngf3

The usual plan for White is the KB fianchetto by means of 4 g3, but Ljubojevic specializes in the text, which is followed by developing the KB on its original diagonal.

4 ...	Bg7
5 c3	

For much of the subsequent play the c-pawn can just as well remain home and thus the immediate 5 Be2! is more accurate, as Ljubojevic played with great success in the middle 1970's. Black's soundest response then is 5 ...Nf6.

5 ...	e5

Here too, 5...Nf6 may be better.

6 a4

Instead of this immediate Queenside demonstration the developmental 6 Be2 Ne7 7 0-0 is more logical. Then, after the premature 7 ...Bg4?! (correct is 7 ...0-0), White gains the advantage with 8 exd5! Bxf3 (8 ...cxd5? 9 Nxe5!) 9 Bxf3 cxd5 10 c4, as in Ljubojevic-Pomar, Las Palmas 1975.

6 ...	Ne7
7 a5	0-0
8 Be2	h6
9 0-0	f5

The battle lines are drawn distinctly; Black will attack on the Kingside; White will try to do something on the Queenside. The position is very unbalanced, but objectively the chances should be equivalent.

10 b3	Kh7

11 Ba3	Rg8
12 Re1	g5

Black's central and Kingside pawn mass looks very imposing so that White decides to reduce it slightly. This, however, brings Black's QB into play.

13 exf5	Bxf5
14 Nf1	Nd7

Trying to bring the QN into the game is logical enough, though at the moment regrouping the Kingside forces is a bit more effective. For this 14 ...Ng6! 15 Ng3 Be6 is in order. Savon then gives the following variation: 16 Bf1 Nd7 17 Nh5 Bh8 18 Nd4! exd4 19 Rxe6 dxc3 20 d4, followed by 21 Bd3 and the obscure position still yields equal chances.

15 Ng3	Bg6
16 a6	

Weakening Black's c-pawn and removing White's a-pawn from the range of Black's Queen.

16 ...	b6

17 d4!

Black's strong center must be challenged, and this and the next moves are quite in order. White's pieces are much too passively placed to expect anything more than equality from the "attacking" 17 h4. After 17 ...g4 18 h5 (18 Nh2?! h5 19 f3 Bf6 gives White *less* than equality.) 18 ..gxf3 19 hxg6+ Nxg6 20 Bxf3 Nf6, Black's active position ensures him good prospects.

17	...	e4
18	Nd2	Nf6
19	f3	Re8!

Black's pawn on e4 exerts a strong cramping effect on White; thus it is in Black's interest to retain, if possible, his presence there.

20	fxe4	dxe4
21	Nc4	Ned5
22	Bb2?!	

The c-pawn has to be protected, of course, but this is both awkward and passive. Logical and correct is 22 Qc1! with about equal chances.

22	...	Qc7!
23	Ne5	Rxe5!

Forced and forcing. For the Exchange, Black receives a pawn and strong attacking chances on the Kingside.

24	dxe5	Qxe5
25	Rc1	Nf4
26	Ba1	Qe7
27	b4	Rd8
28	Qb3	

Up to here Black has played excellently but has used up almost all of his time; in what follows he becomes completely unrecognizable. Quite strong now is 28 ...h5! and 29 ...h4 to continue the attack. White has to defend accurately to hold on. Also reasonable is the "positional" 28 ...N6d5.

28 ...   Nd3??

This is something like chess madness. Black exchanges his active Knight for White's KB (and thereby goes against the general principle that the attacking side should hold on to his pieces), exposes his e-pawn, allows White's Rooks to become active, and even permits an exchange of his own Rook.

29 Bxd3   Rxd3

30 Rcd1   Qd7?

The Queen is poorly placed here. Correct is 30 ... Rxd1 and 31 ...h5. Black then has at least some practical chances for an attack.

31 Qc2   Ng4?

Loses two tempos. At the moment 31 ... h5? is refuted by 32 Nxe4! Bxe4 33 Rxe4! Rxd1+ 34 Re1+!. Black's only try is 31 ... Rxd1 32 Qxd1 Qe6, again aiming for 33 ...h5.

32 Qe2   Nf6
33 c4

All of White's pieces now are trained on Black's center and e-pawn. The latter's days, and thus Black's, are numbered.

33 ...   Rxd1
34 Rxd1   Qe7
35 Bxf6!

This and the following move are a pretty and effective tactical way to win the e-pawn. Black has obviously been left without enough pieces to cover the required ground, so it is not surprising that White has a winning combination at his disposal.

35 ...   Bxf6
36 Nxe4!   Bxe4?!

White's response is so obvious the text is equivalent to choosing to die with one's boots on. If Black doesn't want to resign then he should play 36 ...Qxe4 37 Qxe4 Bxe4 38 Rd7+ Kg6 39 Rxa7 b5, even though White does have a forced win with 40 c5 Bc3 41 Re7 Bd5 42 Rd7! (42 a7?! Bxb4!! 43 a8=Q Bxc5+ followed by 44 ... Bxe7 is not clear) 42 ... Bxb4 43 Rxd5! cxd5 44 c6 and one of White's pawns will Queen.

37 Re1   Bd4+
38 Kh1   Bxg2+
39 Kxg2

Black overstepped the time limit and lost.

White has a decisive material advantage and positional superiority. Black's loss on time here, in lieu of resignation, is just a formality.

GAME 39

White: V. Savon
(U.S.S.R.)

Black: V. Hort
(Czechoslovakia)

Played at Petropolis (Brazil)
Interzonal Tournament, August 11,
1973, Round 13.

Pirc Defense

A fighting opening leads to a
fighting middlegame with balanced
chances. Then inexplicably White
sacrifices (throws away?) his center
pawns for nothing perceivable.
Black accepts the gifts, consolidates
efficiently, and realizes his advantage in good style.

1	e4	d6
2	d4	Nf6
3	Nc3	g6

This is the basic position in the
Pirc Defense, named for Yugoslav
GM Vasja Pirc, who was the first top
master to demonstrate the playability of Black's system. It is a
relatively new opening, having been
taken seriously only after the Second World War and thus has had
a "professional" life of about forty
years. The Pirc can be looked on as
an e-pawn counterpart of the King's
Indian. The key difference between
the King's Indian and the Pirc is that

in positions of the former, White's
c-pawn is on the fourth rank rather
than back home on c2. Therefore, in
the King's Indian White has a more
imposing center (albeit one more
subject to succesful counterplay),
whereas in the Pirc White is a move
ahead in developing his pieces.

4 f4

In the King's Indian this would
be the fourth pawn on the fourth
rank and would risk a shaky center
situation. In the Pirc the move is considered the active positional continuation. A noncommital and popular
strategic plan is 4 Nf3, followed by
5 Be2 and 6 0-0. A sharp fight
follows 4 Bg5 (see Game 59,
Mestel-Tukmakov, Hastings 1972/
73).

4	...	Bg7
5	Nf3	c5

This counter to White's center
prior to Black's castling can lead to
great complications. The faint-at-
heart prefer the safer 5... 0-0, after
which 6 Bd3 gives White a slight
plus.

6 Bb5+

The alternative is 6 dxc5 Qa5 7
Bd3 Qxc5 8 Qe2 0-0 9 Be3. In either
case White can hope to obtain the
usual first move advantage.

6	...	Bd7

7 Bxd7+?!

But this is completely harmless since Black can efficiently recapture with the KN. Correct is 7 e5 Ng4 when White has three logical ways to go for a slight advantage: 8 e6, 8 h3, and 8 Bxd7+ Qxd7 9 d5.

| 7 ... | Nfxd7! |

Only so! After the inferior 7 ...Qxd7?! 8 dxc5! dxc5 9 0-0 Nc6 10 e5 Qxd1 11 Rxd1 Ng4 12 h3 Nh6 13 Be3, White's space advantage gave him a comfortable endgame plus in Hort-Bohm, U.S.Open Championship 1974.

8 d5	Na6
9 0-0	0-0
10 f5	

With the idea of opening the diagonal for the QB, but it carries the significant strategic disadvantage of handing the e5 square over to Black permanently. Savon obviously was not satisfied with the move because a few months later, against Korchnoi at the 1973 U.S.S.R. Championship, he played 10 Qe2. But after 10 ...Nc7! 11 Rd1?! (11 a4 is better) 11 ... b5! 12 Nxb5 Nxb5 13 Qxb5 Rb8 14 Qe2 Bxb2 15 Bxb2 Rxb2, Black's chances in the sharp fight turned out to be superior to White's. The fault I think lies with 7 Bxd7?!.

| 10 ... | Qb6 |

The Queen gets in the way more than it helps in the Queenside play. More accurate is 10 ... Nc7! with the idea of 11 ...b5, as in the previous note.

| 11 Kh1 | Nc7 |
| 12 Ne2 | |

The idea behind this maneuver is unclear. Much more in the spirit of White's tenth move is 12 Qe1! followed by 13 Qh4.

12 ...	c4
13 Ng3	a5
14 Rb1	c3?!

And here more accurate is 14 ... a4 first. When playing the text Black didn't pay sufficient attention to White's 16th and 17th moves.

| 15 b3 | a4 |

Otherwise White plays 16 a4, and Black's advanced c-pawn can turn out to be quite weak.

| 16 Bg5! | Nf6 |
| 17 bxa4 | |

An interesting position. Opening the b-file gives White's Rook pressure against the b-pawn. In addition Black's 16th move has made the protection of his c-pawn difficult. It appears that White will wind up a pawn ahead, and the important question remaining is whether Black will have sufficient compensation.

17 ...	Qa7
18 Nd4	Rab8
19 Nde2!	Qxa4
20 Nxc3	Qa5
21 Bd2	Rfc8

So White has won the c-pawn and is a pawn ahead. Black does have some pressure along the c-file, and White's a-pawn, c-pawn, and e-pawn are inherently somewhat weak. White cannot clearly or simply do anything with his extra pawn; nevertheless Black's compensation for the pawn should not be, theoretically, quite sufficient.

22 fxg6   fxg6

The positional capture is 22 ...hxg6; i.e., toward the center. There is really nothing wrong with that, but Black, cognizant of being a pawn down, prefers to unbalance things and hopes to have some potential play along the f-file in case the c-file turns out unpromising.

23 Qf3

Doesn't seem like a comfortable square for the Queen. 23 a4! instead is good to gain some extra space on the Queenside and neutralize the possible positional threat of ...b5.

23 ...	Qa6
24 e5??	

This throws away both of White's central pawns for no reason. It is not that White overlooked some special or deep response, since all of Black's moves are normal and obvious. The only explanation is the collapse of his chess nerves: White felt he had to do something, and what's more logical than a central advance? 24 a4! is still the correct and indicated move.

24 ...	dxe5
25 Rbe1?!	

White continues to play "thematically." Protecting the d-pawn with 25 Rfd1 is better.

25 ...	Rf8
26 Qd1?!	

Can White have overlooked that 26 Rxe5 allows 26 ...Nfxd5? The passive Queen retreat also can't be right. 26 Qd3, aiming for an endgame in which Black's extra pawn is a doubled e-pawn, is the logical way to head for a draw.

26 ...	Ncxd5

Thank you.

27 Nxd5	Nxd5
28 Qb1?!	

This too is inexact because White's Rook will be misplaced on f1. The accurate move order is 28 Rxf8+! Rxf8 29 Qb1.

28 ...	Rxf1+!
29 Rxf1?!	

Here 29 Nxf1 is better.

29 ...	Rc8!
30 Qb3	

White needs to get the Knight into the game, but here 30 Ne4? fails to 30 ... Rxc2! - showing up the error in White's 28th move.

30 ...	Qc4!
31 Qxb7	

The endgame after 31 Qxc4 Rxc4 32 Rc1 e4 is equally hopeless for White since Black will win the c-pawn and then remain up two pawns.

31 ...	e4!

Black first achieves total domination of the board. He sees that the Queenside pawns won't run away.

32 Qb3	e3!
33 Ba5	e6!
34 Re1	Qxc2
35 Qb7	Qc6
36 Qb3	

A time-pressure reflex which hastens the end. The exchange of Queens, however, would only prolong the game without affecting the outcome. White's a-pawn would go lost and Black's two passed e-pawns would be strong enough to win.

36 ...	Nf4
37 Rg1	Bd4
38 Qd1	Qd5

White overstepped the time limit and lost.

Losing on time is just a formality here, too. There is no way for White to cope with the coming 39 ...e2.

GAME 40

**White: W. Uhlmann
(East Germany)**

**Black: V. Smyslov
(U.S.S.R.)**

Played at Hastings (England) International Tournament, January 3, 1973, Round 7.

English Opening

A model game when played: a modern opening with a piquant tactical shot leads to a strategically superior middlegame, in which positional advantages are transformed by means of beautiful combinations into a direct, decisive mating attack. The passage of time has shown White's opening idea not to be quite correct, nevertheless, this does not decrease Uhlmann's creative and sporting achievements.

	1	c4	e5
	2	Nc3	Nc6
	3	Nf3	Nf6
	4	g3	Bb4

This subvariation of the English Four Knights has been exceedingly popular in the 1970's. The reason is clear: a strategically unbalanced, complicated, full-play position results, in which both sides have excellent winning chances, but neither totters at the edge of an abyss. The major points are: (*1*) Black gets ready to castle and then will be able to use the KR for central purposes on e8; and (*2*) the exchange of the KB will increase Black's central influence and most likely give White doubled pawns. The strategic disadvantages of Black's plan may be that Black's advanced center (particularly if the e-pawn advances to e4) can be liquidated to White's advantage and that White's Bishop pair can exert strong pressure. The course of the game allows White to demonstrate both of these factors.

	5	Bg2	0-0
	6	0-0	

This noncommittal move is the standard choice here, but 6 Nd5 is also playable. We'll see that in Game 43, Smyslov-Mecking, Petropolis Interzonal 1973.

	6	...	e4

This immediate advance is very demanding of Black. More flexible and a shade more accurate is 6 ... Re8.

7 Ng5

Looks great since the triple attack on the e-pawn forces Black's reply. But it has been established that the Knight's location on g5 has more disadvantages than advantages. Thus the modest retreat 7

Ne1! is at present viewed as the only method to gain a slight advantage. A recent example is Petrosian-Rogoff, 1976 Biel Interzonal, which went 7...Bxc3 8 dxc3 h6 9 Nc2 d6 10 Ne3 Re8 11 Qc2 b6, and now instead of 12 Bd2? Ne5! with at least equality for Black (and a draw in 19), White can keep a slight plus with either 12 b3 or 12 f4.

| 7 ... | Bxc3 |
| 8 bxc3 | |

8 dxc3 is pointless here since the KN has no good retreat square.

| 8 ... | Re8 |
| 9 f3?! | |

Works well in this game, but objectively it is not sound because White's King position is weakened too much. Black's e-pawn must be attacked, but hindsight tells us that the correct way is 9 d3! After 9..exd3 10 exd3 d6 the chances are even.

(Despite being used twice by Kasparov in his 1987 World Championship Match against Karpov, the objective value of the move remains uncertain. This is because Karpov both times avoided the theoretical continuations. In Game 4, after 9 ... exf3 10 Nxf3 he played the insipid 10 ...Qe7?! and lost miserably. In Game 2, Karpov tried 9 ...e3!? as a novelty and won in good style even though Kasparov's 10 d3! did lead to an initial edge for White.)

| 9 ... | exf3 |
| 10 Nxf3 | d5! |

Quickly striking at White's center, while developing his own pieces, is the thematic response.

| 11 cxd5 | Nxd5? |

This capture is the losing move. After the debacle here, Smyslov made a searching analysis of the position after White's 11th move and concluded that after 11...Qxd5! Black is fine. His judgment was rewarded next time he was Black in this position; G. Sigurjonsson-Smyslov, Reykjavik 1974, continued 12 Nd4 (12 d4 Qh5 also favors Black) 12...Qh5 13 Nxc6 bxc6 14 e3 Bg4 15 Qa4 Re6 *(After 15 ...Be2, White with the Exchange sacrifice 16 Rxf6! gxf6 could have reached sound equality if instead of 17 Qxc6?!, Pliester-Farago, Lugano 1983, he had played 17 Bxc6! Bf3 18 Bxa8!.)* 16 Rb1? Be2 with advantage to Black, who won on move 24. *(Instead of 16 Rb1?, the developmental 16 Ba3 makes sense. The game Stefanov-Kertesz, Rumanian Championship 1977 continued: 16 ...Be2 17 Rf4 g5 18 Rf5 Bd3 19 Rxf6! Rxf6 20 Qd4 Qg6 21 e4 with good compensation to White for his sacrificed material.)* Uhlmann had not noticed the Sigurjonsson-Smyslov game and allowed Makarichev of the U.S.S.R. to play the same variation at the 1975 IBM tournament at Amsterdam. He did try to improve by playing 15 Bf3, but after 15...Qg6! 16 Bxg4 Nxg4 17 Qe2 Rad8 18 Ba3 h5, Black has a clear advantage because of play in the center and against White's weakened Kingside. Makarichev won in 61 moves, and ever since Uhlmann has switched to 7 Ne1!.

12 e4!!

This tactical shot allows White to build a strong center and a strong attacking position along the f-file. These two factors and the Bishop pair give White a strategically won position, whose exploitation Uhlmann demonstrates with fine tactics. The e-pawn is en prise but can't be taken: 12...Rxe4?! 13 Ng5! Re7 14 Qh5! is devastating. Unsatisfactory also is 12...Nf6 because of 13 e5! Nxe5 14 Nxe5 Rxe5 15 d4 Re8 16 Bg5 with an irreparable weakening of Black's Kingside to follow. Not that what happens in the game is much better for Black.

| 12 ... | Nb6 |
| 13 d4! | |

Thanks to tactics, the building of White's center continues. 13...Rxe4? 14 Ng5 is even worse for Black than on the previous move.

13 ...	Bg4
14 h3	Bh5
15 e5	Nd5
16 Bd2	Qd7
17 g4!	

White's center is secure, his minor piece development complete. Thus it is time to start active play where the attacking chances lie, the Kingside.

| 17 ... | Bg6 |
| 18 Ng5 | Na5?! |

Black is anxious to start something himself, but this gives White the tempo he needs to seriously weaken Black's Kingside. The minor evil is 18...h6 19 Ne4.

| 19 h4! | h6 |
| 20 h5 | hxg5 |

About equivalent is 20...Bxh5 21 gxh5 hxg5 22 Qf3! followed by 23 Bxg5.

21 hxg6	fxg6
22 Qf3	c6
23 Bxg5	

White's advantages are multiple: central space, protected passed e-pawn, two Bishops in an open position, attacking chances against Black's weakened Kingside, superior pawn formation, etc. Even so, Uhlmann's crisp and decisive exploitation of these factors is noteworthy.

| 23 ... | Nc4 |
| 24 Qh3 | Qe6?! |

Allowing White to double Rooks on the f-file speeds Black's demise. 24 ... Rf8, is better though after 25 Be4 Black's prospects are obviously bleak.

| 25 Rf2 | Rf8 |
| 26 Bf3!! | |

This move and the idea behind it are the real crusher. Since Black has no defense against it anyway, he may as well take the c-pawn.

| 26 ... | Nxc3 |
| 27 Raf1! | |

The threat is 28 Rh2!, and there is nothing to do about it but sacrifice the exchange for some temporary relief. Uhlmann gives the following clear line after 27 ...Qd7: 28 Rh2 Qxd4+ 29 Kh1 Rxf3 30 Qh7+ Kf7 31 Rxf3+ Ke6 32 Qxg6+, etc.

27 ...	Rxf3
28 Qxf3!	Nb5
29 Kg2!	

Frees the h-file for a Rook check and thus prepares the coming beautiful combination. Black does not notice it, but he has no defense anyway. For instance, if 29 ...Qd5 30 Qxd5 cxd5 31 e6 followed by 32 e7 and 33 Rf8+, or if 29 ...Qe8 30 e6!! Nxd4 (30 ...Qxe6 allows 31 Qf8+! as in the game)31 Qf7+ Qxf7 32 exf7+ Kf8 33 Re1! with the unstoppable threat 34 Be7 mate!

29 ...	Nxd4
30 Qf8+!!	
Black resigns	

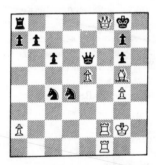

An electrifying finish: 30 ...Rxf8 31 Rxf8+ Kh7 32 Rh1 mate!. It's curious how Black's doubled g-pawns hem in his King.

GAME 41

**White: V. Smyslov
(U.S.S.R.)**

**Black: B. Larsen
(Denmark)**

Played at Hastings (England)
International Tournament, January
4, 1973, Round 8.

Sicilian Defense
(Closed Variation)

Smyslov sees that his attempt to
enter a standard line in the Closed
Variation is foiled and reacts to the
changed circumstances with a lot of
originality and little strategic logic.
In short order Black has a significant
space advantage. When White voluntarily opens a line against his own
King, this adds to Black's prospects.
Black achieves pressure on the
Kingside and then opens the Queenside. Under normal circumstances
White would be hard pressed to
guard all his weaknesses, but in time
pressure he completely falls apart
and offers no resistance whatsoever.

1 e4	c5
2 Nc3	

Smyslov has had many suc-
cesses on the White side of the
Closed Variation and employs it periodically. The usual lines start with
2 ...Nc6 3 g3 g6 4 Bg2 Bg7 5 d3 d6,
etc. Characteristically, Larsen
chooses a less common continuation.

2 ...	e6
3 Qe2?!	

This brute attempt at preventing
Black's ...d5 will fail, and e2 is
hardly the square to which the
Queen should go on move 3. Logical are either 3 g3 to stay in the
Closed Variation or 3 Nf3 and 4 d4
to transpose back into open lines.

3 ...	Nc6
4 Nf3	Nge7!
5 g3	d5
6 Bg2	

6 exd5 exd5 opens the Black
QB's diagonal, forcing White to
worry about ...Bg4 followed by
...Nd4.

6 ...	d4
7 Nd1?!	

The Knight will have no future
here. Correct is 7 Nb1 followed by
8 d3. The QN can then be brought
back into the game via d2.

7 ...	e5!
8 0-0	f6
9 b3?!	

In this early part White's play is
much too passive. A fianchettoed
QB will have nothing to do and the
QN doesn't have much future there

either. 9 Ne1 is better, and then if 9 ...Be6, White can exchange Black's "good" QB with 10 Bh3! Bxh3 11 Qh5+ and 12 Qxh3.

9 ...	Bg4
10 Nb2	Qd7
11 a4	g5

Black obviously has a large space advantage in the center and on the Kingside. White's position is so passive and cramped that he is in no position to attack any of Black's central or Kingside points. Already Black's advantage is unquestionable.

| 12 h3 | Be6 |

White's tactical point was 12 ...Bxh3 13 Nxe5! Nxe5 14 Qh5+ followed by capturing the QB. Black can keep the pin with 12 ... Bh5 but now that White has weakened his Kingside prefers to place his Bishop centrally.

| 13 h4 | |

Otherwise 13 ...g4 is very unpleasant.

| 13 ... | h6 |
| 14 Nd3 | Nc8! |

At the moment there is nothing wrong with 14 ...b6. But Black does not want White to have anything to attack with a5. After Black castles Queenside, this factor has some

importance.

| 15 Nh2 | Rg8 |
| 16 f4? | |

Opening the g-file against his own King has to be completely wrong. I suppose White played it out of frustration with his uncomfortable position. Correct is 16 hxg5 hxg5 17 f3 to try to set up a semi-blockade with 18 Ng4.

16 ...	gxf4
17 gxf4	Qg7
18 f5	Bf7
19 Kh1	Nd6!

With the help of tactics (20 Nxc5 Nxf5!) the Knight returns to the game to prepare ...c4, which will gain additional space while weakening White's Queenside pawn formation. Strategically Black has a won position: he has strong pressure on the Kingside, clear central superiority, and play on the Queenside. In practice the game has still to be won, but at this level of play, the only significant question remaining is where the decisive action will take place.

20 Rg1	c4!
21 bxc4	Nxc4
22 Bb2	0-0-0
23 Bf3	Qh7
24 Rxg8	Qxg8
25 Rg1	Qh7
26 Bc1	h5
27 Nb2	Nb6
28 Qb5	Nd7!
29 Nd3	Bd6
30 a5	a6
31 Qa4	Rg8!

Black has prevented a weakening of his King position and has retained all minor pieces so that White's pawn weaknesses can be attacked. However, Black welcomes the exchange of Rooks since the semi-blockaded nature of the position prevents his Rook from being an effective attacking power, whereas White's Rook can be useful defensively.

32 Ba3	Rxg1+
33 Kxg1	Bxa3
34 Qxa3	Qh6
35 Nf1	Bc4!

Black's attack comes from both the Kingside and the Queenside. There is no way for White to hold all his weaknesses, but affected by time pressure, he does manage to lose the fastest possible way.

36 Kf2?!

Usually King centralization is the right method in the endgame, but the King is more exposed here than back home on g1. The punishment is immediate.

| 36 ... | Bxd3! |
| 37 Qxd3 | |

After 37 cxd3 White's Queen is separated from his King.

37 ...	Qf4
38 Ng3	Qxh4
39 Bxh5	Nc5
40 Qa3?	

A time-pressure blunder, which loses a piece. After the mandatory 40 Qf3, Black has the pleasant choice between taking the a-pawn with 40...Nxa5 or going for more with 40...Nb4.

| 40 ... | Nxe4+ |
| **White resigns** | |

After 41 Kg2 Nxg3 42 Qxg3 Qxh5, Black's up a Knight and pawn.

GAME 42

White: V. Smyslov
(U.S.S.R.)

Black: W. Browne
(U.S.A)

Played at Hastings (England) International Tournament, January 7, 1973, Round 11.

Queen Pawn Opening

After achieving approximate equality out of the opening, Black overlooks a simple combination and drops a pawn. But Smyslov, instead of consolidating his advantage, very uncharacteristically allows a Rook and Knight to be trapped on the seventh rank. His efforts to extricate them are the worst, and he ensures the end by a ridiculous Queen sacrifice. Black takes advantage of every offered chance, but White is solely responsible for the outcome of the game.

1 d4	Nf6
2 g3	c5
3 dxc5	

White's second move was unusual, and this capture is even more so. Smyslov likes positions which are clear, not cluttered, and his move is in the clearing tradition. Whether it can lead to an opening advantage for White is, however, questionable.

3 ...	Na6

Black prepares for a somewhat esoteric recapture. The normal 3 ...e6! is simpler and probably better.

4 Bg2	Nxc5
5 c4	g6
6 Nc3	Bg7
7 Nh3	0-0
8 0-0	d6
9 Nf4	a6

White's c4 has given him a bit more central influence. Therefore Black plans to neutralize it by means of ...b5. Once that is achieved Black will have full equality.

10 Be3	Rb8
11 Rc1	Ng4!

First, though, White's QB must be chased away. The immediate 11 ...b5? loses the Exchange after 12 cxb5 axb5 13 b4 Ne6 14 Ba7.

12 Bd2	b5
13 cxb5	axb5
14 b4	Ne6
15 Nfd5	

Black has good symmetrical equality and would retain it with the developmental 15 ...Bd7. Instead he overlooks White's simple, pretty threat.

15 ...	Ne5?

16 Nxb5!

Black's b-pawn is gone since 16 ... Rxb5? runs into 17 Rxc8 Qxc8?? 18 Nxe7+, winning the Queen. Therefore Black must rush to develop his QB.

16 ...	Ba6
17 Nbc7?	

Normally Smyslov likes clear positions, especially if they are inherently favorable. Thus, White could be expected to play here 17 a4! Bxb5 18 axb5 Rxb5 19 Qa4 with a marvelous position: fine, active piece deployment, the two Bishops and a strong passed b-pawn. The adventurous text only muddies the positional waters.

17 ...	Nxc7
18 Rxc7	

Possible is 18 Nxc7 Bc4 19 Nd5 Bxa2, but Black is obviously better off than in the previous note. Thus Smyslov decides to jump in

the mud with both feet.

18 ...	e6
19 Ra7	Bb5
20 Nc7	

Placing both Rook and Knight in precarious positions from which they do not escape. Theoretically the move is playable, but 20 Ne3 is considerably safer. Black then has some compensation for the pawn, but White is in no noticeable danger.

20 ...	Bc6
21 Qc2?	

And this is a very serious waste of time. Correct is 21 b5!, and whether Black captures the b-pawn or plays 21 ...Bxg2 22 Kxg2 Nc4 23 Bb4! White is still somewhat better (23 ...Rc8 24 b6!).

21 ...	Rb6!
22 b5	

White finally starts to recognize the danger, but it's almost too late.

22 ...	Qb8!
23 Ra3?!	

23 Ra6 has to be better even though after 23 ... Rxa6! 24 Nxa6 Qxb5 Black's active position gives him the advantage.

23 ...	Bxg2
24 Kxg2	Rc8

25 Rc1

25 Rc3? is refuted by 25 ... Nd7.

25 ...   Rxb5

Black has recaptured the pawn and has a significant advantage.

26 Nxb5??

Sacrificing the Queen for nothing is an act of madness. Hastings was not a successful tournament for Smyslov, and the course of this game graphically illustrates why. 26 Rb3! is imperative with some chances for successful resistance. White's Knight does remain clumsily placed, but it is uncertain that Black can win it.

26 ...	Rxc2
27 Rxc2	Qxb5
28 Rc8+	Bf8
29 Raa8	

29 Bh6 allows 29 ...Qb7+, whereas after the text Black can win White's Bishop with 29 ...Qd5+.

Could Smyslov have overlooked these elementary possibilities?

29 ...   Kg7!?

Tempting White to save the piece and run into a mating attack. White decides to oblige.

30 Bc3	Be7
31 f4?!	Qxe2+
32 Kg1	Kh6!
33 fxe5	Bg5
White resigns	

Mate is imminent with 34 ...Be3+ coming up.

GAME 43

**White: V. Smyslov
(U.S.S.R.)**

**Black: H. Mecking
(Brazil)**

Played at Petropolis (Brazil) Interzonal Tournament August 7, 1973, Round 11.

English Opening

The young Brazilian GM handles the stratgeic opening better than his experienced opponent, and thanks to some thematic tactics he carries a clear advantage into the middlegame. Some positionally and tactically sharp play extends the middlegame advantage into the endgame. Then a strategic sacrifice leads to a situation in which the combination of Black's Rook and pawns overwhelms White's minor pieces. A perfect, and impressive game by Mecking.

1 c4	e5
2 Nc3	Nf6
3 Nf3	Nc6
4 g3	Bb4
5 Bg2	0-0
6 Nd5!?	

As mentioned in connection with game 40, the usual move is 6 0-0. The less common text, however, seems to be at least equally good.

| 6 ... | e4! |

With this and the next move Black deflects the White KN and places his KB actively. This is the most exact way to go for dynamic equality.

7 Nh4

Of course not 7 Nxb4?? exf3 8 Nxc6 fxg2 and Black wins.

7 ...	Bc5
8 0-0	Re8
9 d3	exd3
10 Qxd3	Ne5
11 Qc2	

The last moves are easy to understand: White breaks the grip of e4 and Black activates his pieces toward the center. The text is preferable to 11 Qc3?!, which after 11 ...Nxd5 12 cxd5 d6 13 b4 Bb6 14 Bb2 Qg5 led to good play for Black in Kane-Popovych, Marshall Chess Club Championship, New York 1976.

| 11 ... | c6!? |

The fighting approach to the opening, though the passive 11 ... Nxd5 12 cxd5 d6 also seems playable.

12 Nc3??

A completely incomprehensible retreat, leaving a valuable central pawn hanging. Smyslov apparently overlooked some rather simple tactical or strategic point. With the routine 12 Nxf6+ or 12 Ne3 White can retain approximate equality. Strongest, however, is the zwischenzug 12 Be3!, with White reaching a slight plus even after Black's best defense: 12 ... cxd5! 13 Bxc5 d6 14 Bd4 dxc4 15 Rfd1! Nc6!, as in Gheorghiu-Szmetan, Torremolinos 1976.

12 ...	Nxc4

Thank you.

13 Na4?!

Leads to a practically hopeless position for White. Imperative is 13 Ne4 Nxe4 14 Bxe4 d5! 15 Bxh7+ Kh8. Black's center and active piece deployment give him the advantage, but material is even and White has chances to resist. Smyslov correctly evaluated the position as favorable for Black, but what he winds up with after the text is infinitely worse!

13 ...	Bf8
14 Qxc4	b5
15 Qd4	bxa4
16 e4	

The weakness of the e-pawn doesn't allow White to capture the a-pawn. Equally unpromising is 16

e3 because of 16 ...Qa5.

16 ...	Ba6
17 Re1	Qb6!

A winning position for Black: he not only is a pawn ahead but also has the initiative. Obviously undiscussable is 18 Qxb6 axb6 with Black having a perfect pawn chain. There is no time for 18 Qxa4 because of 18 ... Ng4 19 Qc2 Bc5. Therefore White's next is his best try, but Black finds a sparkling rejoinder.

18 Be3	Bb4!
19 Qxb6	

What else? 19 Qd1 Qa5 is obviously pointless for White, while 19 Red1 is parried by 19 ...Qxd4! 20 Rxd4 Bc5 21 Rxa4 Bb5 22 Ra5 Bxe3 23 fxe3 Nxe4.

19 ...	axb6
20 Red1	Be2
21 Rd4	c5!

Sharpest and most accurate.

After 21 ...Bc5 22 Rd2 Bxe3 23 Rxe2 the opposite color Bishops give White some hope for a draw.

22 Rxb4

About equivalent to 22 Rd6 Re6 when White has no compensation for his missing pawn.

22 ...	cxb4
23 e5	Ng4
24 Bxa8	Nxe3
25 Re1	Bc4
26 Be4	Nd5
27 a3	bxa3
28 bxa3	Nc3

Here too, White obviously has no compensation for the pawn, and Black must win in due course. Even so with 29 f4 White can make things more difficult. The erroneous text allows Black a pretty liquidating combination.

29 Bf3?	f6!
30 Rc1	Rxe5!
31 Kg2	

The end is immediate after 31 Rxc3? Re1+ 32 Kg2 Bf1+ 33 Kg1 Bh3 mate.

31 ...	Rc5
32 Rxc3	Bf1+
33 Kxf1	Rxc3
34 Bd5+	Kf8
35 Ke2	Rxa3

The end of the forced play has led to this situation: with a Rook and three pawns for two minor pieces, Black has a decisive material and positional superiority. White could resign in good conscience.

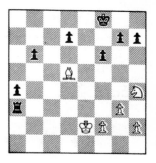

36 Kd2	b5
37 Nf5	b4
38 Ne3	b3
39 Kc3	Ra2
40 Kb4	Rxf2

Black simplifies by trading his Queenside for White's Kingside and receives another pawn in the bargain.

41 Kxa4	b2
42 Ba2	Rxh2
43 Kb3	Rh3
44 Nf1	Rh1
45 Nd2	Rg1
White resigns	

After 46 Kxb2 Rxg3 Black has four passed pawns and an assured win.

GAME 44

White: H. J. Hecht
(West Germany)

Black: B. Spassky
(U.S.S.R.)

Played at the West German International Championship, Dortmund, May, 18, 1973, Round 2.

Sicilian Defense

White does not really get much out of the opening and in the early middlegame would acquiesce to a draw. But Spassky wants more, and to unbalance the position he weakens his central pawn chain. Hecht quickly seizes the offered chance, applies pressure against the weakest spot in the chain, and gets a favorable endgame. Spassky does not defend it well, and Hecht wins in good style. The game is a good practical demonstration of how to defeat a superior opponent.

| 1 e4 | c5 |

Spassky's primary weapon against 1 e4 is 1 ...e5. His choice of the Sicilian shows that he's determined to win.

| 2 Nf3 | Nc6 |
| 3 Bb5 | |

As in Game 24, Kuzmin-

Larsen, Leningrad 1973, in which Black now played 3 ...Nf6. Spassky selects a more common continuation in which the fianchettoed KB controls the key d4 and e5 squares and at the same time helps prepare Black for quick Kingside castling.

3 ...	g6
4 0-0	Bg7
5 Re1	Nf6
6 Nc3	

A more common plan is 6 c3 followed by 7 d4. The text move presages a more closed contest.

| 6 ... | 0-0 |
| 7 Bxc6 | |

In Round 3, Spassky-Kunsztowicz, White tried 7 e5 Ne8 8 Bxc6 but after 8 ...dxc6! 9 h3 Nc7 10 d3 Ne6 11 Ne4 b6 12 Bd2 Qd5 Black had good equality and the game ended in a draw in 29.

| 7 ... | bxc6 |

An unbalancing, thematic (toward the center) recapture. From the standpoint of clearer equality, 7 ...dxc6!, as in the previous note, is simpler.

| 8 h3 | d6 |
| 9 e5 | Nd7 |

Or 9 ...Ne8. White stands somewhat better after 9 ... Nd5?! 10 exd6 exd6 11 Nxd5 cxd5 12 d4.

10	exd6	exd6
11	d3	Rb8
12	Bg5	f6
13	Bf4	Ne5
14	Rb1	

Black has somewhat greater space control at the cost of a weakened Queenside pawn formation and an innate looseness of his position. Black should therefore play aggressively so as not to give White time to build on Black's weaknesses. Hecht gives this line for Black: 14 ...Rb4! 15 Nxe5 fxe5 16 Be3 Rh4!? with approximately even chances. As played, Black achieves no play - and it is therefore impossible to win. When Spassky tries anyway, he gets punished.

14	...	Rb7
15	Ne4	Nf7
16	Bd2!	

The Bishop must find a more useful and safer location. 16 Qd2?! is faulty because of 16 ...g5! 17 Bh2 h6 and Black is ready to really push White back, starting with

18 ... f5.

| 16 | ... | Re8?! |

Overlooking the following small combination. More accurate is 16 ...Re7. Now White is able to temporarily disjoin the cooperation of Black's pieces.

| 17 | Ba5! | Qd7 |

Of course not 17 ...Qxa5? 18 Nxf6+ Bxf6 19 Rxe8+ followed by 20 Rxc8.

18	Bc3	Re6
19	Qd2	Qd8
20	Ba5	Qf8
21	Bc3	

To play for a win, White's last two moves were pointless. Hecht blames them on the inability to properly concentrate because of the sound of rock-and-roll music from a nearby park. This turns out to be a blessing in disguise since Spassky now decides on an unmotivated central push. There is little question that a draw is to be had with 21 ...Qd8 22 Ba5, etc. But Spassky wants more- and comes up with less.

| 21 | ... | d5? |

Weakens the forward c-pawn permanently. White is very effective in immediately starting to line up against it.

22 Ng3	Qd6
23 b3!	Bh6
24 Rxe6	Bxe6
25 Qe2	Bd7
26 Re1	Bf8

Preventing the incursion of White's Queen and protecting the c-pawn.

27 Bb2!	Bc8
28 Qd2	Kg7
29 Ba3	

Already White has the strong threat 30 d4!

29 ...	Qd8
30 Qc3	Rb5
31 d4!	Qa5
32 Qxa5	Rxa5
33 Bxc5	Bxc5
34 dxc5	Kf8

White has efficiently transformed his middlegame edge into a pleasant endgame advantage: Black will be weak on the dark squares, will have a rather impotent QB, will have problems in placing his Rook soundly, and will have difficulties in protecting the c-pawn. Overall, White has some winning chances and no risk of a loss-an excellent practical situation. With his last move, Black prevents White's Rook from getting to his seventh or eighth ranks.

35 Nd4	Nd8!

A good defensive move, whereby Black protects his c-pawn and the important e6 square. The immediate 35 ...Rxc5? is faulty because of the surprising 36 Re6! and White will win a pawn.

36 Nge2	Rxc5
37 Nf4	Bd7?!

Prepares the following move. But the Rook does not find a happy home there. Preferable therefore is 37 ...Kf7, keeping White's Knight out of the hole on e6. Hecht gives this probable continuation: 38 f3 Rc3 39 Re2 Ba6 40 Rd2 g5 41 Nfe2 Bxe2 42 Nxe2 Re3 43 Kf2 Re8 44 Rd4 followed by c4 and a slight plus for White.

38 f3	Ra5
39 a4	c5?

A very serious weakening of the central pawns and for what purpose? Black chases White's Knights where they want to go! The simple 39 ... Kf7 is imperative with White only slightly better.

40 Nde6+	Nxe6
41 Nxe6+	Kg8

Instead 41 ...Bxe6?! 42 Rxe6 Kf7 43 Rc6 leads to a miserable R+P endgame, whereas 41 ...Kf7 leads to a direct loss after 42 Nd8+ Kf8 43 Nb7.

42 Nc7

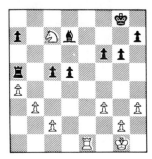

The sealed move and not the best one. Subsequent analysis showed that the Knight was a powerhouse on e6 and there was no need to move it. 42 g4! is the strongest move (taking f5 away from Black's Bishop). Black is then practically in zugzwang.

42 ...   d4?

Spassky has no luck with his pawn moves in this game. Correct is 42 ...c4 43 b4 (43 Rd1?! Bf5! gives Black counterplay) 43 ... Rxa4 44 Nxd5 Ra6 45 Re7 and White is significantly better, but Black may not yet be definitely lost.

43 Ne6!

Spassky overlooked this paradoxical looking retreat in his home analysis and now spent half an hour looking for a satisfactory response. Sacrificing a pawn to free his Rook

is the best practical chance. Ultimately hopeless is further passivity with 43 ...Bc6 44 Kf2 Bd5 because of 45 Nc7 Bf7 46 Ne6! and Black is in a complete bind.

43 ...	c4!?
44 Nxd4	Kf7
45 Kf2	h5
46 h4	Rd5
47 Ke3	

With 47 ...Re5+ 48 Kf2 Rd5 Black can now reestablish the status quo. The definitive winning line is therefore 47 Rd1 Bf5 48 bxc4 Ra5 49 Nxf5 gxf5 50 Ke3 Rxa4 51 Kd4 and a won R+ P endgame (as given by Hecht).

47 ...	g5
48 g3	Re5+
49 Kf2	cxb3
50 cxb3	Rxe1?

Why did Spassky think the resulting pawn-down and minor piece endgame offered drawing chances? To hope to cope with White's Queenside pawns Black will obviously need the services of an active Rook. A reasonable defensive move therefore is 50 ...Rc5.

51 Kxe1	Ke7
52 Kd2	Kd6
53 Kd3	Ke5
54 a5	a6
55 b4	

White prepares to create a

passed pawn with a properly timed b5 break, and there will be nothing Black can do about it. The attempt to get immediate counterplay by 55 ... gxh4 56 gxh4 Kf4 is foiled by the "zwischen-check" 56 f4+!: 56 ...Kd5 57 gxh4 Bh3 58 Nb3 Bf1+ 59 Ke3 Bb5 60 Nd2 f5 61 Nf3 Kc4 62 Nd4! Kxb4 63 Nxf5 Kxa5 64 Nd6! and White will win on the Kingside (analysis by Hecht). Nevertheless this variation offers Black more hope than the game continuation.

55 ...	Kd5?!
56 Kc3!	gxh4
57 gxh4	Ke5
58 Kc4!	Kd6

White's b5 cannot be prevented, and Black is completely lost: If 58 ...Kf4 instead, White wins with 59 Kc5 Kg3 60 Kd6 Bc8 61 Kc7! Bh3 62 b5!.

59 b5	axb5+
60 Nxb5	Ke5
61 Kc5!	Bc8
62 Kb6!	Bh3

Or 62 ...Kf4 63 Nd6!.

63 a6	Bg2
64 f4+!	

White is of course interested in queening the a-pawn for nothing rather than allow Black's Bishop to

sacrifice itself for it. With the elegant text move White deflects Black's King from d6, and White's Knight can then start to block Black's Bishop for the a-pawn.

64 ...	Kxf4

Equally hopeless is the defensive 64 ... Ke6. White plays 65 Nd4+, then Ne2, Ng3, and a7 and either wins the h-pawn or queens his a-pawn.

65 Nd6

There is no way for Black's Bishop to cope with the a-pawn; e.g., 65 ...Ba8 66 Ka7 Bg2 67 Kb8 followed by 68 Nb7, etc.

65 ...	f5
66 Nb7!	Kg3
67 a7	f4
68 a8=Q	f3
69 Qb8+	
Black resigns	

GAME 45

White: B. Spassky
(U.S.S.R.)

Black: J. H. Donner
(Netherlands)

Played at Amsterdam (Netherlands) IBM International Tournament, July 1973, Round 9.

Sicilian Defense (Najdorf Variation)

Spassky allows a sharp variation with which he could be expected to be familiar. But just as the independent thinking should start, he tries an unbelievably unsound combination. Donner gains two pieces for a Rook and wins very easily.

1	e4	c5
2	Nf3	d6
3	d4	cxd4
4	Nxd4	Nf6
5	Nc3	a6
6	Bg5	

The sharpest continuation, showing that Spassky is going for the win. This game follows the course of Game 30 through move 12.

6	...	e6
7	f4	Nbd7
8	Qf3	Qc7

9	0-0-0	b5
10	Bd3	Bb7
11	Rhe1	h6?!
12	Qh3	0-0-0

Up to now like Game 30, Timman-Polugaevsky, Hilversum 1973, in which White was successful with 13 Bxf6! Nxf6 14 Nd5!. Donner was of course familiar with that game, but although it had been played over a month earlier, Spassky was still unaware of it. After some deliberation he played.

13 f5?!

Inferior to 13 Bxf6 and calamitous as a preparation for what follows.

13 ...   e5

Now White has nothing better than 14 Bxf6 Nxf6 15 Nb3, though Black has at least full equality. Instead he continues with his combination/hallucination...

14 Ne6??

With the plan 14...fxe6? 15
fxe6 Nc5 16 Bxf6 gxf6?? 17 e7+,
but he overlooks the simple...

14 ...   hxg5!

Whereby Black gains the decisive material superiority of two
pieces for a Rook in a position in
which White doesn't have a chance
for anything. Since 15 Nxc7 Rxh3
16 gxh3 Kxc7 is now absolutely
hopeless, White has to stay in the
middlegame.

15 Qxh8	fxe6
16 fxe6	Nc5
17 Qh3	g4
18 Qg3	Qe7

Black will smoothly recover the
pawn and then start to exploit his
material superiority.

19 b4

Realizing that he must be lost,
White embarks on an essentially
suicidal opening of the Queenside.
19 Nd5 Qxe6 20 c4!? has to be a
shade better.

19 ...	Nxd3+
20 Qxd3	Qxe6
21 a4	bxa4

21...Qc4 is safe and sound, but
Black feels that opening the position will redound to the advantage of
his two Bishops.

22 Nd5	Kb8
23 Kb2	Nxd5
24 exd5	Qd7
25 c4	Be7
26 Ka3	Rf8
27 Rf1	Rxf1
28 Rxf1	Bf6

Black's KB is now well placed
and his e-pawn is passed. White
therefore hurries for one last try at
Black's King.

29 Rb1	Bc8

With the threat of 30...Qf5. If
now White plays 30 c5, then 30
...Qb5 puts a stop to everything.

30 b5	axb5
31 Rxb5+	Kc7
32 Qd2	

White's attack is only of cos-
metic strength since there is nothing
to back it up.

32 ...	Kd8!
33 Rb6	Qc7
34 Rc6	Qb8
35 Qa5+	Ke7
White resigns	

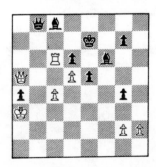

White's "attack" is over and now it's Black's turn; e.g.. 36 Rb6 Qc7 37 Qb4 Bd7 38 Rb7 Qc8 39 Rb6 Qc5 etc.

GAME 46

**White: A. Suetin
(U.S.S.R.)**

**Black: L. Portisch
(Hungary)**

Played at Ljubljana-Portoroz (Yugoslavia) International Tournament, April, 1973.

French Defense (Tarrasch Variation)

Suetin handles the opening soundly and enters the middlegame with a slight advantage. He manages the middlegame quite well and achieves a clearly superior double-Rook endgame. But in time pressure in the endgame he falls apart completely. First he throws away his advantage, then botches an equal position, and by adjournment stands significantly worse in a single-Rook endgame. Upon resumption of play he puts up good resistance in the beginning but falters later on and fails to take advantage of a good drawing opportunity. A good endgame effort by Portisch though White must take the blame for the loss rather than Black the credit.

1 e4   e6

The French is an unbalanced, steady, though somewhat cramped approach to meeting the aggressive

1 e4. Black plans to neutralize White's active e-pawn by a ... d5 and ensures that he can recapture with his e-pawn in case White plays exd5.

**2 d4   d5
3 Nd2**

White's e-pawn is challenged and he must decide what to do about it. The exchange 3 exd5 is harmless and 3 e5 - the Advance Variation - is playable though currently out of fashion. That leaves 3 Nc3 and the text as workable alternatives. The most aggressive choice is 3 Nc3, but since that allows the Winawer Variation (3 ...Bb4) with resultant great complications, many players prefer the more modest text. Originated by Tarrasch, it has two clear advantages over 3 Nc3: the pin on the QN is prevented and the c-pawn can be used for central support with c3. The disadvantages are the QN applies no pressure against Black's center and that the QB is blocked in.

3 ...   Nf6

One of three theoretically significant moves. The Guimard Variation, 3 ...Nc6, immediately applies pressure on the d-pawn but blocks off the c-pawn. Most popular currently is 3 ...c5, an excellent move to go for equality but the positions resulting after 4 exd5 exd5 or 4 ...Qxd5 are almost unwinnable for Black. The text is something in between 3 ...c5 and 3 ...Nc6: Black has a more unbalanced position than after the former and a strategically more flexible one than after the latter.

	4 e5	Nfd7
	5 Bd3	

More modern and currently about equal in popularity is the center-strengthening 5 f4.

	5 ...	c5
	6 c3	Nc6
	7 Ne2	cxd4
	8 cxd4	f6

In this type of position the thematic approaches for Black are to try to undermine White's center with ...c5 and ...f6. Instead of the text 8 ...Qb6 9 Nf3 f6 and 8 ... Nb6 are also playable and popular.

9 exf6

The attempt to attack with 9 Nf4? boomerangs: 9 ...Nxd4! 10 Qh5+ Ke7 11 Ng6+ hxg6 12 Qxh8 Nxe5 and Black has a slight material and significant central advantage.

9 ...   Nxf6

About equivalent is 9 ...Qxf6. In either case Black will try to get in ...e5.

	10 Nf3	Bd6
	11 Bf4	

The exchange of the dark-square Bishops is in White's strategic interest since this will weaken the dark squares in Black's position and leave White with the significantly superior Bishop. However, the exchange is not easy to bring about. Therefore, 11 0-0! is more accurate and only after 11 ...0-0 12 Bf4. If Black tries to prevent this by 11 ...Qc7 then White retains the superior chances with 12 Nc3 a6 13 Bg5.

(The positions after 11 0-0 Qc7 have become since 1984 the main line in the 3 ...Nf6 variation. The defensive resources that have been discovered for Black put him very close to full equality.)

11 ...   0-0?!

Giving White what he wants. Correct is 11 ...Qa5+!, and if 12 Bd2 Qc7 and Black is a tempo ahead of the previous note. If instead 12 Qd2, Black gets an essentially equal endgame after 12 ...Qxd2+ 13 Bxd2 0-0 14 0-0 Bd7, as in Parma-Tatai, Madonna di Campiglio 1974 (draw in 20).

	12 Bxd6	Qxd6
	13 0-0	e5

This is the only way to free Black's position, and Black must hurry with it before White has a chance to prevent it.

	14 dxe5	Nxe5
	15 Nxe5	Qxe5

| 16 Qd2 | Bd7 |
| 17 Rae1 | |

Modern master practice has shown that this type of position invariably favors White. Black's d-pawn, though passed, is isolated and readily blockadeable on d4 and is much more a weakness than a strength. White's Bishop has much more attacking scope than Black's. Overall Black has no prospects for active play and has to defend accurately to prevent White's pieces from penetrating. Theoretically Black is just a shade worse, but in practice his task is unpleasant.

17 ...	Kh8
18 Bb1!	Ng4
19 Ng3	Qd6
20 f3!	Nf6
21 Rd1	Qc5+
22 Qf2!	b6
23 Rc1!	Qd6

With his thoughtful 17th to 23rd moves, White has pushed Black's Queen and Knight around

and simultaneously improved the position of his own forces. Black's Queen is an excellent defender; it is better to keep it than allow the prospectless endgame after 23 ...Qxf2+?! 24 Rxf2.

| 24 Qd4 | Rae8 |
| 25 Bd3 | Kg8 |

Black anticipates the endgame and thus brings his King back closer to the center.

| 26 Ne4! | Qe5?! |

26 ...Nxe4 allows the strong 27 fxe4!; nevertheless, the coming endgame is very bleak for Black, and Suetin therefore feels that Black should stick to the middlegame with 26 ... Qe7! , whose immediate tactical point is that Black need not fear 27 Nxf6+ Rxf6 28 Qxd5+ since 28 ...Be6 recovers the pawn.

27 Nxf6+	Rxf6
28 Qxe5	Rxe5
29 Rc7	Bf5
30 Bxf5	Rfxf5

Up to here White has played perfect chess and after the obvious 31 Rxa7 would have an extra pawn and excellent winning chances. Then 31 ...Re2 is refuted by 32 g4! followed by 33 Rf2, and Black would therefore have to look for counterchances by means of 31 ...d4.

31 Kf2?!

Influenced by time pressure, White completely loses the bearings of the position over the next ten moves. The centralizing King move does keep out Black's Rook, but 31 Rxa7 wins a pawn for nothing!

31	...	Rf7!
32	Rc8+	Rf8
33	Rxf8+	Kxf8
34	Re1	

With the idea of a winning K+ P endgame after 34 ...Rxe1? 35 Kxe1 Ke7 36 Kd2 Kd6 37 Kd3, since White's Kingside pawn majority will yield him the outside passed pawn. But, since Black doesn't have to exchange, to grab the c-file immediately with 34 Rc1! is more efficient. Black then still has a very hard defensive road ahead.

| 34 | ... | Rh5! |
| 35 | Rc1? | |

There is no reason to give Black the h-pawn. Correct is 35 h3! and only then 36 Rc1. Since Black's King remains cut off, the penetration of White's Rook is assured. White would still have a clear advantage.

35	...	Rxh2
36	Rc8+	Ke7
37	Rc7+	Kd6
38	Rxg7	

Considerably simpler for drawing purposes is 38 Rxa7!. White continues to play for a win mostly out of inertia.

| 38 | ... | a5 |
| 39 | Kg1?? | |

Chasing Black's Rook where it wants to go (on h6 it protects the b-pawn and can swing over to c6), and giving up the center to Black's King and d-pawn. Correct is 39 Ke3 with approximate equality.

39	...	Rh6
40	Rg8	Ke5!
41	Rc8	Kd4

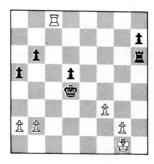

From a clearly inferior endgame, Black has achieved a clearly superior one. Material is equal, but Black's active King and passed d-pawn give him a tangible positional advantage. Black now threatens 42 ...Kd3 followed by 43 ...d4, 44 ... Kd2, etc. White correctly tries to prevent that as long as possible.

| 42 Rc3! | b5 |

43 Kf2	b4

The important factors in the position are Black's Rook, King, and d-pawn, and the move by the b-pawn costs Black a tempo. Immediately activating the Rook with 43 ... Rh1! is stronger.

44 Rc7	Kd3
45 f4!	

White's only hope for counterplay is the passed f-pawn.

45 ...	Ke4
46 Ra7	d4
47 Rxa5	Rc6!

Rook activity is always very important in R+P endgames, and the text is considerably stronger than 47 ...Kxf4?! 48 Rb5!.

48 Ra7	Rc2+
49 Kg3	Rxb2
50 Re7+	Kd5

Black doesn't want to block his d-pawn with 50 ... Kd3, but the game course shows that that must happen anyway.

51 Rxh7	Rxa2
52 Rb7	Kc4

Static evaluation gives White, with connected passed pawns, the superior pawn formation. But the dynamics all favor Black: his pawns are further advanced and his King

is able to assist the pawns' advance.

53 Rc7+	Kd3
54 Rb7	Kc3

The King must do the protecting since 54 ...Rb2? allows the f-pawn to run: 55 f5!, etc.

55 Rc7+	Kd2
56 Rb7	d3!

The b-pawn can't be protected so Black gives it up to mobilize the d-pawn advance.

57 f5	Ke2!

57 ...Kc3?! is fruitless since after 58 Kf3! White's King can help to stop the d-pawn: 58 ...d2 59 Ke2!

58 Rxb4	d2
59 Rb1!	

The only way to stop the d-pawn. Immediately losing is 59 Re4+? Kd3 60 Re8 Ra4! 61 Rd8+ Rd4.

59 ...	Ra4!

In order to win the coming R vs. 2P endgame, Black must prevent White's King from assisting in the advance of the f- and g-pawns for as long as possible; i.e.; until Black's King can get back in time. Only drawing is 59 ... d1=Q? 60 Rxd1 Kxd1 61 Kf4! Rxg2 62 f6, etc.

60 Rh1!   Re4?!

Here too 60...d1=Q? gives White a draw after 61 Rxd1 Kxd1 62 f6! Ra6 63 f7 Rf6 64 Kh4 Rxf7 65 g4, etc. Correct, however, is 60 ...Rc4! 61 Rb1 Rc1 62 Rb2 Rf1! 63 Kg4 Ke3 64 Rxd2 Kxd2 and compared to the above line, Black's King and Rooks are effectively placed and can stop the pawn (s).

61 Ra1   Kd3
62 Rd1?

White allows a variation of the previous line, and this is quite hopeless. The only chance is 62 f6!? Re1 63 f7! Rxa1 64 f8=Q d1=Q 65 Qd6+, and White has perpetual check, according to Suetin.

62 ...   Re1!
63 Rxd2+   Kxd2
64 Kf4   Kd3
65 f6   Kd4!

Black's King gets back very quickly, and the end is in sight.

66 Kf5   Kd5
67 g4   Rf1+
68 Kg6   Ke6
69 g5   Rf5
70 Kh6   Kf7
White resigns

The pawns have been stopped and 71 Kh5 Rf4! 72 Kh6 Rh4 is mate!

GAME 47

White: A. Suetin
(U.S.S.R.)

Black: J. Smejkal
(Czechoslovakia)

Played at Ljubljana-Portoroz (Yugoslavia) International Tournament, April 1973.

Dutch Defense
(Leningrad Variation)
(By transposition)

Uncharacteristically, Suetin opens with the c-pawn and soon doesn't really know what to do. He allows the doubling of pawns for nebulous chances along the b-file, fears to undertake anything in the center, and finds himself contained all across the board. Black has a strong grip on the center and after judicious preparation starts a positional Kingside attack. White is so disgusted at his position that he resigns while he still has material equality.

1 c4?!

The losing moment! Objectively, of course, there is nothing wrong with the English, but Suetin is an inveterate e-pawn man and will not feel at ease in the coming strategic waters. On the other hand,

Smejkal is a fine positional player and feels at home on both sides of this opening, as Games 6 and 14, for example, demonstrate.

1 ...   f5

An offer to enter the Dutch Defense by means of 2 d4. The text (and the Dutch Defense) has the strategic point of acting on the important e4 central square and preparing an attack along the f-file (occurring in this game on move 32!). The disadvantages are that the move does nothing to further development and carries with it a slight weakening of the Kingside.

2 Nc3	**Nf6**
3 g3	**g6**
4 Bg2	**Bg7**
5 d4	

This two-square advance of the d-pawn transposes the game into the Leningrad Variation (characterized by the fianchetto of Black's KB rather than its development on e7) of the Dutch Defense. A formation with 5 d3 retains the characteristics of the pure English.

5 ...	**0-0**
6 Nf3	**d6**
7 0-0	**c6**
8 Rb1?!	

Already White shows himself to be unfamiliar with the specifics of the opening. The correct and theoretical move is 8 d5! which leads to a slight plus for White.

| 8 ... | Ne4! |

Now after 9 Nxe4 fxe4 10 Ng5 Black has 10 ...d5.

9 Bf4	h6
10 Qc2	Nxc3
11 bxc3?!	

The doubling of the c-pawns gives White an inferior pawn formation without any noticeable compensation. The hoped for pressure along the b-file comes to nothing since White has no way to weaken Black's b- and c-pawns. Correct is the modest 11 Qxc3 with approximate equality.

| 11 ... | g5! |

With White in no attacking shape of any kind, Black can afford to expand his Kingside influence with a gain of time.

| 12 Bc1 | e5 |

And now Black has excellent influence in the center also.

| 13 Ba3 | Rf7 |
| 14 Rfd1 | |

White's edge in development is a mirage because he is too passive to be able to undertake anything of value. Thus 14 dxe5?! (opening the position) leads to nothing but a further weakening of the pawn formation (isolated, doubled c-pawns) after 14 ... dxe5 15 Rfd1 Qe8.

14 ...	e4!
15 Nd2	Qc7
16 e3	Nd7

A position containing significantly more opportunities for Black than for White. Black has superior central influence and characteristic chances for an attack on the Kingside. White's doubled pawns are a fundamental weakness, and his chances for play are nowhere in sight. If White continues to do nothing Black will complete his development with ... Nf6, ... Be6 ... Raf8 and then be ready for a decisive thrust on the Kingside. White must, therefore, undertake something.

17 f3!

The direct elimination of Black's advanced e-pawn is White's best course. 17 g4?! is too risky because of 17...Nf6! 18 gxf5 d5, when Black's e-pawn is safe whereas White has a seriously weakened Kingside.

17 ...	exf3
18 Bxf3	Nf6
19 Qd3?!	

White's position needs breathing room and thus 19 e4! is correct, after which White is only slightly worse.

19 ...	Be6
20 Rf1?	

Here was the last chance for 20 e4!.

20 ...	d5!

Fine strategic play by Black. He voluntarily allows White to liquidate his doubled pawn but gets a complete grip on the important e4 and c4 central squares in return. This will mean that White will be without chances for active play and that Black will be able to prepare the thematic attack on the Kingside at his relative leisure.

21 cxd5	cxd5!
22 Rbc1	Rc8!
23 Be2	Qa5
24 Bb4	Qa4!

Surely not 24...Qxa2??, losing the Queen after 25 Ra1 Qb2 26 Rfb1.

25 Qc2	Qe8!

Black wants to keep the Queen for attack and is not about to lighten White's load by an exchange.

26 Qd3	a6
27 Bd1	Bd7!

The Bishop on e6 is like a glorified pawn, and Black obviously wants to bring it to a more useful location.

28 Bb3	b6!
29 Rfe1?!	

Black's last is not so much to protect the c5 square as to prepare the a-pawn advance, which will cause a complete misplacement of White's forces. Therefore White has to play 29 a3! After 29... a5 30 Bd6 a4 31 Ba2 b5 the bind on White's position continues , but at least White's pieces have reasonable locations.

29 ...	a5
30 Ba3	a4
31 Bd1	Bb5
32 Qb1	f4!

At last Black starts his Kingside attack; White's disorganized army is in no condition to resist.

33 gxf4	gxf4
34 Nf3	Ne4
White resigns	

White still has material equality but resigned here in disgust at the helplessness of his position. A probable continuation is 35 Bb4 (to protect the c-pawn) 35 ...Rc6 36 Qb2 (36 Rc2 allows 36 ...Bd3) 36 ...Rg6+ 37 Kh1 fxe3 38 Rxe3 Ng3+ 39 hxg3 Qxe3, etc.

GAME 48

White: A. Suetin
(U.S.S.R.)

Black: B. Ivkov
(Yugoslavia)

Played at Ljubljana-Portoroz
(Yugoslavia) International Tournament, April 1973.

Ruy Lopez
(Steinitz Deferred
Variation)

White plays an interesting opening novelty and, when Black does not defend correctly, achieves a significant advantage. He gains a pawn for nothing and could safely consolidate his material plus. Instead, in a moment of chess blindness, he plays a faulty combination. Black wins a piece and thereafter the game. The swing from a winning to a losing position is immediate and drastic.

1	e4	e5
2	Nf3	Nc6
3	Bb5	a6
4	Ba4	d6
5	0-0	Bd7
6	d4	

In Game 3 White played 6 Re1 instead. The text is the more common choice, though ultimately the same position is usually

reached. Not in this game, however!.

6 ...	Nf6
7 c4!?	

An interesting and theoretically successful novelty. White's usual plans are 7 c3 and 7 Re1; also good is the less frequent 7 Bxc6 Bxc6 8 Re1. The idea of the text is to gain an immediate spatial advantage on the Queenside. Black must react resolutely to thwart White's plans.

7 ...	Be7?!

This move allows White to accomplish his objective. The correct way was demonstrated subsequently in Suetin-Knaak, Polinica Zdroj 1974: 7 ...exd4 8 Nxd4 b5! 9 Bb3 Nxd4 10 Qxd4 Be7 11 Nc3 0-0 12 Re1 b4 13 Nd5 Nxd5 14 cxd5 a5 with full equality for Black.

8 d5!	Na7

A more useful retreat square is b8!, and after 9 Bxd7+ Black has 9 ... Nbxd7, thereby controlling the c5 square.

9	Bxd7+	Qxd7
10	Nc3	c5?!

Black wants to make it more difficult for White to get in b4 but allows something considerably worse. The normal 10 ... 0-0 is preferable.

11 dxc6 e.p.   Qxc6?!

Unfortunately 11 ... bxc6? allows 12 c5! and a permanent weakening of Black's Queenside pawn formation. Therefore Black must acquiesce to allowing White complete control of the d5 central square. Even so the text is difficult to comprehend. Why not get the QN back into the game with 11 ... Nxc6?

12 Bg5!

Immediately going after the d5 square.

12 ...   Qxc4?!

Until he gets the wondrous gift from White, Black seems overly fatalistic about his ultimate chances for resistance. It is difficult to believe that as fine a positional player as Ivkov doesn't realize that the c-pawn capture is unsafe. The minor evil is 12 ...0-0.

13 Bxf6   Bxf6

After 13 ...gxf6 White has the pleasant choice between 14 Nd5 and 14 Nh4 followed by 15 Nf5.

14 Qxd6

Black's backward d-pawn is gone, but now his e-pawn is weak, his King is caught in the center, and White's Knight is ready to ensconce itself on d5.

14 ...   Nc8
15 Qa3   Ne7?!

This makes a bad situation even worse. Black has to get his King to safety and protect the e-pawn with 15 ...Be7 16 Qa5 f6 17 Rfd1 0-0, although White keeps a pleasant and significant advantage after 18 Rac1.

16 Rac1   Rc8

16 ...0-0? loses to 17 Nd5.

17 Nxe5!

The tactical punishment for Black's strategic errors. The Knight is inviolate since 17 ... Bxe5?? allows 18 Nd5 Qxc1 19 Qxe7! mate.

17 ...   Qe6
18 Qa4+??

Instantaneously transforming a won position into a lost one. After the modest retreat 18 Nd3, Black has nothing better than 18 ...Bxc3 19

Rxc3 Rxc3 20 Qxc3 0-0, after which
White plays 21 Qb4 and remains a
sound pawn up.

| 18 ... | b5 |
| 19 Nxb5 | |

Intending 19 ...axb5?? 20
Qxb5+ Kf8 21 Nd7+ Kg8 22 Rxc8!
Nxc8 22 Rc1 and White wins. As
Suetin tells it, he was horror-
stricken when he noticed, as he was
playing this move, that it's legal for
Black now to castle.

| 19 ... | 0-0! |

Now both of White's Knights
are en prise and one must go lost.

20 Rxc8	Nxc8
21 Nc4	axb5
22 Qxb5	Qxe4

White has two connected
passed pawns for the piece, but the
pawns cannot be quickly mobilized,
whereas Black's forces rapidly come
into play. White's situation is hopeless.

| 23 b3 | Qe2 |
| 24 a4 | Rd8! |

Threatening an immediate end
with 25 ... Rd1.

| 25 h3 | Bd4 |

26 Qf5	g6
27 Qf4	Qe6
28 Qf3	Nd6!
29 Na5?!	

29 Nxd6 Qxd6 ensures that
White's Queenside pawns won't
be able to advance, but allowing the
Black Knight to live guarantees an
accelerated end.

29 ...	Ne4
30 Qe2	Bxf2+!
31 Rxf2	Rd2

Moving the attacked Queen
away loses the Rook, and 32 Qxd2
Nxd2 33 Rxd2 Qe1+ or 32 Qxe4
Qxe4 33 Rxd2 Qe1+ leads to the loss
of the Queen and Rook. So ...

| 32 Nc4 | Rxe2 |
| White resigns | |

33 Rxe2 f5, etc., is obviously
hopeless for White.

GAME 49

**White: E. Ungureanu
(Rumania)**

**Black: M. Taimanov
(U.S.S.R.)**

Played at Bucharest (Rumania) International Tournament, March 1973.

King's Indian Defense (Normal Variation)

Taimanov tries an off-beat line in the King's Indian, but his opponent's strong and consistent strategy quickly demonstrates that it is White who gains from Black's experimentation. He puts Black in a bind on the Kingside, establishes control of key squares in the center and Queenside, and achieves control of the d-file. This soon leads to a gain of decisive material, and the rest is a mop-up operation.

1 Nf3	Nf6
2 c4	g6
3 Nc3	Bg7
4 e4	0-0
5 d4	d6

Because Taimanov does not usually play the King's Indian when he expects his opponent to play the main lines, he must have something particular in mind.

6 Be2	c6

We have reached the Normal Variation by transposition. Black's "normal" move is now 6 ...e5. see Game 21).

7 0-0	a6?!

So this is Black's off-beat plan! It is superior to the ridiculous 7 ... Qb6? of Game 23 but inferior to the usual 7...e5. The idea behind the text is to start action on the flank by means of ...b5.

8 a4!	

Immediately putting a stop to Black's plans. 8 Bg5 is not bad either, and after 8 ... b5 9 e5 Ne8 10 Re1 White was better in Uhlmann-Doda, Polonica Zdroj 1967.

8 ...	a5

Forced because of the threat of 9 a5. But Black's a-pawn has taken two moves to reach a5, and thus it is White's turn to move again. The Queenside weaknesses are about equivalent, but White has gained without cost a tempo for development.

9 h3	Na6
10 Be3	Nd7
11 Qd2!	

This and the following moves are unquestionably White's most

active approach. Also good is 11
Nd2, and after 11 ... e5 12 d5 White
had a slight advantage in Bobotsov-
Sakharov, Sochi 1966.

11 ...   Re8?!

Neither this nor the next pre-
paratory move adds punch, and as a
result White can build a more active
position. Correct is the immediate
11 ...e5.

12 Rad1	Qc7
13 Nh2!	e5
14 f4!	exd4
15 Bxd4	

A   marvelous position for
White has been reached soon after
the opening. White's development
is complete, and he has significant
superiority in the center, good
pressure against Black's weak d-
pawn, and excellent attacking
chances against Black's Kingside.
Black has no prospects for active
play and hasn't even developed his
Queenside.

15 ...   f6

The exchange of Bishops ir-
reparably weakens   Black's
Kingside; e.g., 15 ... Bxd4+?! 16
Qxd4 Ndc5 (or 16 ...Nac5 17 Ng4!)
17 f5!, in either case with an
exceedingly strong attack for White.

16 Ng4	Nac5
17 Qc2	Ne6
18 Be3	Nef8?

Black's position is very
cramped and therefore nearly critical. Exact maneuvers are required,
and so imperative is 18 ...Nd8! followed by 19 ... Nf7, which allows
the Knight to protect the d-pawn and
the important h6 square. After the
inexact text move, Black is caught in
a bind from which he never recovers.

19 f5!   Ne5

Even worse is 19 ...gxf5? 20
Nh6+! Bxh6 21 Bxh6 fxe4 22 Nxe4
and   Black's   Kingside   soon
crumbles.

20 Nxe5   dxe5

20 ...Rxe5? loses to 21 Bf4 and
20 ...fxe5? to 21 f6.

21 c5!	Rd8
22 Nb1!	

Black's Kingside is immobile,
the   Queenside still undeveloped,
and there are lots of weaknesses in

his camp. White prepares to send his Knight to c4 and from there to d6, b6, or a5, depending on the situation. Black is strategically lost; but giving White's Knight the e4 square a move later amounts to driving another nail into his own coffin.

22 ...	Kh8
23 Nd2	gxf5?!
24 exf5	Bd7
25 Ne4!	

25 Nc4 isn't bad but the text completely paralyzes Black.

25 ...	Be8
26 Bc4	Rd7
27 Rxd7!	Nxd7?!

Overlooking White's plan. Some resistance can be mounted with 27 ... Qxd7.

28 Ba2!

Threatening 29 Qb3 followed by mate on g8. There is no defense to this threat.

28 ...	b5
29 Qb3	Bh5
30 g4	

Since the attacked Bishop can't afford to retreat, White wins a clear piece.

| 30 ... | bxa4 |

31 Qc4	Qb7
32 gxh5	h6
33 Rf2	

Black is totally busted, and only White's time pressure gives Black the nerve to continue the game.

33 ...	Qb4
34 Rd2	a3
35 bxa3	Qxa3
36 Kf2	Rb8

If 36 ...Rd8, 37 Rxd7! anyway.

37 Rxd7

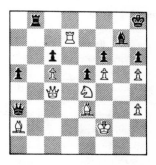

Now Black is two pieces down in a hopeless situation. If 37 ... Rb2+ 38 Rd2. Still he braves it to move 40.

37 ...	Qb2+
38 Nd2	Rf8
39 Rf7	Rd8
40 Rd7	Rf8
41 Qg4	

Black resigns

GAME 50

White: R. Byrne
(U.S.A.)

Black: M. Taimanov
(U.S.S.R.)

Played at Leningrad (U.S.S.R.) Interzonal Tournament, June 16, 1973.

Sicilian Defense (Taimanov Variation)

Both players handle the opening creatively, with White perhaps emerging with a tiny edge. The middlegame is, however, all Byrne's. Some deep strategy backed by ultrasharp tactics leads to White's decisively gaining material. A time-pressure slip by White affords Black the opportunity to gain a problem draw in an endgame in which he has Rook and pawns against White's Queen and pawn. After missing this opportunity, he is quickly extinguished. Overall an excellent effort by Byrne, showing the creative and sporting form which enabled him to reach the Candidates matches.

1	e4	c5
2	Nf3	Nc6
3	Nc3	a6
4	d4	

Instead 4 g3 d6 transposes into our Game 3. Byrne prefers the normal waters that result after the text.

4	...	cxd4
5	Nxd4	e6

With some transposition of moves we've reached one of the positions of the Taimanov Variation. Black establishes some central presence and plans to start something soon on the Queenside. The whole approach in the Taimanov is to have a fluid, if not to say ambigous, situation. Such an approach forces White to start independent thinking early on. The slight disadvantage to Black's approach is that his moves are often not the most logical for central development.

6 g3

The fianchetto of the KB is strategically sound. Other good moves are 6 Be2 and 6 Be3.

6	...	Nge7

Somewhat esoteric looking, though with the reasonable plan of conveniently exchanging Knights with 7 ...Nxd4 8 Qxd4 Nc6. More common is 6 ... Qc7.

7 Nb3

Preventing the above plan is White's most common response. Worth considering, however, is 7 Be3 since then 7 ...Nxd4 8 Qxd4 Nc6

allows White to bind down Black's
Queenside with 9 Qb6!.

| 7 ... | b5?! |

This immediate Queenside
demonstration has quickly gone out
of master practice since it carries no
concrete threats, loses time, and
weakens the Queenside without
significant benefit. Also not quite
successful is the further attempt to
exchange Knights with 7 ... Na5,
since after 8 Qh5! White obtains a
very active position. The modern
move is the developmental 7 ...d6
followed by 8 ...Bd7 (9 Qxd6??
loses the Queen after 9 ...Nd5).

8 Bg2	d6
9 f4	Bb7
10 Be3	g6

A plan that succeeds in this
game. Even so, the more modest
development 10 ... Ng6 11 0-0 Be7
is somewhat sounder.

| 11 Qd2 | Qc7 |
| 12 Qf2 | |

After this Black has enough
time to consolidate. The only way to
seriously question Black's setup is
the active 12 0-0-0! Rd8 13 Qf2! Rd7
14 e5! and Black is exposed to a
dangerous attack.

| 12 ... | Bg7 |
| 13 0-0 | 0-0 |

| 14 Rad1 | Rfe8 |
| 15 Rd2 | Nc8! |

Black has approximate equality
after this fine multi-purpose move,
whereby Black protects the d-
pawn, allows his Queen to help
protect the Kingside in case of a f5
by White, and allows the KR pressure on the e-file in case it is
opened. White has no immediate
active course available; e.g., 16 f5
Ne5!, 16 e5 Nd8! or 16 Rfd1 Na5 17
Nxa5 Qxa5 18 a3 b4 and Black is the
one attacking! Therefore White
quite soundly takes timeout for a
preventive move on the Queenside.

| 16 a3! | Rb8! |

Black strives to get lines
opened on the Queenside, his
thematic attacking side.

17 Rfd1	b4
18 axb4	Nxb4
19 Bd4!	

Black's KB is an excellent defensive and offensive piece, and it is in White's interest to exchange it.

19 ...	Bxd4
20 Qxd4	Ba8
21 Bf1	

Keeping a watch on Black's a-pawn at the cost of some weakening of his own e-pawn. A good alternative is 21 Qf2 with the plan 22 f5.

| 21 ... | e5 |

Possible is 21 ...Nxc2 22 Rxc2 Rxb3 but it appears that, after 23 Bxa6, White's passed b-pawn gives him a slight plus.

| 22 fxe5 | Rxe5 |
| 23 Qf2!? | |

Both a good move and a trap. It works like a charm.

| 23 ... | Bxe4? |

Taimanov felt that Byrne had simply left a pawn en prise. This seems like a naive approach against a world-class GM. Correct is 23 ...Qe7 or the sharper 23... f5!?, in either case with approximate equality.

| 24 Nxe4 | Rxe4 |
| 25 c3 | Nc6?? |

When one doesn't search he can't be expected to find anything. Black is still ignorant of White's threat(s). The surprising 25 ...Nc2! is imperative even though White still has a clear advantage after 26 Bd3 Ne3 27 Bxe4 Nxd1 28 Rxd1 Rxb3 29 Bd5 Rb8 30 Rf1 since he recovers his pawn and retains the superior position.

26 Nc5!!

This should mean the end for Black. The dual threats 27 Nxe4 and 27 Nxa6 force the capture and then...

| 26 ... | dxc5 |
| 27 Rd7 | |

...wins the Queen because of the threat of 28 Qxf7+.

27 ...	Qxd7
28 Rxd7	Re7
29 Rd1?!	

White's position is quite won, but in incipient time pressure he starts taking things too lightly. Easily winning is 29 Rxe7 N8xe7 30 Bxa6. Instead White wants to retain his Rook for attacking purposes; in practice only Black can gain from thus complicating the position.

29 ...	N8a7
30 Bxa6	Ne5
31 Bf1?!	

And this makes things even

more uncertain. Winning by force is 31 Qxc5! Rxb2!? 32 Rd8+! (in time pressure White considered only 32 Qxe7?? whereupon Black draws with 32 ...Nf3+) 32 ... Kg7 33 Qxe7 Nf3+ 34 Kf1 Nxh2+ 35 Ke1 Nf3+ 36 Kd1- White's King now has access to this square.

| 31 ... | c4 |
| 32 Bg2?! | |

Allowing Black access to d3 and a surprising chance for a draw. After 32 Rd5! White should still win- slowly but surely.

32 ...	Nd3
33 Qd4	Nb5
34 Qxc4	Nxb2
35 Qf4	Rbe8
36 Rb1	Nd3?

Leads to additional material loss. In time pressure and seeing, in effect, nothing over the last part of the game, it is not at all surprising that Taimanov misses the problem draw available with 36 ...Nxc3!! 37 Rxb2 Re1+! 38 Bf1 (38 Kf2?? Nd1+) Ne2+ 39 Rxe2 R8xe2 40 Qc4! Rxf1+!! 41 Kxf1 Rxh2. Black does have a significant material disadvantage, but the presence of pawns on only one side of the board does not allow White a winning ma-

neuver; e.g., 42 g4 Rh4! 43 Qc8+ Kg7 44 Qc3+ Kg8 45 Qg3 g5 followed by ...Rh6 (Zuckerman) and how is White to makes progress?

| 37 Qd2 | Na3 |
| 38 Ra1 | |

The Knights are in an untenable situation. If now 38 ...Ne1 39 Rxa3 Re2, White scores with 40 Ra8!

38 ...	Re1+
39 Rxe1	Nxe1
40 Qd7	Re2
41 Bd5	Kg7

Black sealed his 41st move but then resigned without continuing the game. After 42 Qxf7+ Kh6 43 Qf8+ Kh5 44 Bf3+ he loses his house.

GAME 51

White: M. Taimanov
(U.S.S.R.)

Black: J. Smejkal
(Czechoslovakia)

Played at Leningrad (U.S.S.R)
Interzonal Tournament, June 23,
1973, Round 15.

King's Indian Defense (Yugoslav/Panno Variation)

By a deft move order, Smejkal
is able to catch Taimanov in a variation which Taimanov does not normally play as White. The results are
not long in coming: White falls into
an opening trap and loses a pawn for
nothing. Smejkal takes the pawn and
brings home the point in a matter-of-technique endgame.

1 c4	Nf6
2 Nc3	c5
3 Nf3	Nc6
4 g3	

An invitation to the Tarrasch/
Reti complexes after 4 ...e6 5 Bg2 d5
or the English after 4 ...d5.

4 ...	g6

Black prefers a symmetrical
approach, showing himself to be
ready for the Yugoslav Variation of
the King's Indian.

5 Bg2	Bg7
6 0-0	0-0
7 d4	

7 d3 is harmless; thus the text
transposes into a normal d-pawn
opening, the Yugoslav Variation of
the King's Indian Defense. Objectively it's O.K. for White, but as
White Taimanov invariably plays
the Normal Variation against the
King's Indian. He's not familiar
with the Yugoslav.

7 ...	d6

The pure Yugoslav. 7 ... cxd4
leads to the Semi- Yugoslav (see the
next game!).

8 d5	

The full-play approach. The
exchanging 8 dxc5 dxc5 leads to a
minute plus for White after either 9
Be3 or 9 Bf4.

8 ...	Na5
9 Nd2	

At first glance this may look
awkward, but over twenty years of
master experience has shown it to be
the only satisfactory way to defend
the c-pawn.

9 ...	a6

With this Black voluntarily enters a variation possible in the Panno (see Game 60), in which White continues with 8 d5 Na5 9 Nd2 and Black plays 9 ...c5. With the text Black aims for quick action along the b-file with ...b5. The alternatives 9 ...e5 and 9 ...e6 keep the game in the pure Yugoslav.

10 Qc2	Rb8
11 b3	b5
12 Bb2	

The two most common plans for Black now are 12 ...e6 and 12 ...e5. But Smejkal has a better idea: speculating on White's lack of expertise in the variation he decides on a more trap-ridden plan.

| 12 ... | bxc4 |
| 13 bxc4 | Bh6!? |

With the obvious threat 14 ... Bxd2 followed by 15 ...Nxc4. White has two good responses: the dynamic 14 f4! and the strategic 14

Ncb1!, in both cases with a slight advantage. But isn't there a sound, simple method like

14 e3??

NO because of ...

| 14 ... | Bf5! |
| 15 e4 | |

White must lose a pawn no matter what he does: e.g., 15 Qc1 Bd3 followed by 16 ...Nxc4 or 15 Nce4 Nxe4 16 Bxe4 Bxe4 17 Nxe4 Nxc4.

| 15 ... | Bxd2 |
| 16 Nd1 | |

No better is 16 exf5 Nxc4 17 Nd1 Nxb2 18 Nxb2 Bh6 and White's a pawn down for nothing, as in Foguelman-Panno, Buenos Aires 1968.

16 ...	Bd7!
17 Bxf6	exf6
18 Qxd2	Nxc4
19 Qc3	Nb6

Black is up a sound protected passed c- pawn, and White has no compensation for it. Black's doubled f-pawns are no problem since White can't attack them, and the Black Kingside is fully defensible. This allows Black to work on his strength - the Queenside - and Smejkal does a workman like job there. White does not get the slightest chance anywhere.

20	Re1	Na4
21	Qd2	Kg7
22	Rc1	Rb4!
23	Ne3	Bb5!
24	Nc2	

24 Ng4?! is foiled by 24 ... f5! since 25 exf5?? is not feasible because of the hanging Knight.

24	...	Rb2
25	a3	c4

The c-pawn is safe here and later on c3, and it restricts White's piece deployment. Thus, for this middlegame position, passed pawns should be pushed.

26	Qd4	Qb6
27	Qxb6	

The endgame is hopeless, the middlegame untenable.

27	...	Nxb6
28	Bf1	Rc8
29	Nd4	Rc5
30	Kg2	c3!
31	Nxb5	axb5
32	Bd3	Ra2
33	Ra1	Rd2!
34	Red1	Rxd1
35	Rxd1	Nc4
36	Ra1	

White's on his last legs. After 36 Bxc4 Rxc4 37 Kf3 Ra4 White loses another pawn.

36	...	Nb2
37	Bc2	f5!

The undermining of the d-pawn soon leads to its gain, and then at the very least Black will have connected passed c- and d-pawns. White could resign here with a clear conscience.

38	Kf3	Nc4
39	Ke2	fxe4
40	Bxe4	f5
41	Bd3	Nb2
42	Rc1	Kf6
43	f4	Rxd5
44	Bb1	

The pawn-down K+P endgame after 44 Rxc3 Rxd3 45 Rxd3 Nxd3 46 Kxd3 Ke6 is hopeless.

44	...	Rd2+
45	Kf3	Nd1
46	g4	fxg4+
47	Kg3	

47 Kxg4 c2, etc.

47 ...   d5
White resigns

Enough is enough. Taimanov was under no illusions after his blunder on move 14 and, realizing the hopelessness of his position, played the rest of the game at virtual blitz tempo, using only 2 hours and 5 minutes for it all. Smejkal, wanting to make the win sure, spent a whole hour more.

GAME 52

White: M. Tal
(U.S.S.R.)

Black: E. Torre
(Philippines)

Played at Leningrad Interzonal Tournament, June 4, 1973, Round 2.

King's Indian Defense (Semi-Yugoslav Variation)

Tal considers that he must beat the youthful Philippine master but obtains little out of a closed opening. A balanced middlegame quickly leads to a balanced endgame, and at exactly this moment Tal's psychological need to win reasserts itself. He eschews normal good moves and to unbalance the position puts his pieces on ridiculous squares. Torre penetrates Tal's camp, wins a pawn, and brings home the full point in a well-played, though not too difficult R+P endgame. One more example in which unmotivated playing to win leads straight to a loss.

1 Nf3

Tal is one of the great, creative attacking players of all time. He also has a very broad repertoire and frequently plays the strategic text. In this game the choice works badly.

White obtains no attacking chances at all, and neither does he achieve a position offering winning chances.

1	...	Nf6
2	c4	g6
3	Nc3	Bg7
4	g3	0-0
5	Bg2	c5
6	d4	

White must play this soon; otherwise the position becomes quite symmetrical. By transposition the game has entered the Yugoslav Variation of the King's Indian Defense.

6	...	cxd4

This central capture leads to the Semi-Yugoslav. The normal Yugoslav follows 6 ... d6 (see the previous game).

| 7 | Nxd4 | Nc6 |
| 8 | 0-0 | Nxd4 |

The slight strategic problem with the Semi-Yugoslav is that Black has to give up more central space to White in order to complete the normal development of his Queenside; e.g., 8 ... d6?! is a dubious pawn sacrifice.

9	Qxd4	d6
10	Qd3	a6
11	Be3	

A good active developing

move, with the point that 11...Rb8?!
is met by 12 Ba7! Ra8 13 Bd4! Also
playable for White are 11 e4 and 11
Bd2.

11 ...	Ng4
12 Bd4	Ne5
13 Qd1!	Rb8!

Black's correct approach is to
aim immediately for counterplay
with ...b5. Instead 13...Be6? proves
to be an unsound pawn sacrifice
after 14 Bxb7 Rb8 15 Bxa6 Rxb2 16
Nd5, and 13...Nxc4?? loses the
Knight after 14 Bxg7 Kxg7 15
Qd4+ Ne5 16 f4.

14 Rc1

The usual move, but worth
considering is the preventive 14
a4!?. It was successfully used in
Shamkovich-Zuckerman, New
York International 1977, in which
after 14...Be6 15 Nd5 b6 16 b3 a5 17
e4 Nd7 18 Bxg7 Kxg7 19 f4 White's
central superiority gave him a small
though steady edge.

| 14 ... | Be6 |
| 15 Nd5 | |

15 b3 has often been recommended but has not so far been tried
in actual practice.

| 15 ... | b5 |
| 16 cxb5 | |

White gets nothing from 16 c5

Bxd5! 17 Bxd5 e6 18 Bg2 d5.

| 16 ... | Bxd5 |

Played regularly, though 16
...axb5 also seems to be O.K. since
after 17 Nc7 Black has 17...Bxa2!?.

| 17 Bxd5 | axb5! |

This seems stronger than 17 ...
Rxb5 18 Bg2 Qa5 19 a3, and White
had a slight advantage in
Tukmakov- Smejkal, Erevan 1976.

18 Qd2?!

White not only does nothing
about Black's plan but also makes
sure that Black can execute it with
gain of time. White has two logical
approaches. He can play 18 b3 or
the sharper 18 f4!?. Then after 18 ...
Ng4 White retains some edge with
19 Bf3 Bxd4+ 20 Qxd4 Nf6 21 Rc6
(Zaitsev) but 18...Nd7! 19 Ba7 Rc8
20 Qd2 Nc5! 21 b4 Qc7! is quite

equal, Ribli-Gheorghiu, Las Palmas
1973.

18 ...	e6!
19 Bg2	Nc4
20 Qc3	Bxd4
21 Qxd4	d5
22 b3	Qb6!
23 Rfd1	

Leads to a completely unwinnable endgame. If White truly wants
to win, then he should keep the
Queens on the board.

23 ...	Qxd4
24 Rxd4	Nd6
25 Rc6	Rfd8

Black can also play actively
with 25 ...Nf5 26 Rb4 Ra8 27 Rc2
Rfc8!, but having full respect for his
opponent, he prefers a safer route.

26 e3??

It's not clear what this has to do
with the game. A normal continuation is 26 Rd1 Rbc8 27 Rdc1 with
equality. Larsen has correctly
pointed out that because White's
Bishop is inactive, White's safest
route to a draw is 26 e4.

| 26 ... | Rbc8 |
| 27 Rb6?? | |

Truly incomprehensible;
moreover, Tal spent a considerable
amount of time both on this and his
previous move. White allows Black

to walk right in, and for what
purpose? The obvious 27 Rxc8
Rxc8 28 Bf1 is correct, and there is
no reason for the game not to end
in a draw.

28 ...	Rc1+
29 Bf1	Ne4!
29 Kg2	

29 Rxb5 loses the Exchange
after 29 ... Nc3 30 Rb7 Ne2+. Not
that what happens is any better. With
the text White hopes for 29 ...Rc2?!
30 Bd3! Rxf2+ 31 Kg1 Rd2 32
Bxe4 and White is safe. But the following zwischenzug spoils White's
dream.

| 29 ... | e5! |
| 30 Rb4 | Rc2! |

Material loss now is
unavoidable. The only remaining
question is whether White can save
himself after all the exchanges are
completed and the number of Black
pawns has been greatly reduced.

31 a4	bxa4
32 bxa4	Rxf2+
33 Kg1	Ra2
34 Rb8	

Since White has no realistic
prospects of pushing his a-pawn, he
tries to get at Black's central
pawns.

| 34 ... | Rxb8 |
| 35 Rxb8+ | Kg7 |

36 Rb5	Nc3
37 Rc5	Nd1

Black heads for a R+P endgame, in which he will be up a pawn and will have various positional pluses. The next few moves are forced.

38 Rxd5	Nxe3
39 Rxe5	Nxf1
40 Kxf1	Rxh2!

The position Black had in mind. Using the technique seen later in the game, he plans to create two connected passed pawns on the Kingside. Meanwhile, the active location of Black's Rook and the passive location of White's King mean that White's a-pawn is no threat.

41 Re7?!

The sealed move and nothing but a waste of time. With the immediate 41 Re2! Rh1+ 42 Kf2 Ra8 43 Re4 White's King could at least get off of the back rank.

41 ...	Ra2
42 Re4	

A sad retreat, but 42 Ra7 immobilizes White's Rook and allows Black's King readily to get to White's Kingside.

42 ...	h5
43 Rh4	f6
44 Kg1	Kf7
45 Kf1	Ke6
46 Re4+	Kf5
47 Rf4+	Ke5
48 Rh4	Rd2!

With the threat 49 ...Rd4! since Black's King is close enough to the a-pawn. Therefore White's Rook must move away and Black's g-pawn can advance.

49 Rb4	g5
50 Rb3	Ra2
51 Rb4	Kf5
52 Kg1	Kg6
53 Rc4	g4

Black is building up for a properly timed ...h4, which will make his f-and g-pawns connected and passed.

54 Rb4	f5!
55 Rb8	

Otherwise 55 ... Kg5 and 56 ... h4.

55 ...	h4!

Ensuring that Black will get connected passed pawns is the clearest method of winning.

56	gxh4	Rxa4
57	Kg2	Ra3
58	Rg8+	

If 58 Rb6+ Kh5 59 Rf6, then 59 ... Rf3 spells the end.

58	...	Kf7
59	Rg5	Kf6
60	Rg8	Rh3
61	Rh8	Ke5
62	h5	

Leads to the loss of the pawn, but otherwise 62 ... Kf4 is decisive.

62	...	Kf6!
63	h6	Kg6
64	Rg8+	Kxh6
65	Kf2	

Equivalent to resignation. But no better is 65 Rh8+ Kg5 66 Rxh3 gxh3+ 67 Kxh3 Kf4! 68 Kg2 Ke3! with a routine K+P endgame win.

65	...	Ra3
66	Kg2	Kh5
67	Kf2	Kh4
White resigns		

The threat is 68 ...Ra2+ followed by 69 ... Kg3, and 68 Rh8+ allows Black's King to go to g5 and then to f4.

GAME 53

White: G. Estevez
(Cuba)

Black: M. Tal
(U.S.S.R.)

Played at Leningrad (U.S.S.R.)
Interzonal Tournament, June 5,
1973, Round 3.

Sicilian Defense
(Scheveningen Variation)

Tal allows his opponent the
kind of attacking position that Tal
himself would like to have. While
Estevez meaningfully improves the
position of his pieces, Tal flutters to
and fro with little consistency of
thought. He gets his Rook caught in
the center of the board, and while
both players are in time pressure
Estevez finally administers mate.
The kind of game in which Tal, not
his opponent, would seem to be playing the White pieces.

1	e4	c5
2	Nf3	e6
3	d4	cxd4
4	Nxd4	Nf6
5	Nc3	d6

Tal has chosen the Scheveningen Variation, a relatively safe way
to handle the unbalancing Sicilian
Defense. Black establishes a modest but clear central presence and
plans to mobilize his Kingside
forces before initiating Queenside
activity.

6 Be2

White's normal continuation.
Sharper are Keres' 6 g4!? and 6 Bc4.

6 ...   a6

Now in many lines we get
something like a cross between the
Najdorf and the Scheveningen.
There is no immediate need for this
move; the usual Scheveningen pro-
ceeds with 6 ...Be7 (see Game 58,
Westerinen-Tukmakov, Hastings
1972/73.)

7 a4

There is even less need for this
precaution since Black is surely not
threatening ...b5. The normal good
moves are 7 0-0 and 7 f4.

7 ...   Qc7

It's also too early for the
Queen to head here since the c-file
may be more useful for the QR, especially if Black chooses a setup
with ... Nbd7. 7 ...Be7 or 7 ... Nc6
is preferable.

8 Be3   b6

Here too, Black has an easier
time equalizing with 8 ...Nc6.

9 f4	Bb7
10 Bf3	Nbd7
11 Qe2	Be7

11 ...g6?! is too dangerous because of 12 e5! dxe5 13 fxe5 Nxe5 14 Bxb7 Qxb7 15 Bg5!: 15 ...Nfd7 16 Ne4! or 15 ...Ned7 16 Nxe6!. And 11 ...Nc5 12 Bf2 will probably transpose into the game continuation.

12 0-0	0-0
13 Kh1	Nc5
14 Bf2	

White has harmoniously developed his pieces and is ready to proceed with the central advance 15 e5!. Black has two reasonable choices, the blockading 14 ...e5, which allows 15 fxe5 dxe5 16 Nf5 with some advantage to White, or the text move.

| 14 ... | d5 |

In theory a desirable move, but it will lead to an isolated d-pawn. Black is O.K. after 15 e5 Nfe4 16 Bxe4 Nxe4 17 Nxe4 dxe4, but White plays better.

| 15 exd5! | Nxd5 |
| 16 Bxd5! | exd5 |

Black's QB will remain rather dead for the rest of the game, but 16 ...Bxd5 17 Nxd5 exd5 suffers from the disadvantage of giving Black an isolated pawn and no prospects of active play.

17 Qg4!

White's KN has access to f5, and thus White will have a strong attacking formation. Black must show that he can equalize.

| 17 ... | Bf6 |
| 18 Nf5 | Ne6 |

It's logical to overprotect the crucial g7 square. 18 ... Ne4?! is very dangerous because of 19 Bh4!.

19 Bh4!

Removing the strong Black Bishop is the right idea for both tactical and strategic reasons.

| 19 ... | Bxh4 |
| 20 Qxh4 | Rfe8?! |

Black prevents Ne7+ and places his Rook on an open file. After the loss in the previous round to Torre, Tal is anxious to win against the young Cuban, especially since Estevez lost his first two games and is the lowest rated participant. 20...Rad8? is worse than the text because of 21 Rf3!, and now 21...d4 (with the idea 22 Rh3? Bxg2+!) is refuted by 22 Ne7+ Kh8 23 Qxh7+!! Kxh7 24 Rh3 mate. However, Black does not really have time for the text and should continue with the immediate 20...d4!. After 21 Nd5! Bxd5 22 Ne7+ Kh8 23 Nxd5 Qc5 24 c4 dxc3 e.p. 25 Nxc3, White has only a slight advantage, according to Estevez.

21 Rad1!	Qc5
22 Qg3!	Kh8
23 Ne2!	Qf8?!

Moving backward is hardly in Tal's style and in general cannot lead to good results. Perhaps he has to risk 23...Qxc2 24 Ned4 Qc7! (24 ... Qxb2?? 25 Rb1 followed by 26 Nxe6). Then 25 Rc1 Qd7 26 Nxe6 fxe6 27 Qxg7+ Qxg7 28 Nxg7 allows White to recover his pawn, but after 28...Re7! Black has no worries. In the game he has nothing to compensate for his suffering.

24 Ned4	Nc5
25 Qh4	Re4?!

The Rook occupies an untenable position here. 25...Ne4 is more in the spirit of his previous move.

26 Ng3	Qe7?

Retreating the Rook is unpleasant because of 27 f5, but leaving it exposed in the center is worse.

27 Qg4!

Now Black is hopelessly lost, since 27...Re3 fails to 28 Ngf5.

27 ...	Bc8
28 Qh5	g6
29 Qh6!	

White is interested in much bigger game than the d-pawn. If now 29...Re3, then 30 f5 is the killer. So Tal tries tactics, but Estevez is right on the ball.

29 ...	Bg4
30 Nxe4	Qxe4??

Allowing his Queen to be trapped in the middle of the board is unforgivable. Not much better is 30...Bxd1?! because of 31 Nf5! Qf8 (31... gxf5 32 Nf6) 32 Ng5! Qxh6 33 Nxf7+ Kg8 34 N5xh6+ Kg7 35 Rxd1 and White is a safe piece ahead. 30... Nxe4 is the best there is, though after 31 Rde1 Black is theoretically quite lost.

31 Rfe1

The end.

31 ...	Bxd1
32 Rxe4	Nxe4
33 f5	

White is up a decisive amount of material and has a killing

Kingside attack. Only both sides' severe time pressure causes the game to be continued.

	33 ...	Re8
34	fxg6	fxg6
35	Ne6!	Rg8
36	Qf4	

With the threat 37 Qe5+ followed by mate on g7. Tal "prefers" a different end.

	36 ...	h5
37	Qh6 mate!	

An excellent game by Estevez, played in an active style characteristic of a Tal.

GAME 54

White: M. Tal
(U.S.S.R.)

Black: R. Hubner
(West Germany)

Played at Leningrad (U.S.S.R.) Interzonal Tournament, scheduled for June 7 but because of Tal's illness actually played on June 10, 1973, Round 4.

Sicilian Defense
(New Taimanov Variation)

Smarting from the previous two losses, Tal is gung ho for a victory and plays sharply for a mating attack. But Hubner's defense is perfect, and the best that White has is to reach for an even endgame. Tal disdains that and is soon forced to accept a middle-game in which his opponent not only gets the material edge of two Rooks and a pawn for a Queen but also retains the overall superior chances. When White plays inexactly he gets hit by an unstoppable attack against *his* Kingside. A fine example of the hunted's suddenly changing roles and becoming the hunter.

1	e4	c5
2	Nf3	e6
3	d4	cxd4
4	Nxd4	a6
5	Nc3	

By transposition the same New Taimanov position has been reached as in Game 18, Keres-Popov, Dortmund 1973. Master practice of the middle 1970's has shown that the flexible 5 Bd3! is more unpleasant for Black, for it leaves open the possibility of c4, which would strengthen White's central control.

5 ...	Qc7
6 Be2	

This is more promising than the 6 g3 of Game 18.

6 ...	b5!?

An interesting psychological moment: Hubner realizes that Tal is hungry for a win, and he therefore chooses a most enterprising plan in the hope that Tal will overpress an attack. The risk, of course, is that Black can be killed by a sharp attack, but Hubner has concluded that Tal's play in this tournament is too unsure to present much real danger. The normal steady move is 6 ...Nf6, and after 7 0-0 Black usually switches to the Scheveningen with 7 ...d6.

7 a3?!

Since there is no immediate threat to the e-pawn, this move is essentially a loss of time. Either 7 0-0 or 7 f4 are more useful.

7 ...	Bb7
8 f4	Nc6
9 Be3	Nxd4
10 Qxd4	Ne7!

Hubner is handling the opening creatively and well. Black has good space on the Queenside, and the KN heads to c6 to dislodge White's Queen from its active post.

11 Rd1	Rd8?!

However, this move is neither necessary nor beneficial. The Rook may not be well placed here (a Bb6 by White would catch Black's Q and R in a scissor) and can well find a better home on c8. The obvious 11 ... Nc6 equalizes after both 12 Qb6 Qxb6 13 Bxb6 f6 and 12 Qd2 d6.

12 0-0	Nc6
13 Qd2	

Because of Black's misplaced QR, 13 Qb6 now leads to a slight endgame plus for White. However, the text is also O.K.

13 ...	Be7
14 Qe1	

The fancy 15 Nd5?! leads to nothing but equality after 14 ... exd5 15 exd5 Qd6.

14 ...	d6

Unfortunately 14 ... 0-0 is met by the annoying 15 Qf2!- see the comment to Black's 11th move. With the text, Black frees the d7 square for his Rook.

15 f5!?

Tal grabs the first opportunity at a direct attack and already envisions the followup Exchange sacrifice. Black must allow it since 15 ... Ne5?! 16 Qg3 Bf6 17 fxe6 fxe6 18 Bh5+ gives White an attack at no cost.

Nevertheless the text is somewhat premature. The attack after 15 Qf2! Rd7 16 Bb6 Qb8 17 Rd3! followed by 18 Rh3 is more easily sustainable, as Hubner's second at Leningrad, GM Hecht, recommended.

15 ...	0-0
16 f6	

The only logical followup since Black otherwise continues with ... Ne5 and ... Bf6 and stands better because of the control of the e5 square.

16 ...	Bxf6
17 Rxf6	gxf6
18 Qh4	

White must go for a direct attack since there is no time for 18 Rd3? on account of 18...Ne5! 19 Bh6 Ng6 20 Rg3 Qc5+ 21 Kh1 Kh8 22 Bxf8 Rxf8, and White has no compensation for his missing pawn.

18 ...	Qe7

The f-pawn must be protected. Losing is 18...Ne5? 19 Qxf6 Ng6 20 Nd5!! exd5 21 Bh6, with mate to follow.

19 Rd3?!

With a cute threat (19...Kh8?? 20 Bd4!! and White wins), but Hubner's perfect defense stamps the move as not fully satisfactory. Correct is the obvious 19 Bh6 Kh8 20 Rd3 f5! (Black has no time for 20 ...Rg8?? 21 Rh3 f5 because of 22 Bg5!, and White wins), and now best play leads to an even ending after 21 Qxe7 Nxe7 22 Bxf8 Rxf8 23 Rxd6 Nc8! 24 Rd7 Bxe4 25 Nxe4 fxe4 26 Kf2! Nb6 27 Ra7 Na4!.

19 ...	f5
20 Bg5	f6
21 Bh6	fxe4!

Ensuring a fine center and an extra pawn, and showing admirable coolness under fire.

22 Rg3+	Kh8
23 Bg7+	

White can regain some of the sacrificed material but not all of it. Black now winds up with two Rooks and a pawn for his Queen, a definite material advantage. But the inherent looseness of the position allows White's Queen much freedom of action, and thus White's prospects are only slightly inferior. The text is much better than 23 Bxf8? Rxf8 24 Nxe4 Ne5, when Black has both a material and positional advantage.

23 ...	Qxg7
24 Rxg7	Kxg7
25 Nxe4	

Worse is 25 Qg4+ Kh8 26 Qxe6 Ne5!, and Black's remaining e-pawn is farther advanced than in the game and quite secure on e4.

25 ...	Ne5
26 Ng3	Ng6?!

Hubner considers this inaccurate since the Knight stood quite well and removing it only serves to chase the White Queen toward the Queenside, where White's *real* attacking chances lie. The accurate plan is 26...Kh8! and only after 27 Qh6 Ng6.

27 Qd4	Kh8
28 Nh5	Ne5!

28 ...Rd7? clearly is bad because of 29 Nxf6 e5 30 Qg4 when Black has lost a pawn for nothing. White also gets too much play after 28 ...e5?! 29 Qb6 Rd7 30 c4! bxc4 31 Bxc4 d5 32 Bxa6 Bxa6 33 Qxa6 d4 34 Qc6 Re7 35 Qd6.

29 Qh4?

Heading in the wrong direction again. Tal dreams of his opponent's King, but his chances lie on the Queenside! White can try either of these plans: 29 Nf4 Bc8 30 a4 or 29 Qb6 Rd7 30 a4, and in either case he has good play and stands almost equal.

29 ...   Rd7!
30 Nxf6

Taking the f-pawn here opens the gates for Black's Rooks. The Knight should have been left where it was in favor of starting action on the Queenside with 30 a4.

30 ...   Rg7!

Black has the attack now, and it is decisive. Check the following lines:

(1) 31 g4 Bf3;

(2) 31 g3 Rgf7 32 Ne4 Rf1+ 33 Kg2 R1f2+;

(3) 31 Ng4 Bxg2! Kxg2 Nxg4 33 Bxg4 Rxg4+! 34 Qxg4 Rg8, with a won K+ P ending.

Tal's move is equally hopeless.

31 Qh6   Rxg2+
32 Kf1   Rf7
33 Bh5   Ng4!
34 Bxg4   Rxg4
White resigns

The coming 35 ...Rg6 will win White's Knight and leave Black with a huge material superiority.

GAME 55

White: J. Rukavina
(Yugoslavia)

Black: M. Tal
(U.S.S.R.)

Played at Leningrad (U.S.S.R.)
Interzonal Tournament, June 25,
1973, Round 16.

King's Indian Defense

Tal decides that to play for a win
he must produce a series of unusual,
antipositional, confusing opening
moves. It soon turns out, however,
that the only one confused is Tal
himself. Rukavina takes note of all of
Black's weaknesses, lines up on
them, and is about to start the harvest
when, after adjournment, Tal resigns. White demonstrates perfectly
that the best way to handle unusual,
antipositional moves is with good
positional play.

1 Nf3	Nf6
2 g3	g6
3 b3	

White's choice of a double fianchetto against the King's Indian
setup is a slightly passive but positionally sound plan.

3 ...	a5?!

It's somewhat outlandish to

move the a-pawn so quickly, but the
move is probably playable if Black
follows up consistently. However,
Tal is much more interested in
creating confusion rather than
achieving consistency, and the text
therefore works out poorly.

4 Bb2	Bg7
5 Bg2	d6?!

The point behind 3 ...a5 should
be to play on the light squares. Thus
a logical plan is 5 ... 0-0 6 0-0 d5 with
an opportune ...a4 to follow. Trans-
posing into the King's Indian with
the text means that Black's 3rd move
was a waste of time and weakened
the Queenside.

6 d4	c6
7 0-0	0-0
8 Nbd2	a4
9 a3	Nbd7?!

A sensible light-square policy
still consists of 9 ...axb3 10 cxb3 d5!.

10 Rb1	Qc7
11 Re1	

An immediate 11 e4! is more
than playable. However, White's
moves are deliberately slow and safe
in the correct expectation that Black
will hang himself.

11 ...	e5?!

Leads to new weaknesses; e.g.,
d6. The minor evil is 11 ...d5!.

| 12 e4 | Re8 |
| 13 h3 | b5? |

Impatient, Black creates a very serious new weakness on the Queenside: either the b-pawn or the c-pawn will now be weak. The only sensible way to develop the QB is by means of 13 ...b6.

14 b4!

A strategically won position for White. His development is complete, and his pieces, though apparently modestly placed, are well trained toward the center. White will soon get in c4, thereby opening the holes in Black's Queenside.

| 14 ... | Nb6 |
| 15 dxe5! | |

Ensuring that White's dark-square Bishop will be the superior one, and making Black's e-pawn a new weakness in Black's position.

| 15 ... | dxe5 |
| 16 Bf1! | Ba6 |

| 17 c4! | Nxc4 |

Not capturing allows 18 cxb5 making Black's b-pawn a permanent weakness.

| 18 Nxc4 | bxc4 |
| 19 Qc2 | c3 |

Forcing the exchange of the light-square Bishops is no accomplishment at all, but Black has no satisfactory continuation. To attempt pawn exchanges with 19 ...c5 is zapped by 20 b5! Bxb5 21 Bxe5!.

20 Qxc3	Bxf1
21 Kxf1	Qb7
22 Qc4	Nd7
23 Red1	Nb6
24 Qe2	

White's basic strategy should be quite clear: to pile up against the isolated c-pawn. Pleasant adjuncts to this are pressure along the d-file and against the e-pawn. Rukavina is already starting to feel the time shortage, and thus his play is not the most efficient in realizing his advantages. Thus 24 Qc2! is simpler, and after 24 ... Qa6+ 25 Kg2. Nevertheless Black's prospects are nonexistent, so Tal isn't able to generate an ounce of counterplay, anyway.

24 ...	h6
25 Rbc1	Re6
26 Ne1!	

Aiming for d3 and then c5.

26 ...	Nd7
27 Qd3	Nf8
28 Qc2	h5
29 Nd3	Nd7
30 Qe2	Bf8
31 Rc2!	

A flexible move with three possible uses: doubling on the c-file, doubling on the d-file, and bringing the Bishop to the excellent e3 central location.

31 ...	Qb5
32 Bc1	Rd6
33 Be3	Rd8
34 Nb2!	

White's Bishop prevents a Black ...c5; thus White can offer the exchange of Queens and a pair of Rooks. No matter what course Black chooses, positionally he remains quite lost.

34 ...	Nf6
35 Rxd6	Bxd6
36 f3	Be7
37 Qxb5	

There was, of course, no need to exchange Queens in this manner and remove the pressure on the c-pawn.

But in time pressure the text looked good and safe to White. The control of the c-file will allow White to attack Black's b-pawn, and Black's e-pawn also remains weak. Thus White still retains a winning position. More thematic, however, is 37 Qc4! followed by 38 Kf2.

37 ...	cxb5
38 Ke2	Nd7
39 Nd3	Bd6
40 Rc6	Bb8
41 Nc5	
Black resigns	

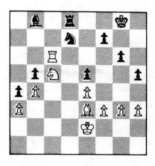

Black can't prevent material loss and will continue to have the inferior position. Tal actually sealed 41 ...Nf8 but resigned without continuing the game. Indeed, White mops up, starting with 42 Rb6.

GAME 56

White: W. Hartston
(England)

Black: V. Tukmakov
(U.S.S.R.)

Played at Hastings (England) International Tournament, December 27, 1972, Round 1.

Sicilian Defense (Velimirovic Attack)

White obtains a slight edge out of the opening but, by undertaking a premature attacking sortie, allows Black central counterplay. Black, however, fails to follow up correctly, and White achieves a strong attacking formation. Black defends poorly and White quickly obtains a winning position.

1	e4	c5
2	Nf3	Nc6
3	d4	cxd4
4	Nxd4	Nf6
5	Nc3	d6
6	Bc4	

This move is usually credited to Soviet master Sozin, who played it a few times- mostly unsuccessfully- from 1929 to 1931. It was, however, Bobby Fischer who showed the world how to handle the variation, and this was Fischer's main line from the late 1950's through the 1972 match against Spassky. Thanks to Fischer's innovations the move received at least equal prominence with the Richter-Rauzer Attack (6 Bg5).

6	...	e6
7	Be3	a6
8	Qe2	

Fischer's "attack" consisted of castling Kingside and an early f4. The text is an idea of the creative and dangerous attacking master of Yugoslavia, GM Velimirovic. White is going to castle Queenside and then unleash a pawn storm against Black's Kingside. Bobby tried this plan only once: unsuccessfully against Larsen at the Palma de Majorca Interzonal.

8 ...	Na5?!

This premature acentral jump allows White a very successful regrouping at no risk whatever. Black should postpone the move until White has castled Queenside and Black has achieved some development. Correct therefore is either 8 ...Be7 or 8 ...Qc7.

9 Bd3!

Exactly! White now will castle on the Kingside and achieve strong pressure against Black's center. The QN will be quite obviously out of the way.

9 ...	Qc7

After 9 ...Be7 also comes 10 f4, and 9 ...b5?! allows the surprising 10 b4! with advantage to White: 10 ...Nb7 (10 ...Qc7? 11 Ncxb5!) 11 0-0 e5 12 Nb3 Qc7 13 Bd2 Bd7 14 a4 as in Mestrovic- Polugaevsky, Varna 1972.

10 f4	b5
11 0-0	Bb7

11 ...b4 12 Nd1 weakens Black's Queenside and achieves nothing. Now, however, White must prevent 12 ...b4.

12 a3	Be7
13 Rad1	Rc8
14 Kh1	0-0
15 Bc1	

White has achieved very harmonious development, every one of his   pieces is well placed and his King is safe enough on h1. His immediate threat is 16 e5, and Black must work to prevent it.

15 ...	Nc4
16 Rf3?	

This King Rook sortie only serves to misplace the Rook. The key central plan is e5; therefore, the correct move is 16 b3!. Then Black has no time for pawn grabbing with 16 ... Nxa3? because 17 Bxa3 Qxc3 18 e5 Ne8 19 Bxh7+! Kxh7 20 Rd3 followed by 21 Rh3+ and 22 Qh5 leads to a winning attack. Therefore Black would have to retreat with 16 ...Nb6, when with 17 Bb2 White safeguards his Queenside and reestablishes 18 e5 as the threat. After 17 Bb2 White has a pleasant, risk-free advantage.

16 ...	g6!

Safeguards the h7 square and by controlling f5 prepares the following central thrust. Black already is better.

17 Rh3

Hardly an attractive location for the Rook, but something had to be done to give the KN a reasonable retreat square.

17 ...	e5!
18 Nf3	

18 fxe5 dxe5 opens the diagonal of Black's KB, so that White prefers to sacrifice his f-pawn.

18 ...	exf4

19 Rf1!

Of course not 19 Bxf4? because of 19 ...Nxb2. With the text White hopes for some action on the Kingside. After his erroneous 16th move, White chooses the best practical alternatives.

19 ...   Qc5?

Overlooking the response. 19 ...Nh5 ? is much too risky because of the sacrifice 20 Rxh5! In order is the positional 19 ... Ne3! 20 Bxe3 fxe3 21 Qxe3 h5! with Black having some advantage: his King is safe, he has a nice two-Bishop game, and White's KB looks like an overgrown pawn.

20 b4   Qb6
21 Bxf4

White has won back his pawn under reasonable circumstances, and chances are roughly even. Now it is quite dangerous for Black to go after the a-pawn since after 21 ...Nxa3? 22 Be3 Qc7 23 Bd4 White has a very strong attack. 21 ...Rfe8! is correct to apply pressure to the e-pawn. Then after 22 Bg5 Black has 22 ...Nd7, and 22 e5?! is met by 22 ...Bf8.

21 ...   Ng4?

In principle it is good to establish control over e5, but Black overlooks the obvious reply.

22 Bxc4   bxc4

If 22 ...Rxc4? 23 Nd2 and White threatens both 24 Nxc4 and 24 Qxg4.

23 Nd2   h5

The Knight has to stand its ground. Worse is 23 ...Ne5?! 24 Bxe5 dxe5 25 Nxc4 Qd4 26 Na5 since 26 ...Rxc3 is refuted by 27 Rd1! (Hartston).

24 Nxc4   Rxc4?

This "combination" leads to a hopeless situation in short order. It is imperative to retain the KN and continue 24 ...Qd4!. White retains the edge with 25 Na5, but Black is not without chances.

25 Qxc4   Nf2+
26 Rxf2   Qxf2
27 Rf3   Qxc2
28 Bh6

Black's Queen has no checks, and his Rook can't move. Black is quite lost.

| 28 ... | d5 |
| 29 Qd4 | |

Not bad, but immediately winning is 29 Qc7!: 29 ...dxe4 30 Qxe7! or 29 ...Re8 30 Qd7.

| 29 ... | f6 |
| 30 Bxf8 | |

Good enough to win, but with the zwischenzug 30 Rf2! White retains the e-pawn.

30 ...	dxe4
31 Rf1	Kxf8
32 Nd5	Bxd5
33 Qxd5	Qe2
34 Qd1	

White's material advantage is sufficient to win in an endgame, and the looseness of Black's King position means that Black has no practical chances in the middlegame. White needs to do little more than safely reach the time control at move 40.

34 ...	Qb2
35 Qc1	Qa2
36 Qh6+	Kf7
37 Qh7+	Kf8
38 Qxg6	Qxa3
39 Qxe4	Kf7

After 39 ...Qxb4 White can choose to win with either 40 Qxb4 or 40 Rxf6+.

40 Qh7+	Kf8
41 Qh8+	
Black resigns	

GAME 57

White: V. Tukmakov
(U.S.S.R)

Black: M. Stean
(England)

Played at Hastings (England) International Tournament, December 28, 1972, Round 2.

Sicilian Defense
(Accelerated Dragon Variation)
(by transposition)

A game of ups and downs. An unbalanced opening leads to a middlegame of equal chances. When Black is careless for a moment, White gains a very strong attack with a creative piece sacrifice. Black defends inexactly, and White first misses a forced win and then a chance for a superior position. Suddenly almost all White's pieces are en prise, and he cannot prevent Black from getting a material advantage and repulsing White's attack. Once the advantage is his, Stean plays exactly and with full confidence.

1	Nf3	c5
2	c4	g6
3	d4	cxd4
4	Nxd4	Nc6
5	Nc2	Bg7
6	e4	

By the kind of transposition common in master chess, a position has arisen which is completely different than that we would have been expecting from the first moves. Instead of a Reti-English, we have a King pawn opening, specifically the Accelerated Dragon Variation of the Sicilian Defense, which White has met with the Maroczy bind. The normal move order is 1 e4 c5 2 Nf3 Nc6 3 d4 cxd4 4 Nxd4 g6 5 c4 Bg7 and now White has played 6 Nc2. This Knight retreat has a long history but is not currently given a high rating because it is antidevelopmental and acentral and it allows Black's KB to dominate his central diagonal. Best for White is 6 Be3! with a slight but definite plus.

6	...	Nf6
7	Nc3	d6
8	Be2	Nd7!

Black plays the opening moves in exact order and thus achieves very strong pressure against White's center. After the routine 8 ...0-0?! 9 Be3 White is slightly better.

9 Be3

Very double edged. Safer is 9 Bd2, but the passivity of that move does not give White much hope for an opening advantage.

9	...	Nc5?!

But this is inaccurate. In order

is the sharp 9 ... Bxc3+! 10 bxc3 Qa5 11 Qd2 Nc5 with equal chances for Black- we'll see this soon in the game.

10 Qd2?!

White reciprocates. Correct is 10 Nd4! 0-0 11 0-0 with White slightly better after either 11 ...Nxd4 12 Bxd4 Be6 13 Bxg7 Kxg7 14 Qd4+, as in Portisch-Gheorghiu, Teeside 1972, or 11 ... Bd7 12 Qd2 Nxd4 13 Bxd4, as in Portisch-Reshevsky, Palma de Majorca 1971.

10 ... Qa5!

Now all is well for Black again because 11 Nd4? loses to 11 ...Nxd4! 12 Bxd4 Nxe4!. Therefore White's response is forced.

11 f3 Bxc3!
12 bxc3

An unbalanced position, but inherently quite satisfactory to Black. Of course, he does miss the

Dragon Bishop, but in dying the Bishop ruined White's Queenside pawn formation. Black's Knights and Queen are exceedingly well placed to take advantage of this factor. Most accurate now is 12 ...f6!, as in Polgar-Forintos, Kecskemet 1972, because the normal 13 0-0?! loses a pawn after 13 ...Na4 14 Nb4 Nxc3!. Also good is 12 ... Qa4 13 0-0 Be6 14 Nb4 Rc8, as in Portisch-Deze, Vrsac 1971.

12 ... Be6

Probably sufficient for equality but not as accurate as either of the above moves. Now, by playing 13 Nd4!?, White could force Black to think. Instead he continues routinely with ...

13 0-0 f6

Everything's fine again.

14 Nd4	**Bf7**
15 Nb3	**Qa3**
16 Rab1	**b6**
17 Nd4	**Rc8**
18 Bh6	**Ne5**
19 Rb4	**Na6?!**

This acentral retreat gives White the opportunity for a surprising combination. Correct instead is 19 ...Nc6! with equality since neither side has anything better than to repeat the position with 20 Nb5 Qa6 21 Rbb1 Ne5 22 Rb4 Nc6 etc.

20 Nb5	Qa5
21 Bg7!	Rg8
22 Bxf6!	exf6

This capture is forced because 22...Nxb4? is much worse: 23 cxb4 Qa6 24 Nxd6+! exd6 25 Qxd6 Nc6 26 b5 and White's attack is decisive.

| 23 Nxd6+ | Ke7 |
| 24 Nb7! | Qa3? |

By being too greedy Black risks a certain loss. As Tukmakov points out it is necessary to get Black's Queen into the game with 24 ...Nxf3+!. Then White can retain a slight edge with either 25 gxf3 Qg5+ 26 Qxg5 fxg5 27 Ra4 or 25 Rxf3 Qe5 26 Ra4 Nc5 27 Nxc5 Qxc5+ 28 Qd4. Of course, 24 ...Rfd8? is also unsatisfactory for Black because of 25 Qb2!.

25 Qd6+?!

White correctly smells victory but is too careless in the execution of his plan. The text allows Black's Queen to pin the Rook, and this presents some difficulties for White. Correct is to first chase Black's Queen away from protecting the d6 square with 25 Rb3! Qa4, and then 26 Qd6+ Ke8 27 Qxf6 wins by force since there is no way to protect the e5 Knight, and it can't move away because of 28 Nd6+.

| 25 ... | Ke8 |
| 26 Rxb6! | |

26 Qxf6 is playable, but after 26 ... Qxc3! the KN is protected and White's QR remains en prise. Apparently White can't get more than equality after 27 Nd6+, when Black has the choice between 27...Kf8 and 27...Kd7.

26 ...   Nc5!

And not 26...Qxa2? 27 Rxa6 Qxe2 28 Qxf6 and White's attack can't be repulsed. After the text we get the critical position in the game.

27 Rb3??

Putting the Rook en prise leads to a material disadvantage too large for White to recover enough of. Tukmakov correctly gives 27 Rb5! as retaining White's advantage. Then 27... Ned7? loses to 28 Nxc5 Nxc5 29 Rb7!. The best Black can achieve is an unfavorable endgame-like position with 27...Qa6 28 Qxa6 Nxa6 29 Nd6+ Ke7 30 Nxc8+ Rxc8 31 Ra5 Rc6 32 c5!.

27	...	Qxa2
28	Qxf6	

Suddenly White has no satisfactory continuation. Thus 28 Nxc5 fails to 28 ....Qxe2, and there is no time for 29 Rb7 because of 29 ... Qe3+ 30 Kh1 Qxc5 31 Re7+ Kf8!.

28	...	Ncd7!
29	Nd6+	Kf8
30	Qg5	Qxb3
31	Nxc8	Kg7

The blood bath is over and Black is a piece up. White's three-pawn compensation is inadequate because the doubled c-pawns are indefensible and Black's a-pawn is a very strong passed pawn. Black handles the following part quite well, both defending and attacking. It is soon clear that White is fighting a lost cause.

32	Ne7	Re8
33	Rd1	Bxc4
34	Nf5+	Kh8

35	Nd4	Qxc3
36	h4	Bxe2
37	Nxe2	Qc5+
38	Kh1	Qe7
39	Qg3	Nf6
40	Nf4	a5!
41	Ra1	Ra8
42	Nd5	Nxd5
43	exd5	Nf7
44	Qf4	Qe5!

White resigns

Both the middlegame after 45 Qa4 Qxd5 and the endgame after 45 Qxe5+ Nxe5 are hopeless.

GAME 58

White H. Westerinen
(Finland)

Black: V. Tukmakov
(U.S.S.R.)

Played at Hastings (England) International Tournament, January 9, 1973, Round 12.

Sicilian Defense (Scheveningen Variation)

After a perfectly played opening, White achieves a very strong Kingside attack in the middlegame. Nevertheless, one inaccuracy is sufficient to enable Black to escape into an approximately even endgame. By now both sides are in severe time pressure and the play becomes very inexact. First White allows Black the somewhat superior chances, and then Black, by underestimating a passed pawn, allows a combination which gains White a full Rook.

1	e4	c5
2	Nf3	e6
3	d4	cxd4
4	Nxd4	Nf6
5	Nc3	d6
6	Be2	Be7
7	0-0	Nc6

Compared to Game 53 in which Black played an early ...a6, Tukmakov here chooses to work first on his development.

| 8 | Be3 | Bd7?! |

Posting the QB here is premature. More in the spirit of his previous play is 8...0-0.

| 9 | f4 | 0-0 |
| 10 | Nb3! | |

By preventing the exchange of this Knight, White makes Black's QB look rather impotent on d7. If instead 10 Qe1 Nxd4 11 Bxd4 Bc6 and Black has good central influence.

| 10 | ... | a6 |
| 11 | a4! | Na5?! |

White was of course threatening to fix Black's Queenside with 12 a5, and the text was a popular method in the early 1970's to prevent that. Nowadays 11...b6 is accepted as Black's best, though White does obtain strong attacking chances with g4 either on move 12 or shortly thereafter.

12 e5!

This central thrust shows up the disadvantage of Black's last move. Impossible is 12...dxe5? 13 fxe5 Ne8 because 14 Nxa5 wins a piece. Therefore Black's KN must retreat immediately.

| 12 | ... | Ne8 |

13 Nxa5	Qxa5
14 Qd2!	Rc8

The obvious 14 ...Bc6?! allows the tactical 15 b4! when Black's Queen and Queen Bishop will be pushed back because 15 ...Qxb4? loses to 16 Nd5!. The alternative to the text is 14 ...Qc7 with White, similarly to the game, retaining the advantage after 15 Bd4.

15 Bd4	Bc6
16 Qe3	Nc7

Black looks for counterplay with the help of tactics; e.g. 17 b4? is parried by 17 ...Qxb4 18 Rfb1 Qa5 19 Bb6 Nd5!. Instead of the text, in Westerinen-Sanz, Torremolinos 1974, Black tried the retreat 16 ...Qc7, but, after 17 Bd3 g6 18 f5! dxe5 19 Bxe5 Bd6 20 Bxd6 Qxd6 21 Rad1 Nf6 22 Be2! Qe7 23 fxe6 Qxe6 24 Qd4, White had a clear advantage.

17 Bd3

A position significantly favoring White: he has superiority in the center, both of his Bishops are trained on Black's King, and White's Queen and Knight can soon join in the attack. To stem the tide, Black's defensive efforts must be Herculean.

17 ...	Nd5
18 Qh3	h6

The other pawn move, 18 ...g6, loses after 19 exd6 Bxd6 20 Qh6 f6 21 Bxg6! with a winning attack.

19 f5!?

Very much in Westerinen's aggressive attacking style- as sharp a move as possible at every turn! Less aggressive souls would have played 19 Ne4!, thereby bringing another piece against Black's King. In either case, it is questionable whether Black can hold the position.

19 ...	Qb4

Not satisfactory, but what is? Thus 19 ...dxe5 is met 20 fxe6!, and now 20 ...exd4? loses immediately to 21 Qf5. And against the recommended 20 ...f5 White has this promising sacrifice: 21 Rxf5! exd4 22 Nxd5! Bxd5 23 Raf1! and White seems sure to at least win back the piece with advantage.

20 Ne2	dxe5
21 fxe6	f5

This should not be sufficient but at least has the practical advantage of bringing about complications. The only alternative loses simply: 21 ...exd4 22 exf7+ Kh8 23 Qf5 Nf6 24 Nf4! g5 25 Ng6+ Kg7 26 Nxe7, etc.

22 c4?

By being too materialistic White gives up all his advantage. Yugoslav GM Bukic has shown that after 22 Bxe5 Bc5+ 23 Kh1 Ne3 24 Nf4! Nxf1 25 Rxf1 White's attack is devastating.

22 ...	exd4
23 cxd5	Bxd5
24 Bxf5	d3!

If now 25 Bxd3 Qb6+ followed by capture of the e-pawn, and Black has a lovely two-Bishop game. Therefore White allows Black's d-pawn to live and again heads for Black's King.

25 Nf4	Qd4+
26 Kh1	d2
27 Qg4	Rf6

The threatened 28 Qg6 had to be prevented.

28 Nh5	Qxg4
29 Nxf6+	Bxf6
30 Bxg4	Rc2

The d-pawn gives Black full compensation for the Exchange. By now both sides are in severe time pressure and the play shows it.

31 Rad1	Bb3
32 Rf3?!	

This turns out to be the winning move because Black misses White's diabolical plot. Nevertheless, the move risks White's being left with the worst of it. The accurate way is 32 Rf2! Rc1 33 Rfxd2 Bxd1 34 Rxd1 Rxd1 35 Bxd1 Bxb2 with a fully equal opposite-color-Bishop endgame.

32 ...	Rxb2
33 e7	

The critical moment in the game. Black can't play the obvious 33 ...Bxe7?? because 34 Rxb3! Rxb3 35 Be6+ wins the Rook. Correct is 33 ...Bxa4! 34 Rd3 Bxe7 35 R3xd2 with Black, who has two connected passed pawns for the Exchange, better, but White has good drawing chances. Instead, Black selects the "logical," "automatic" choice ...

33 ...   **Kf7??**   **Black resigns**

... and loses exactly as after the   The choice is between losing
"obvious" 33 ...Bxe7??.   the Rook and allowing a new Queen
                                       after 35 ... Kxe6 36 e8=Q+, which is
34 Rxb3!   **Rxb3**   no choice at   all.
35 Be6+!

GAME 59

White: J. Mestel
(England)

Black: V. Tukmakov
(U.S.S.R.)

Played at Hastings (England) International Tournament, January 11, 1973, Round 14.

Pirc Defense

Immediately out of the opening, Black stands well, but very quickly loses his bearings. White achieves some advantage, and then Black inconceivably acquiesces to a completely lost endgame. White does make things rather difficult for himself all the way through but finally wins the game. Some positions are just so inherently lost that almost nothing can save them; this can be said about the course of this game from move 23 on.

1	e4	d6
2	d4	Nf6
3	Nc3	g6
4	Bg5	

The quietest way to meet the Pirc is 4 Nf3 (Karpov's move!), an in-between method is 4 f4 (see game 39), and White's sharpest approach is the text.

4 ...	Bg7

5 f4

White again selects the most ambitious move. Less hurried is 5 Qd2.

5 ...	c6

But Black prefers not to respond in kind. Almost incalculable complications can result after 5 ...h6 6 Bh4 c5!?.

6 Nf3

Black shows very nicely that it is quite important for White to play the next few moves in the right order. The accurate way is 6 Qd2!, then 7 Bd3, and thereafter 8 Nf3.

6 ...	0-0
7 Qd2?!	

Black shows up this routine move. Required first is 7 Bd3.

7 ...	d5!!

Instead the usual lines go 7 ...b5 8 Bd3, and White is O.K. Theoreticians have paid no attention to the text either before or after this game, but it is very strong. White does not have the normal response 8 e5 now because after 8 ...Ne4 9 Nxe4 dxe4 Black gains lots of time from the attack on the KN.

8	Bd3	dxe4
9	Nxe4	Bg4

10 c3

White must allow the ruination of his Kingside pawn formation because 10 Ne5?! Qxd4 11 Bxf6 exf6 12 Nxg4 f5 is worse since Black regains the piece with clear advantage.

| 10 ... | Bxf3 |
| 11 gxf3 | Qd5?! |

This gives White the chance, by means of simple tactics, to get rid of the isolated, double-pawn liability. As Mestel recommends, 11...e6! followed by 12...Nbd7 leads to a position slightly preferable for Black, since White has no compensation for the doubled f-pawns.

| 12 f5! | Nbd7 |

12...Qxf5?? drops the Queen after 13 Nxf6+, and 12...gxf5? 13 Nxf6+ exf6 14 Bh6 is simply horrible.

| 13 fxg6 | hxg6 |
| 14 0-0! | |

After White's fine last move the position is in dynamic equilibrium: the partial looseness in White's Kingside is balanced by some greater central influence and the two Bishops.

| 14 ... | Rfd8?! |

Starting here, Black loses all resolve to do anything. It is unquestionably proper to start challenging White's center immediately with 14 ...c5 or 14...e5. In either case chances remain even.

15 Qe3!	Rac8
16 b4!	Re8
17 f4!	b6
18 f5!	

While White has been moving resolutely forward, Black has had difficulty deciding what to do. Even so, after the thematic 18 f5!, White's advantage is relatively small.

| 18 ... | gxf5?? |

But this is just madness. The best Black can hope for now is a completely chanceless endgame. What kind of choice is that for a practical game?

| 19 Rxf5 | Qxf5 |

After 19...Qe6 20 Qg3! the risk is great that Black will be mated; e.g., 20...Nxe4 21 Bxe4 Qxe4 22 Bh6!.

20	Nxf6+	exf6
21	Bxf5	Rxe3
22	Bxe3	

A hopeless endgame for Black. White is effectively a pawn up, has the two Bishops in an open position, and has a very strong, mobile passed h-pawn.

22	...	Re8
23	Re1?!	

Up to here White has played with real gusto, but from now on he hardly knows what to do. The only reason he wins is that Black's position is totally lost. Instead of the incomprehensible text, 23 Kf2! followed by 24 Rg1!, etc, is obvious, logical and decisive.

23	...	Nf8
24	Bf2	

24 Kf2!

24	...	Ne6
25	Bg3	Bf8
26	Kf2	b5
27	Be4	Rc8
28	Bf5	Re8
29	Bh4	Bg7
30	Be4	Rc8

With time somewhat short White repeats moves, but now he needs a plan. Black is still in a complete bind; therefore, it is logical to activate the King with 31 Kf3!, followed by 32 Kg4 and 33 Kf5. Black's resistance would then be very short.

31 Rb1?!

On the face of it, the move looks pointless. It turns out to have a plan behind it, even though the plan is rather clumsy.

31	...	Nf4
32	Rb3	Nd5
33	Ra3	Bh6?!

Why let in White's Rook? Surely 33 ...Rc7 is better.

34	Rxa7	Nxc3
35	Bf3	Nd5
36	Bxd5	cxd5
37	Bxf6	

White has now transformed the positional advantage into a material one. Black must embark on a counterattack, but that will leave his King insufficiently protected.

37	...	Rc4
38	a3	Rc2+
39	Kg3	Bc1
40	Ra5?!	

On the last move before time control, White misses the right plan.

Correct is the immediate 40 h4!,
planning a mating net after 41 h5,
42 Ra8+, 43 Rh8 mate !.

40 ...	Rc3+
41 Kg4	Bxa3
42 h4!	Kh7

Black is almost at the end of the
rope. The end is immediate after 42
...Bxb4? 43 Ra8+ Kh7 44 h5.

43 h5?

This automatic move allows a
surprising defense. Mestel subsequently demonstrated that there was
a forced win with 43 Ra8! Kg6 (43
...Rc6 44 Kf5) 44 Ra6! followed by
45 h5+! and 46 Ra8. This way White
prevents the defensive maneuver
available to Black in the game.

43 ...	Rc6!
44 Kf5	Bb2!
45 Rxb5	

The problem is that 45 Ra8?!
allows 45 ...Rxf6+! 46 Kxf6 Bxd4+
47 Kxf7 Bc3 followed by 48 ...Bxb4
and a theoretically drawn position
results.

| 45 ... | Rc2 |
| 46 Ke5! | |

There is no time for 46 Rxd5?
because of 46 ...Rf2+ 47 Ke5 Re2+
with a draw because 48 Kd6? allows
48 ...Re6+.

46 ...	Rh2
47 Kxd5!	Rxh5+
48 Kc4	Rh3

The B+P endgame resulting
after 48 ...Rxb5?! 49 Kxb5 is lost: 49
...Kg6 50 Bh8! Kh7 51 Be5 Kg6 52
Kc4, etc.

49 Rb6

And so White is still up a pawn
and has two passed pawns. Black's
best chance now is to try to activate
his King with 49 ...Kg6!?. As
played, his King remains shut off,
and this ensures the loss.

49 ...	Rf3?!
50 Be5	f5
51 Rf6	Rc3+
52 Kb5	Rf3
53 Kc5	Rc3+
54 Kd5	Rb3
55 Bd6	Rf3
56 Ke5	Re3+
57 Kd5	Rf3
58 b5!	

After saving time to reach the
time control on move 56, White
starts to use his passed pawns. The
end appears close, but White actually wins quite securely.

| 58 ... | Rb3 |
| 59 Kc4 | Rc3+ |

Or 59 ...Bxd4 60 Kxb3! Bxf6 61
b6 Bd4 62 b7 Ba7 63 Kb4 followed
by 64 Kb5 and 65 Ka6.

60 Kb4	Rd3
61 Be5!	Bxd4
62 Bxd4	Rxd4+
63 Kc5	

help his passed pawn's advance, whereas Black's King is shut off from his pawn. Therefore White wins very easily.

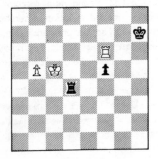

63 ...	Rf4
64 b6	Kg7
65 Rc6	Rf1
66 b7	

Black resigns

The cardinal difference in this position is that White's King can

A probable continuation is 66 ...Rc1+ (66 ...Rb1 67 Rb6) 67 Kb6 Rb1+ 68 Kc7 Rxb7+ (otherwise 69 Rb6) 69 Kxb7 and Black's f-pawn can never advance; e.g., 69 ... f4 70 Rc4, etc.

GAME 60

White: M. Quinteros
(Argentina)

Black: V. Tukmakov
(U.S.S.R)

Played at Leningrad (U.S.S.R.)
Interzonal Tournament, June 9,
1973, Round 6.

King's Indian Defense
(Panno Variation)

White carries a tiny edge out of
the opening into the strategic middlegame. However, Black's careful
defense does not allow White to
increase his advantage. Late in the
middlegame, White decides to trade
his Queen and pawn for two Rooks.
But Black's active Queen keeps the
game in balance. So it remains until
Black blunders on move 39, and
allows a Rook sacrifice which leads
either to mate or the decisive loss of
material. A shocking sudden end to a
game well played by both sides.

1	Nf3	Nf6
2	c4	g6
3	d4	Bg7
4	g3	0-0
5	Bg2	d6
6	Nc3	Nc6
7	0-0	a6

White has selected a sound
positional approach, the KB fianchetto, against the King's Indian.
With his 6th and 7th moves Black
entered the Panno Variation, named
after the Argentine GM Oscar
Panno. The Panno is a fighting,
flexible, sound variation, whereby
Black's QN applies pressure against
the d-pawn and Black gets ready
to advance on the Queenside with
a ...b5. Now with 8 d5 Na5 9 Nd2,
White could enter variations akin to
the Yugoslav, which was discussed
in conjunction with Game 51. Instead White prefers a more independent approach.

8 h3

For the play to come, it is useful
for White to prevent both ...Bg4 and
...Ng4.

8	...	Rb8
9	e4	

This centrally active push
leads to main-line variations.
Korchnoi has had success with the
flexible 9 Be3 b5 10 Nd2!.

9 ...   b5

Black has no choice: he must be
active. Inferior is 9 ...Nd7?! 10 Be3
b5 11 cxb5 axb5 12 Qc1! e5 13 Rd1
and the many weaknesses in Black's
position lead to a clear plus for
White in Hubner-Naranja, Palma de
Majorca 1970.

10 cxb5

Sharpest play possible results after 10 e5! Nd7! 11 cxb5 axb5 12 Ng5 dxe5! 13 Bxc6 exd4 14 Nb5 Rb6! with something like even chances in an unclear position, though Black won in Szekely-Weinstein, Budapest 1976.

10 ...   axb5
11 Be3!?

Of course, here 11 e5 Nd7 can lead to the variation given above. White has also tried 11 Re1, though 11 ...e6!, as in Portisch-Adorjan, Budapest 1975, allows Black eventually to equalize.

A theoretical novelty when played in 1973. The Bishop is developed immediately to an excellent central square,   and White gets ready for rapid play along the c-file. Resolute action by Black is required.

11 ...   b4
12 Ne2

(Works well in this game. Yet 12 Na4 may well be better to inhibit Black's ...c5.)

12 ...   e5

Not 12 ...Nxe4?? 13 Qc2 and White's Queen skewers both unprotected Knights.

(However, the text is too passive to lead to full equality. With the active 12 ...Na5! 13 Nd2 Nd7 14 Rc1 c5! Black obtained at least equality in Belyavsky-Ligterink, Le Havre

1977.)

13 dxe5   dxe5
14 Qc2

A position slightly, though pleasantly, in White's favor. He is devoid of weaknesses himself and has play against various weak spots on Black's Queenside.

14 ...   Bb7!

The only   correct defense. Wrong is 14 ...Bd7? 15 Rfd1 Qc8 16 Rac1, and there is no satisfactory defense to the threat 17 Rxd7! followed by 18 Qxc6.

15 Rfd1   Qc8
16 Nd2!   Re8
17 Nb3   Ba8
18 Nc5

So White's first   strategic achievement is full control of the important c5 square. Black also must be careful to guard his weak b- and c-pawns.

18 ...   Bf8

19 Nc1!

The Knight heads for b3 where it will reinforce c5 and also keep watch over the d4 square.

19 ...	Bd6
20 N1b3	Nd7
21 Rd2	Nxc5
22 Nxc5	Nd8!

Here and following, Black defends very accurately. The text brings the Knight to a good defensive post and allows the QB to start participating in the play. White, on his part, starts to activate his hitherto passive KB.

23 Bf1!	Bc6
24 Kh2	Ra8

Black cannot yet afford to offer the exchange of the light-square Bishops because after 24...Bb5? 25 Bxb5 Rxb5 26 Qc4! his position is too holey; e.g., 26...Rb8 27 Na6 winning at least a pawn, or 26 ...Qb8? 27 Nd7 followed by 28 Nf6+.

25 Bc4	Nb7
26 Nb3	Bd7
27 h4	Be6!
28 Bxe6	Qxe6
29 Qc6	Na5
30 Nxa5	Rxa5

With some judicious exchanges Black has succeeded in lightening his defensive load. White still has a

minute advantage because of the superior Bishop and the weakness of Black's Queenside pawns. However, since White's a-pawn is under attack, White decides to exchange it for Black's b-pawn and thereby creates a passed a-pawn for himself.

31 a4	bxa3 e.p.
32 bxa3	Rea8

White's a-pawn only looks to be en prise; it is actually quite safe since attempts to capture it fail. Thus 32...Rxa3?? loses a piece after 33 Rxd6! and 32...Bxa3? loses the exchange to 33 Qxe6 Rxe6 34 Rda2 Rea6 35 Bd2! Ra4 36 Bc1.

33 a4	R5a6

Black can't afford to go after the b-pawn with 33...Qb3?! because of 34 Bh6! since then 34...R5a6 35 Qd7 Rxa4? allows White a mating attack: 36 Rxd6! cxd6 37 Qxd6!!.

34 Qb7	Kg7

Instead 34...Rxa4 35 Qxa8+ Rxa8 36 Rxa8+ Kg7 leads to the same type of position with Black a tempo behind. With the text he hopes to do better.

35 Rd5

The resulting exchanges are fine for Black. The only way to try to retain a slight advantage is 35

Rda2! followed by 36 a5. Even then it is not clear how White can strengthen his position.

35	...	Rxa4!
36	Qxa8	Rxa8
37	Rxa8	Qg4
38	Ra4	f5!

Black's Queen is active and he has good play against White's weakened King position. The chances are balanced.

39 Ra7!

With the obvious threat 40 Rxd6, which Black decides to "prevent," much to his sorrow. Correct now is 39 ...f4! with even chances, since White has nothing better than 40 Bb6 Kh6! 41 Bxc7 Bxc7 42 Rxc7 fxg3+ 43 fxg3 Qxe4 44 Rd2! followed by 45 Rcc2, with a stable position. Attempts to win achieve the opposite; e.g., 40 Rxd6 fxe3 41 Rxc7+ Kh6 42 Rdd7?? (42 fxe3 transposes into a drawing line) 42 ...Qxd7!! 43 Rxd7 e2!, and Black gets a new Queen.

39 ...   Kf6??

Black had ten minutes left for the last two moves, so time can't be blamed for this blunder. It's simply a reflection of Tukmakov's poor sporting form throughout the Interzonal.

40 Rxd6+!
Black resigns

He loses a piece since 40 ...cxd6 41 Bg5+ Ke6 allows 42 Re7 mate.

GAME 61

White: R. Byrne
(U.S.A.)

Black: V. Tukmakov
(U.S.S.R.)

Played at Leningrad (U.S.S.R.)
Interzonal Tournament, June 13,
1973, Round 8.

Ruy Lopez
(Breyer Variation)

Black plays the opening better
than White and, as a reward, comes
out a pawn ahead. But, starting with
the middlegame, White shows more
assurance than Black. Though still a
pawn down, White is able to activate
his pieces so as to get fair compensation for the missing button. In time
pressure, Black sees ghosts and
promptly allows an elementary
combination which nets White a full
piece. An excellent example of how
a player in top sporting form can
recover from an unpleasant position,
whereas one in poor shape can do
nothing with the offered chances.

1	e4	e5
2	Nf3	Nc6
3	Bb5	a6
4	Ba4	Nf6
5	0-0	Be7
6	Re1	b5
7	Bb3	d6
8	c3	0-0

9	h3	Nb8
10	d4	Nbd7
11	Nbd2!	

Up to here the game has followed the same course as Game 13,
in which White played the impetu-
ous 11 c4. The text is the usual and
best choice. White already has a
space advantage; he now will complete his development and only then
look for a more definitive plan.
Black is clearly in no condition to
attack White, so why shouldn't the
first player strengthen his position
before starting active operations?

11	...	Bb7
12	Bc2	

A good multi-purpose move.
By protecting the e-pawn, the
Bishop allows the QN to move to f1
and makes way for the b-pawn to be
used for Queenside play.

12	...	Re8

Black aims to safeguard his e-
pawn and possibly threaten White's
after a timely ...exd4. The alternative, often played by Gligoric, is to
challenge White's center immediately with 12 ...c5. At present this is
less common because White can
achieve a significant space advantage with 13 d5, after which Black is
hard pressed to find breathing room.

| 13 | b4 | |

Karpov invariably prefers to play 13 Nf1 and 14 Ng3 first, thereby usefully deploying the QN. The text is an active alternative.

13 ...   Bf8

13 ...d5?! is premature because of 14 Nxe5 Nxe5 15 dxe5 Nxe4 16 Nxe4 dxe4 17 Qg4 with good attacking chances for White in Kavalek- Robatsch, Sarajevo 1968.

14 Bb2

Not bad, but a more consistent followup to the previous move is 14 a4!, and after 14 ...Nb6 15 a5, with space advantage for White, as in Fischer- Spassky, Match Game 10, 1972, for example.

14 ...   Nb6!

Now it will be difficult for White to get his Queenside going. Inferior are both 14 ...a5?! 15 Bd3! c6 16 a3 Nb6 17 Rc1 exd4 18 Nxd4 Nfd7 19 N2b3 with White better in Tal-Karpov, Leningrad Interzonal 1973 (played in this same round!), and 14 ...g6?! 15 c4 exd4 16 cxb5 axb5 17 Nxd4 d5 18 exd5 Rxe1+ 19 Qxe1 Bxd5 20 a3 c6 21 Ne4 and the better pawn formation and superior piece mobility give White a slight plus, as in Dueball- O'Kelly, West Germany 1971.

15 a3   Nfd7

Possible also is the prophylactic 15 ...h6. Then after 16 c4 Nxc4!? 17 Nxc4 bxc4 18 dxe5 dxe5 19 Nxe5 c5 20 Nxc4 cxb4!, as in Parma- Unzicker, Berlin 1971, Matanovic rates the position even.

16 Rc1	**g6**
17 Bb1	**Bh6**
18 Rc2	**a5**

White's pieces momentarily give the appearance of being in a hedgehog formation. However, White's pawns do control more space, and he can now snap out of his shell with 19 bxa5! Rxa5 20 c4! and thereby keep a tiny edge; e.g., 20 ...bxc4 21 Nxc4 Nxc4 22 Rxc4.

19 c4?

The right plan all right but the wrong execution. Instead of having a secure a-pawn, White will now have a weak b-pawn, and this gives Black time to activate his pieces with great force.

19 ...   axb4!

20 axb4	exd4
21 Bxd4	

21 Nxd4?! leads to the loss of the c-pawn for nothing after 21 ...Bxd2.

21 ...	bxc4
22 Ba2	

22 Nxc4 leaves the e-pawn hanging.

22 ...	Ra4!
23 Qb1	Qa8!

The pressure along the a-file, against the b-pawn, and against the e-pawn is very unpleasant for White. A defensive move such as 24 Rb2 is met strongly by 24 ...Qa6!, threatening 25 ...Ra8. Therefore White decides to chuck a pawn and get some breathing room.

24 Nxc4	Rxe4!

The complications after 24 ...Bxe4?! 25 Rce2 are fine for White since 25 ...Bxb1? 26 Rxe8+ Qxe8 27 Rxe8+ Nf8 28 Nxb6! Rxa2 29 Nd7 f5 30 Ng5! leads to a winning Kingside attack, despite the absence of Queens.

25 Ne3	c5?!

The series of exchanges starting with this move accomplishes nothing for Black while serving to activate White's pieces. Much more annoying for White is for Black to keep the bind, by 25 ...Rf4!, for example.

26 bxc5	dxc5
27 Bc3	

It's possible that 27 Bxc5!? is playable, but by now both sides are in acute time pressure and, on general principles, the text looks like the correct move for White.

27 ...	Nd5
28 Nxd5	Bxd5
29 Bxd5	Qxd5

With White's pieces becoming active, Black can't interpolate 29 ...Rxe1+? 30 Qxe1 Qxd5 because of 31 Qe8+ Bf8 (31 ...Nf8?? leaves the Rook hanging) 32 Rd2 and White wins.

30 Rd1	Qe6
31 Rb2!	

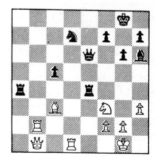

The active location of White's pieces and the inherent looseness in Black's King position make it very doubtful whether Black can do anything with his extra c-pawn. White is threatening to play 32 Rb7 and, after the Knight moves, 33 Rb8. Therefore 31 ...Bf4! is a worthwhile move for Black, since then 32 g3? fails to 32 ...Qxh3 33 gxf4 Qg4+ 34 Kf1 Qxf3 35 Rb8+ Nf8, and Black's attack will come first. But in time pressure, Black sees ghosts rather than simple tactics and plays ...

31 ...	Ra8??
32 Rxd7	

Thank you. If now 32 ...Qxd7 33 Qxe4, and whatever gets played,

White will be up a piece. Only the mutual time pressure extends the game to move 40. Otherwise Black would resign on the spot.

32 ...	Re8
33 Rd1	Bf4
34 Rb6	Qc4
35 Qb3	Qe2
36 Rb7	c4
37 Qb1	Be3
38 Rf1	Bc5
39 Rb8	h6
40 Rxe8+	Rxe8
41 Qb5	

Black resigns

GAME 62

White: V. Tukmakov
(U.S.S.R.)

Black: J. Smejkal
(Czechoslovakia)

Played at Leningrad (U.S.S.R.)
Interzonal Tournament, June 21,
1973, Round 13.

Grunfeld Defense

A game in which White is better
in the first part, Black in the last. But
whereas White can do nothing with
his advantage, Black is able to win
his superior endgame. White has a
theoretical draw for a while, but bad
form also means losing drawable
endgames. This Rook and pawns
endgame appeared in nearly all the
chess magazines of the world.

1	d4	Nf6
2	c4	g6
3	Nc3	d5
4	Nf3	Bg7
5	Qb3	

About thirty years ago this was
the main line of the Grunfeld, but it
is currently out of fashion. The
present fashion is to look for flexible
and strategic approaches, and the
active text is too sharp and complicated. A strategic buildup with g3
was discussed in connection with
Game 2.

*(The 1986 and 1987 World
Championship matches have con-
siderably increased interest in 5
Qb3.)*

5 ...		dxc4

The point of the Grunfeld is to
launch an attack against White's
center in the hope of bringing it
down. The play after the text is
therefore consistent. 5...c6?! is self-
cramping.

6	Qxc4	0-0
7	e4	Bg4

This direct way to apply pressure against White's d-pawn is
originally an idea of Smyslov's.
Currently more popular are the flexible 7...a6!? and 7...c6!?

8	Be3	Nfd7

Part of the plan associated with
7...Bg4: the KN will go to b6 to chase
away White's Queen, and the QN
will go to c6 to attack the d-pawn.

9	Rd1

The main-line variations start
with 9 Qb3 Nb6 10 Rd1 Nc6. The
text gives both sides a chance to
vary.

9 ...	Nc6

Black can enter the line above
with 9...Nb6 10 Qb3 Nc6. Now

White can try something else.

10 Be2!

But here 10 Qb3?! is inferior because of 10...Bxf3! 11 gxf3 e5! and Black has at least equality.

10 ...	Bxf3
11 gxf3	

This center-building recapture is generally the correct method in this variation. After 11 Bxf3?! e5! Black again stands well.

11 ...	e5?!

But here this thematic push doesn't seem to work out well. Abramov and Botvinnik recommended 11...Nb6!? 12 Qc5 f5! 13 d5 Ne5 14 Nb5!? here, with approximately even chances in a very complex position.

12 dxe5	Ncxe5
13 Qa4!	Qc8
14 h3	

But the need for this defensive move (to keep Black's Knight from g4 and Black's Queen from h3) is unclear. Abramov and Botvinnik recommend the immediate 14 f4! Nb6 15 Qb3 with White judged to be better after either 15...Ng4 16 Bc5 or 15...Nc6 16 h4! Rd8 17 f5. This looks correct, but a practical test is needed to confirm this analysis.

14 ...	Nb6
15 Qb3	Rd8
16 Rxd8+	Qxd8
17 0-0	

This position is also somewhat advantageous for White. He has the two Bishops and the greater central influence and will have the more active Rook. Black's counter-chances must rest with the White King's somewhat weakened position. However, there seems to be no direct way of exploiting this factor; e.g., 17...Qh4 18 Kg2! (not 18 f4? because of 18...Qxh3!) 18...Bh6 19 Nb5!, and after 19...Bxe3 White can play 20 fxe3 with advantage. Therefore with the next move Black ensures a good location for his Knight at e5 by preventing White's f4.

17 ...	g5!?
18 Nb5	Ng6
19 Rd1	Qe7
20 a4	Nf4
21 Bf1	Be5
22 Nd4	

The threat of 23 Nf5 forces the

following exchange alright, but Black is just able to safeguard his weak spots. Considerably stronger is the direct 22 a5!, and after 22 ...Nd7 23 Nxa7, whereas after 22 ...Nc8 White has 23 a6! bxa6 24 Nd4.

22 ...	Bxd4
23 Rxd4	Rb8
24 Qd1	

After 24 a5 Black has 24 ...Nd7, but now Black must prevent the serious threat of 25 a5.

24 ...	a5
25 Rd2	Re8
26 Bxb6	

White does win a pawn this way at the cost of being left with the significantly inferior minor piece. Overall that turns out to be no bargain for White. More in the strategic spirit of the opening are 26 Qc2! and 26 Qb3! with the threat 27 Qb5.

26 ...	cxb6
27 Rd7	Qf6
28 Rxb7	Ng6!
29 Qd7	Rd8
30 Qf5	

By now both players are out of time and the next ten moves take place at blitz tempo.

| 30 ... | Qxf5 |
| 31 exf5 | Nh4 |

32 f6

A move which looks more terrifying than it is. 32 Rxb6! is simpler and good for full equality.

| 32 ... | h6! |
| 33 Be2? | |

"Developing" the Bishop thusly is pointless. If White wants to move his Bishop, then 33 Bc4 is correct, probably followed by 33 ...Nxf3+ 34 Kg2 Ne5 35 Bb3 Rd6 36 Re7 Nd7 37 Rxf7 Kh8 and 38...Nxf6 and approximate equality. Also perfectly playable is 33 Rxb6 Rd1 34 Rb5. Black then has a draw by perpetual check starting with 34 ...Nxf3+ 35 Kg2 Nh4+, etc, but he has no more than that.

33 ...   Rd6

Already Black is better. His b-pawn is safe, and he'll regain the missing pawn and be left with the double advantage of better pawn formation and superior minor piece.

34 f4!?

White doesn't want to be left in a very passive position after 34 Rc7 Rxf6 35 Rc3 Rf4 and thus prefers to sacrifice a pawn in such a way as to give Black isolated doubled pawns.

| 34 ... | gxf4 |
| 35 f3 | Rxf6 |

White gets fine play after 35 ...Rd2?! 36Kf1 Rxb2?(36 ...Rd6!) 37 Bc4.

36	Rd7	Rc6
37	Rd4	Rc2
38	Kf2	Ng6

After 38 ...Rxb2 39 Rxf4, it's difficult to see how Black can hope to advance the backward b-pawn.

39	b4	Ra2
40	bxa5	bxa5
41	Kf1	

The sealed move. Black is obviously better, but the weakness of his pawn formation (four isolated pawns) makes ultimate success questionable.

41	...	Kg7
42	h4	h5
43	Bd3	Ra3
44	Kf2	Nxh4
45	Rxf4	Rxd3

Home analysis apparently convinced Black that the coming R+P

endgame offered better chances to win than keeping the minor pieces on after 45 ...Ng6 46 Rd4.

46	Rxh4	Kg6
47	Rc4	Ra3
48	Kg3	Kg5!

Black must activate his King; otherwise there is no hope of making progress.

49	Rc5+	f5
50	Rxa5	h4+
51	Kg2	Ra2+
52	Kh3	Rf2
53	Ra8	Rxf3+

Not surprisingly, Black has won back the pawn, but he is now left with the f-and h-pawn combination which, if White's King and Rook are correctly placed, is a theoretical draw. Not that the draw is easy—many master games have been lost by the weaker side. Even so, White's simplest approach is to give up the a-pawn and achieve a theoretically drawn position. The way he plays, he eventually winds up with the worst of both worlds. The a-pawn will not do anything positive but will tie down White's Rook to its defense.

54	Kg2	Rg3+
55	Kh2	Ra3
56	Rg8+	

Perhaps the fact that this is the last move before the time control explains this needless check. Improving White's King position with 56 Kg2! is the soundest approach.

56	...	Kf4
57	Rh8	Kg4
58	Rg8+	Kf3
59	Ra8	f4
60	a5	Kf2
61	a6	f3
62	a7	Ra1

The only try. After 62 ...Kf1?! 63 Rf8, it's an instantaneous draw, and after 62 ... Ra4?! 63 Kh3, Black is in zugzwang and, again, has nothing better than to allow 63 ... Kf1 64 Rf8 Rxa7 65 Rxf3+.

63 Kh3?!

This does not throw the draw away but does make White's task more difficult. As GM Flohr points out, here is the most opportune time to activate White's Rook with 63 Rb8!. The following moves are then pretty much forced, and White's Rook can check Black's King away from the scene of action: 63 ...Rxa7 64 Rb2+ Ke3 65 Rb3+ Kf4 66 Rb4+ Kg5 67 Rb5+ Kg6 68 Rb6+ Kg7. Now White reverses gears and plays 69 Rb3! Rf7 70 Kg1 f2+ (otherwise 71 Kf2) 71 Kf1 and will win the f-pawn for a draw: 71 ...Kg6 72 Rh3 Kg5 73 Rh2, etc.

63 ...   Ra4

Black is trying to put White in zugzwang. Another try at winning

is 63 ... Rh1+ 64 Kg4 Rg1+! 65 Kxh4 Rg7. Then, as Keres points out, White can draw only with 66 Kh5! (66 Rb8? loses to the simple 66 ...Rxa7 67 Rb2+ Kg1 68 Kg3 f2! 69 Rxf2 Rg7+ 70 Kf3 Rf7+, winning the Rook) 66 ...Kg2 67 Kh6!, since then 67 ...f2? (67 ...Rxa7 is a draw) 68 Kxg7 f1=Q 69 Rg8! is good only for White.

64 Kh2   Ra3
65 Kh1??

It's only this horrible blunder that seals White's fate. There were still two (!) ways to draw: (1) 65 Rb8, as in the note to White's 63rd move (after 65 ... Rxa7 we have the same position as there); and (2) 65 Kh3 Kf1 66 Rb8!, as Keres pointed out. Again after 66 ...Rxa7 Black's King will have no satisfactory way to get out of checks.

65 ...   Ra2!

Now, because of the miserable position of White's King, Black has a forced win.

66 Kh2   Kf1+

Because this occurs *with check,* White has no time for the "drawing" 67 Rf8.

67 Kh1

67 Kh3 f2 68 Kxh4 Kg2 leads to the variation shown in the note to

White's 69th move.

| 67 ... | f2 |
| 68 Kh2 | h3!! |

But not 68 ...Ra3? 69 Rb8!, and again White's Rook will have enough checks to reach a drawn position.

69 Kh1

White can only choose between losing prosaically and losing poetically. The text leads to a normal finish, as does the immediate 69 Rb8. The winning method for Black after 69 Kxh3 is prettier. Then Black wins as shown in a 1890 study by Emanuel Lasker: 69 ...Kg1 70 Rg8+ Kh1 71 Rf8 Ra3+ 72 Kh4 Kg2 73 Rg8+ Kh2 74 Rf8 Ra4+ 75 Kh5 Kg2 76 Rg8+ Kh3 77 Rf8 Ra5+ (note how Black forces White's King forward) 78 Kh6 Kg3 79 Rg8+ Kh4 80 Rf8 Ra6+ 81 Kh7 Rxa7+ (this can now be played with check- the whole point of Lasker's

maneuver) 82 Kg6 Kg3. Black has won White's passed pawn and will queen his own.

69 ...	Ra6
70 Kh2	Ra1!
71 Rb8	

71 Kxh3 Kg1 loses as in the above note, whereas 71 Kh1?! allows 71 ...Ke2+.

71 ...	Rxa7
72 Rb1+	Ke2
73 Rb2+	Ke3
74 Rb3+	Ke4
75 Rb4+	Ke5
76 Rb5+	Ke6
77 Rb6+	Ke7
78 Rb1	Ra3

The difference between this position and those shown earlier as draws is that the Black pawns are so far advanced that White has no defensive flexibility; e.g., White's King does not have access to either g2 or g1. If now 79 Rf1 Rf3, and since White can't move his Rook, Black's King will march in with decisive effect. As played White gives a few spite checks and then resigns.

79 Rb7+	Ke6
80 Rb6+	Ke5
81 Rb5+	Ke4
82 Rb4+	Kf3
White resigns	

After 83 Rb1 a simple win is 83 ...Re3 followed by 84 ...Re1.

GAME 63

White: E. Torre
(Philippines)

Black: V. Tukmakov
(U.S.S.R.)

Played at Leningrad (U.S.S.R.)
Interzonal Tournament, June 22,
1973, Round 14.

Sicilian Defense

A difficult and somewhat frustrating game for the annotator. By
now Eugenio Torre is a fine grandmaster, but Leningrad was his first
big international tournament and his
unsteady play showed this. And
Tukmakov was in simply atrocious
form. The net results were many,
many incomprehensible moves.
First White was better, then Black,
then White again; finally Black's
blunders ensured his loss.

1	e4	c5
2	Nf3	e6
3	d3	

A fairly popular approach
against the Sicilian, which no one
less than Bobby Fischer uses
periodically if Black has played 2
...e6. The idea is that, now that
Black has weakened the f6 square,
his KB fianchetto, the usual method
of meeting White's buildup, may
have certain disadvantages. The
positions which result are like those
of the King's Indian Reversed and
can also arise by transposition from
the French Defense.

3	...	Nc6
4	g3	d5

This straightforward central
approach is preferred by Anatoly
Karpov, among others. Playable too
is 4...g6.

5 Qe2?!

Why put the Queen here?
Normal variations continue 5 Nbd2
Bd6 6 Bg2 Nge7 7 0-0 0-0 8 Nh4!,
with perhaps a slight edge for White.

5	...	Nge7
6	Bg2	g6
7	h4	

The threat of 8 h5 forces a
weakening in Black's Kingside
pawn formation, though at the cost
of some weakening in White's
Kingside, too.

7	...	h6
8	e5	Nd4?!

Why accept an unwieldly
doubled pawn? 8...Nf5 is normal,
and after 9 c3 Black can start Queenside play with 9...b5!.

9	Nxd4	cxd4
10	Nd2	Nc6
11	0-0	Bd7

12 Nf3   Bg7

If Black's plan is to castle Queenside, then this move has no point and can be replaced with the immediate 12 ...Qc7.

13 b3   Qc7
14 Re1   0-0-0

Black has some difficulty knowing where to put his King. The Kingside seems dangerous because Black is short on defenders there, and the center is clearly inappropriate, therefore the Queenside looks to be the best there is.

15 Bf4   Kb8
16 a3   Rc8?!

What's Black planning to do on the c-file? More logical is 16 ...Ka8, getting the King out of a possible pin, and then ...Rce8 aiming for an eventual ...f6.

17 Qd2   a6?!

Why voluntarily create an attacking object for White's b-pawn?

18 b4   Bf8

Black has no concrete plan and many weaknesses. The paradoxical text, though, meets with instantaneous success.

19 Rec1??

White plans to open the c-file with c3 or c4. He wants to leave the QR on a1 so that it can be used to advance the a-pawn and or the b-pawn.

The overall idea is fine, but the correct execution is 19 Rac1! with a clear advantage to White. The careless, naive, acentral text move allows Black to grab the initiative.

19 ...   f6!!

With the primary threat of 20 ...g5 trapping White's QB. Thanks to Black's 18th and White's 19th moves, the obvious 20 exf6 is answered by 20 ...e5, when White again will lose a piece. Therefore White has to try something desperate.

20 c4!?   dxc3 e.p.

This is not bad, but considerably stronger is 20 ... dxc4!. Then 21

Rxc4?! loses to 21 ...g5. Therefore White must play 21 dxc4, but after 21 ...fxe5 he has no satisfactory continuation. For instance, 22 b5 exf4 23 bxc6 Bxc6 gives Black an excellent, pawn-plus middlegame, and after 22 Nxe5 Nxe5 23 Re1 Bg7 24 Qe2 d3! 25 Qe3 d2!, Black keeps a significant material advantage.

21	Rxc3	g5
22	hxg5	hxg5
23	Be3	fxe5
24	Bxg5	Bg7

Even though Black has not gained any material, his positional advantage here is considerable. He has a marvelously strong center and some attacking chances along the h-file.

25	Re1	Rhf8?

But what does this have to do with the game? Why leave the QR on c8? What can it hope to do there? Correct is the fairly obvious 25 ...Rcf8!, thereby retaining the advantage and even looking forward to some play along the f-file. Inadvisable, however, is 25 ...e4?! since after 26 dxe4 White has ample compensation for the Exchange.

26 Bh6!

Exchanging the dark-square Bishops severely undermines the pride of Black's center, the advanced e-pawn. The chances are now roughly in balance.

26	...	Bxh6
27	Qxh6	Qd6
28	Rc5	Rf5?

In time pressure Black overlooks a simple tactical possibility. Required is 28 ...Rh8 29 Qe3 Rh5, and winning the e-pawn with 30 g4 Rh7 31 Nxe5 entails certain dangers for White after 31 ...Rg8.

29	Nh4	Rff8
30	Rxd5!	Qe7?

True, Black has lost an important pawn for nothing, but is that reason voluntarily and immediately to lose a lot more? There is nothing but 30 ... Qc7.

31	Ng6	Qf6

Or 31 ...Qf7 32 Rxd7 Qxd7 33 Nxf8. In severe time pressure Black tries a desperate attack. Since his position remains miserable, the attack must fail.

32	Rxd7	Qxf2+
33	Kh2	Rf3
34	Qh3	Qd2
35	Nxe5	Nxe5
36	Rxe5	Rf2

After 36 ...Rc2 the simplest is 37 Rc5 Ra2 38 Rcc7.

37	Rxb7+	Ka8
38	Ra7+!	

Black resigns

White has no shortage of wins, but the text is the most elegant. After 38 ... Kxa7 White mates with 39 Qh7+ Kb6 40 Qb7.

GAME 64

White: V. Tukmakov
(U.S.S.R.)

Black: W. Browne
(U.S.A.)

Played at Madrid (Spain) International Tournament, November 27, 1973, Round 2.

Sicilian Defense (Najdorf Variation)

A fascinating fight. A creative, sharp opening leads to an unbalanced middlegame, with White generally always a bit better. The real excitement starts around move 25, when, with both sides in severe time trouble, Black starts to really complicate things. First both sides match blows, but then a serious blunder by White on move 31 allows Black to mop up in a walk. A game in which bravery is rewarded.

1 e4	c5
2 Nf3	d6
3 d4	cxd4
4 Nxd4	Nf6
5 Nc3	a6
6 Bg5	e6
7 f4	Nbd7
8 Qe2	Qc7
9 0-0-0	

This has followed Game 37, in which White played the less flexible 9 g4. The logical text gets the King to relative safety and allows the QR to start taking part in the battle. With his next typical move, Black also shows off his aggressive notions.

| 9 ... | b5 |
| 10 f5!? | |

The most popular moves for White have been the precautionary 10 a3 and the attacking and developmental 10 g4 with the plan of meeting 10 ...b4?! with the sharp 11 Nd5!. The text is a specialty of Tukmakov's, which, for reasons unclear to me, has had no followers. It looks like a good idea since White immediately attacks the most vulnerable point in Black's center, the e-pawn.

| 10 ... | e5 |

Black decides to keep the center closed, at the cost of weakening the d5 square. The only alternative worth discussing is 10 ...b4, after which White plays 11 fxe6 bxc3 12 exd7+. Black has two reasonable ways of capturing:

(1) 12 ...Bxd7?! 13 Bxf6 gxf6 14 Qc4! Qxc4 15 Bxc4 Bh6+ 16 Kb1 Bf4 17 b3 Ke7 18 Rd3 Rhg8 19 g3 Be5 20 Rhd1 with a clear advantage to White, since Black has serious difficulties with his weak pawns, as in Tukmakov-Averkin, 1973 U.S.S.R. Championship; and

(2) 12 ...Nxd7 13 Qc4! cxb2+ 14 Kb1 Qxc4 15 Bxc4 Ne5 16 Bd5 Rb8 17 Bf4 f6 18 Rhe1 Be7 19 Re3 Bd8 20 h3 Bd7 21 Rb3 with a slight advantage to White who'll recover his pawn and keep the freer position, as in Tukmakov-Polugaevsky, 1973 U.S.S.R. Championship.

11 Nd5	**Nxd5**
12 exd5	

Intriguing but unsatisfactory is 12 Ne6?! fxe6 13 Qh5+ g6 14 fxg6 N7f6!, with clear advantage to Black.

12 ...	**Nc5**
13 Qh5!	**Be7**

As Tukmakov points out, Black must try to consolidate his King position quickly. Immediately losing is 13 ...exd4? because of 14 Re1+, and little better is 13 ...g6?! because of 14 Qf3! exd4? 15 Re1+ Kd7 16 fxg6, with White again winning.

14 Nc6	**Bxg5+**
15 Qxg5	**f6**
16 Qh5+	**Qf7**
17 Qf3	

The opening phase has led to a middlegame position somewhat favorable to White. White's Knight plays an inhibiting role on c6 and Black can hardly ever afford to exchange it, since that will open the way for White's QR and KB. White also has good chances of opening either the Kingside or the Queenside for play against Black's somewhat cramped position. Black's only pride is the protected, passed e-pawn, but this can be of importance only in a far-off endgame.

17 ...	**Bb7**
18 Kb1	**0-0**
19 g4	**Rac8**
20 Bg2	**Na4?!**

White's reply stamps this as a waste of time. Correct is to activate the Queen immediately with 20 ...Qc7. If White does nothing, Black can try to carry out the plan ...Na4 ...Nb6, ...Kh8 followed by ... Nxd5, as given by Browne.

21 Qa3	**Nc5**

The d-pawn must be protected, and 21 ...Qc7 allows White to get his Queenside play going at no risk: 22 c4! Nb6 23 c5 Nc4 24 Qb4!.

22 Rhe1	**Rfe8**
23 Re3	**Qc7**
24 Rc1	**Qb6**
25 b4!?	

White has been preparing to

open up the Queenside and does so
now. Objectively the plan is fine,
though in the existing mutual time
shortage the practical risk is considerable. Of course not 25 c4?? first
since White's Queen is trapped
after 25...Bxc6 26 dxc6?! b4.

25 ...	Na4
26 c4	bxc4

Black has no interest in allowing the smothering 27 c5. At the
moment his Knight is safe since 27
Qxa4? allows 27...Qxe3.

27 Rxc4   a5!?

Starting here Black shows
great creativity and courage by complicating the position as much as
possible. In time pressure this gives
good practical winning chances
while not really significantly increasing one's losing chances. It's
true that 27...Qb5 28 Qb3 Nb6 is
safer, but after 29 Rc1 White is
better in a no-risk situation.

28 Qb3!

With the simple threat 29
bxa5. Wrong is 28 Nxa5? Qb5! 29
Rxc8 Rxc8 30 Nxb7 Qc4!, and
Black's attack is decisive.

28 ...	Ba6!
29 b5!	Bxb5
30 Rxa4	Rb8!!

Both sides have been trading
blow for blow. Now correct and
necessary is the obvious 31 Nxb8
Rxb8. The play thereafter can become very complicated, and lengthy
analysis after the game showed best
play to be 32 Rae4 a4 33 Qb4 Qc7 34
Ka1!! Bd3! (34...Qc1+ 35 Qb1
Qxb1+ 36 Kxb1 Bf1+ 37 Kc2 Bxg2
38 Rxa4 Bxd5 and thanks to the
passed a-pawn White must be better)
35 Qxb8+ Qxb8 36 Rxd3 Qb6 37
Re2 a3! White does have a significant material advantage here, but his
pieces and King are in a bind so it
is not at all easy to make progress.
Overall Black must be considered
to have good practical drawing
chances. Instead White plays...

31 Rae4??	a4
32 Qb4	Bxc6

So White has not only failed to
take Black's Rook but has also, in
effect, left his Knight en prise. A
tragedy in time presure, but it is also
Black's reward for brave practical
play.

33 Qxb6	Rxb6+
34 Kc1	Bxd5

And so Black is sure of a huge material advantage in a completely secure position. The only practical question remaining is whether he can reach the time control on move 40. Once he does, White immedi- ately resigns.

35 Rd3	Rc8+
36 Kd2	Rb2+
37 Ke3	Bxe4
38 Bxe4	Rb6
39 Rd5	Rc5
40 Rd3	Kf8
White resigns	

GAME 65

**White: T. Ujtumen
(Mongolia)**

**Black: R. Vaganian
(U.S.S.R.)**

Played at Dubna (U.S.S.R.)
International Tournament, December 1973, Round 4.

Alekhine Defense
(Four Pawns Attack)

Both sides are quite willing to
discuss a modern sharp variation.
After the forced variations are finished, White should be able to look
forward to the slight initiative of the
first player. But Black can't get
himself to accept this situation and
continually insists on sacrificing a
piece. In due course White accepts
the sacrifice, consolidates his material advantage and wins in good
style. A good example of steady
nerves winning over impetuousness.

1 e4	Nf6

The Alekhine Defense is
named for former World Champion
Alexander Alekhine, who introduced it into modern tournament
practice against A. Steiner at
Budapest 1921. Its strategic point
is to force White's center pawns
forward, then challenge in the hope
of annihilating them. This kind of
"hypermodern" approach became
popular in the 1920's. The debit side
of the strategy is that, unless Black
is able to destroy White's center,
this center will severely cramp
Black's game. The Alekhine has
never achieved broad popularity, but
Fischer's two successes (one win
and one draw) in his 1972 match
against Spassky means, to me, that
this defense must be fundamentally
sound.

2 e5	Nd5
3 c4	

In conjunction with the next
two moves, this is White's sharpest
approach. Also quite good and very
popular in the 1970's is the modern
variation 3 d4 d6 4 Nf3; White keeps
some central superiority and is less
exposed than in the Four Pawns Attack.

3 ...	Nb6
4 d4	d6
5 f4!	

This decidedly establishes the
Four Pawns Attack. Four of
White's Pawns are at present in
essentially total control of the
center. However, this means that
White has been neglecting piece
development. Can Black take advantge of this factor? This is the
whole crux of the variation. Instead
of the text, the Exchange Variation,
5 exd6, is harmless.

5 ...	dxe5
6 fxe5	Nc6

Much too sharp is 6 ...c5?! because of the simple 7 d5, but a completely good (and in fact more common) alternative is 6 ...Bf5.

7 Be3	Bf5
8 Nc3	e6
9 Nf3	Be7

A relatively quiet move in the Four Pawns. Sharper are 9 ...Qd7 and 9 ...Nb4. The latter seems equivalent to the text in quality, but the former (with the plan ...0-0-0) is too risky. The idea behind the text is simply to castle Kingside and then challenge White's center with ...f6. To hope for any advantage White must play sharply before Black's development is complete. The older 10 Be2 0-0 11 0-0 f6! allows Black eventually to achieve full equalization.

10 d5!	Nb4

The obvious alternative is the interpolation of 10 ...exd5 11 cxd5 and only then 11 ...Nb4. According to the latest theory, this works out to White's benefit after 12 Nd4 Bd7 13 e6!.

(The above sequence has become the main line in the Four Pawns Attack. The evaluation is somewhere around "Black gets eventual equality- the position remains unclear.")

11 Rc1

But here, without the center-clarifying pawn exchange, 11 Nd4 is not quite as effective, and Black gains good counterchances after 11 ...Bg6 12 a3 c5! 13 Nxe6 fxe6 14 axb4 cxb4.

11 ...	exd5

Black has nothing better. Interesting is 11 ...f6, but after 12 a3 Na6 13 g4! Bxg4 14 Rg1, White establishes a very strong attacking position, as in Velimirovic-Gipslis, Havana 1971, for example.

12 a3	c5!?

Black's most active attempt to counterattack. Somewhat in White's favor are both 12 ...Na6 13 cxd5 0-0 14 Bxb6 axb6 15 Qd4! and 12 ...Nxc4!? 13 Bxc4 dxc4 14 axb4 Qxd1+ 15 Rxd1 Bxb4 16 0-0 Bd3 17 Rf2.

13 axb4	d4
14 Bxd4!	

White must give back part of the bounty. 14 bxc5?! is unsatisfactory because after 14 ...dxc3 the strength of the c-pawn gives White no time for 15 cxb6, and after the defensive 15 bxc3 Qxd1+ 16 Rxd1 Na4, Black is all right.

14 ...	cxd4
15 Nxd4!?	

An interesting psychological moment. According to analysis by Hort, White can obtain a safe, slightly superior position with 15 Qxd4 Bxb4 16 c5 Nd5 17 Bb5+ Bd7 18 Bxd7+! Qxd7 19 0-0. The double-edged text shows that he's going for more.

15 ...   Bg6?!

Black apparently has no time for this "defensive" move. The critical line is 15 ...Qb8!? 16 Qe2 Bg6 17 c5 Nd7, and now both 18 c6! and 18 Nd5! should lead to some practical advantage for White. Practical tests are, however, in order.

(I am not aware of any tests with the above recommendations. However, tested and recognized as leading to a slight advantage for White after 15 ... Qb8 16 Nxf5 Qxe5+ 17 Be2 Qxf5 18 c5 Nd7 19 Nd5! Bd8 20 Rc3 0-0 21 Ne3 Qe6 22 Bg4, Velimirovic-Marovic, Yugoslavia 1977.)

16 c5

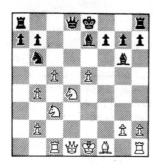

What is Black to do now? He's

already a pawn down, 16 ...Nd7?! 17 e6 is miserable, and 16 ...Nd5?! 17 Bb5+ Kf8 18 0-0 with the threat of 19 Ne6+ is plain horrible. 16 ...Bg5 is possible, however, though after 17 Ra1! Nd7 18 Nf3!, the best that Black can hope to achieve is the game continuation.

16 ...   0-0!?

A suggestion of Timman's with the idea that after 17 cxb6 Bxb4 Black's active pieces have good practical chances of bothering White's uncastled King. This doesn't mean that Black's piece sacrifice is fully sound, but he does get real practical chances.

17 Nf3!

After ten minutes of thought the Mongolian IM decides on the best psychological and practical course; i.e., why give Black any chances at all?

17 ...   Nd7
18 Bb5!   Bg5?!

This does not work out well, but Tal's suggestion of 18 ...Nb8 is hardly the kind of course that he himself would choose in a game. After 19 0-0, White is better.

19 Ra1!

What now, Knight? 19 ...Nb8 is worse than before since after 20

Qxd8 Black must recapture with the Bishop. Objectively this is probably the way to go, but it goes too much against Vaganian's grain. Therefore he prefers to ditch the Knight with...

19 ...	Nxe5?!
20 Nxe5	Qf6
21 Nf3	Rad8

Black has a lovely position, *except* that he's a whole piece down.

22 Qb3	Bh4+?

Voluntarily exchanging one of the attackers soon leads to a halt of Black's attack. Considering that White's KB takes away the important e8 square from a Black Rook , it is logical to put a question to the Bishop with 22...a6!?

23 Nxh4	Qxh4+
24 g3	Qh3
25 Ne2	Qg2
26 Rg1	Qe4

This "centralization" leads to naught, but any hope after 26...Qxh2 27 Qf3, etc, is also very meager.

27 Kf2	a6
28 Bc4	Rd2
29 Rgd1!	Qd4+
30 Qe3!	

This puts a definitive end to Black's attack and hopes. The incautious 30 Ke1? allows 30...Re8!!

with good attacking prospects for Black because 31 Rxd2? is refuted by 32...Qg1 mate!

30 ...	Qf6+
31 Qf4	Qxf4+

Forced to save the Rook but practically chanceless.

32 gxf4	Rxb2
33 Rd4	Re8
34 Ra2!	Rxb4?!

Of course, 34...Rexe2+ 35 Bxe2 Rxa2 allows 36 Rd8 mate! With the text, Black hopes to tempt White into 35 Bxf7+?? Bxf7 36 Rxb4 Bxa2, with Black better. But White has a neat zwischenzug.

35 f5!
Black resigns

Additional material loss is unavoidable since 35...Bxf5 is met by 36 Bxf7+, and 35...Bh5 fails to 36 Ng3. In the game Black apparently did play on a few more moves, but my Soviet source didn't deem them worth publishing.

GAME 66

White: E. Vasiukov
(U.S.S.R)

Black: Z. Ribli
(Hungary)

Played at Wijk aan Zee (Netherlands) International Tournament, January 1973, Round 8.

Pirc/Modern Defense

A perfect game by the young Hungarian master (long since a grandmaster). With original and creative play he comes into the middlegame with some advantage. White realizes that his position is inferior and, by throwing caution to the winds, starts a sharp, dangerous attack against Black's Kingside. Combining defense and counterattack to an exquisite degree, Black holds White off long enough to generate his own winning combination.

1	e4	g6
2	d4	Bg7
3	Nf3	

A somewhat less active approach than the 3 Nc3 d6 4 f4 of Game 36.

3	...	d6
4	Bc4	

That Black has not yet developed his KN gives White a broader range of possible set-ups. The text followed by 5 Qe2 is a favorite of Tal's, among others. White strives to get in an early, active e5.

4	...	Nf6
5	Qe2	Nc6!?

Rarely played, either before or after this game. Black issues an immediate challenge to White's center and is unafraid of the coming e5. More cautious, and common, are 5 ...c6 and 5 ...0-0.

6 e5!?

A logical attempt to refute Black's last move. Safe and sound is 6 c3, but it is questionable whether White can then achieve more than the tiniest of edges.

6	...	dxe5

Forced, since after 6 ...Nd7? Black gets hit by 7 Bxf7+ Kxf7 8 Ng5+, and Black is lucky to come out with only one black eye after 8 ...Ke8 9 Ne6 Nxd4! 10 Nxg7+ Kf7 11 Qc4+ Kxg7 12 Qxd4.

7	dxe5	Ng4
8	Bb5??	

This is completely incomprehensible. White misplaces the KB and pays the price of a lost tempo for the "privilege." This can already be considered the losing move. Thematic and correct is unquestionably, 8 e6!, as in Kotkov-Razuvaev, Moscow 1972. Black then must prove that he can equalize.

8 ...	Bd7
9 Bf4	0-0
10 Nc3	

The punishment was severe in Vogt-Szymczak, Lublin 1974, after the further time-wasting 10 h3? : 10 ...Ngxe5! 11 Bxe5 Bxe5 12 Bxc6 (12 Nxe5 loses to 12 ...Nd4) 12 ...Bxb2 13 Qb5 Bxa1 14 Bxd7 c6 15 Qd3 Qc7, and Black went on to win easily. The text, by protecting the KB, prevents this tactical possibility.

10 ...	a6
11 Ba4	b5
12 Bb3	b4
13 Na4	Na5
14 0-0-0	Qe8

Black has been pushing White around on the whole board and now

threatens the obvious 15 ...Bxa4 winning the strayed Knight. After the "normal" 15 Nc5 comes 15 ... Bb5 16 Qe1 Nxb3+ 17 axb3 a5 followed by 18 ...a4 and a strong attack for Black. Even though White's position is in theory defensible, in practice such an approach is very often chanceless. Therefore, Vasiukov decides on a radically different course: White sacrifices material to get the attack. True, in the end this will fail, but only because the young Ribli plays as the Great Ribli.

(In the "Modern Defense" published in 1979 GM Hort continues the line given above and concludes White is better after 18 h3 Nh6 19 g4. Such a conclusion is far from clear after Black's 19 ...a4 or 19 ...Qc6 or 19 ...Bc6. It may be more accurate, however, to play 17 ...Qc6 or 17 ...Bc6 in place of the immediate 17 ...a5.)

| 15 h3!? | Bb5 |

The first small mine to be avoided is 15 ...Nxf2? 16 Rxd7!, and it is White who gains material.

16 Qd2	Nxf2!
17 Qxf2	Bxa4
18 Qc5	

There is absolutely no future in 18 Qh4? Nxb3+ 19 axb3 Bc6 20 Ng5 h6 21 Nf3 Bxf3 22 gxf3 g5, etc.

| 18 ... | Nxb3+ |

19 axb3	Bc6
20 Nd4!?	

Continuing his reckless policy, White throws two more pawns into the fray. True, 20 Qxb4 reestablishes material equality, but after 20 ...a5 followed by 21 ...a4 Black's attack rolls on and White's prospects are bleak.

20 ...	Bxg2
21 Rhg1	Bxh3
22 Nc6	Kh8!
23 Rd2	a5!!

A brilliant concept: Black's QR now will be able to defend the Kingside and to attack the e-pawn. In addition, Black will be ready for a timely ...a4 advance.

24 Rh2	Ra6!
25 Nxe7	Re6
26 Nd5	Bf5
27 Qf2!?	

White again finds the best practical chance; i.e., bringing the Queen over to the Kingside. Clearly unsatisfactory is 27 Nxc7?! because of 27 ...Rxe5 28 Nxe8 (28 Bxe5?! Qxe5 29 Qxe5 Bxe5 with a fork on the Rook and the Knight) 28 ...Rxc5 29 Nxg7 Kxg7 30 Bh6+ Kg8 31 Bxf8 Kxf8, and Black's three connected Kingside passed pawns are a winning advantage.

27 ...	Qd8?

Black must prevent White's threatened Qh4. Losing is 27 ...Rxe5? 28 Qh4 h5 29 Nf6 Qe7 30 Qxh5+!! and White mates. After the text White's Knight is en prise.

28 Nf6!?

A last try aiming at weakening the dark squares around Black's King. The sacrifice 28 Rxh7+ is unsound after 28 ...Kxh7 29 Qh2+ Kg8 30 Rh1 g5!, and 28 Rd1 is met by the simple 28 ...Bxe5! (Ribli)

28 ...	Bxf6
29 exf6	Qxf6
30 Bg5	Qe5
31 Qh4	h5

Black is up a whole Kingside, three pawns, but his Kingside is now full of holes. White has four pieces trained along open lines against it. If left alone, White can create dangerous threats. But Black sees that White's King position is also inherently loose, and combines attack and defense so adroitly that the game is over in fewer than ten moves.

32 Bf4	Qe4
33 Qg5	Rfe8!
34 Kb1	

34 Rxh5+ Kg8 35 Rh2 gives Black time for the decisive 35 ...Rc6!. Therefore White tries to get his King to relative safety.

34 ...	a4!

No rest for the weary! Now 35 bxa4 allows 35 ...b3, and 35 Rxh5+ Kg8 36 Qh4 is met by 36 ...Qd4!, with White's attack stopped and Black's ready to accelerate. What White selects is no better.

35 Qh6+	Kg8
36 Qxh5	Qe1+
37 Ka2	

Obviously 37 Rxe1? Rxe1+ followed by 38 ... gxh5 costs White a Rook. And after 37 Bc1 Black has another tactical shot: 37 ...Bxc2+! 38 Kxc2 (or 38 Ka1 Qxc1+) 38 ...Rc6+, etc.

37 ...	axb3+

38 Kxb3	Re3+!
39 Bxe3	Qxe3+
40 c3	Be6+
White resigns	

It's either mate or a decisive loss of material.

GAME 67

White: K. Langeweg
(Netherlands)

Black: E. Vasiukov
(U.S.S.R.)

Played at Wijk aan Zee (Netherlands) International Tournament, January 1973, Round 13.

King's Indian Defense

White chooses an unassuming buildup against the King's Indian. By leaving the c-pawn back home, White renders his center less vulnerable to attack. Black is not able to come up with a coherent plan for counterplay and soon finds himself in a cramped, prospectless position. White is able to bring about a favorable two-Bishop endgame, in which he also gets an outside passed pawn. When Black plays too passively in the endgame, he is ground down with zugzwang motifs. Overall a pleasant game for White all the way through. At no time is he in the slightest danger of losing but always has good winning chances. This is an excellent situation for defeating a superior opponent.

1	Nf3	Nf6
2	g3	g6
3	Bg2	Bg7
4	0-0	0-0
5	d4	d6

6 Nc3

Of course the "normal" 6 c4 leads to one of the usual variations in the King's Indian- see, for example, Game 60. The text is an unassuming approach to the coming play. White voluntarily neglects to exert fuller central influence, thereby giving Black fewer chances for central counterplay. In addition, White saves a tempo for development. White's approach is not at all harmless for practical play, and Black must defend correctly not to land in a passive, constrained situation.

6	...	Nbd7

Aiming for ...e5 is both good and logical. Bobby Fischer once made the claim that, after 6 ...d5, Black was better. With all due respect, such a conclusion is rather extravagant, and after 7 Re1, aiming for e5, White still has the usual first-move advantage.

7	e4	e5
8	a4	exd4?!

By giving up the center, Black unquestionably hands over central superiority to White. Such action should be taken only when a clear and immediate benefit can be derived, and that is not the case here. The strategically proper approach for Black is 8 ...a5! 9 Be3 Re8 10 Re1 c6! 11 dxe5 dxe5 12 Nd2 Nb6 13 f3 Be6 14 Qe2 Nfd7 with equality, as in Sosonko- Dueball, Mannheim 1975.

9 Nxd4	Re8?!

Trifunovic correctly points out that White's next should be prevented by 9...a5. As played Black runs into the danger of being suffocated because of a lack of room.

10 a5!	Nc5
11 Re1	Ng4?!

Achieves nothing for Black except loss of time, whereas White gets a very strong center. Trifunovic again is right in suggesting 11...Bg4!? 12 f3 Bd7 as a more workable plan of development.

12 h3	Ne5
13 f4	Ned7
14 Be3	Nf8
15 Qd2	a6
16 b4	Ncd7
17 Nb3	Nf6
18 Rad1	

A position of striking contrasts. White controls more space on the Queenside, in the center, and on the Kingside, whereas about the only thing that Black controls is his back rank! White's development is complete, his pieces in attractive, purposeful locations, whereas Black still has much to do to get his forces out. White can methodically prepare for action along several fronts; Black has no prospects for action- only for reaction to hold off White. Despite his obvious advantages, White must still work to win the position; Black is very cramped but he has no fundamental weaknesses.

18 ...	Be6
19 Qd3	Qc8
20 Kh2	Bxb3?!

One of the general principles of defending cramped positions calls for exchanging pieces to lighten the defensive task. Black's move is in accordance with this general approach but suffers from the specific disadvantages of giving White the two Bishops and weakening Black's light squares. Creation of the doubled b-pawns is also more in White's favor since he can now expect to develop pressure along the c-file. Black's best plan is to try to keep the status quo with 20...Bd7, for example.

21 cxb3	Qe6
22 Nd5	Nxd5

23 exd5	Qd7
24 Bf2	h5
25 Rxe8!	

White plays the whole game in excellent practical style. The exchange of Rooks will ensure that Black gets no attacking chances whatever. This will allow White's Queen and Bishops unperturbed play against Black's Queenside.

25 ...	Rxe8
26 Re1	Rxe1
27 Bxe1	Nh7
28 Qc4!	Bb2

Hardly a great spot for the Bishop, but Black wants to continue ...Nf6 without blocking off the Bishop.

29 Bf1

With the plan b5, and not bad. Considerably stronger, however, is 29 Bf2!, as Langeweg pointed out, logically going after the accessible c-pawn with Ba7 and Bb8. If Black plays similarly to the game, 29 ...Nf6?!, his Bishop runs the risk of getting trapped after 30 Qc2! Ba3 31 Be1.

29 ...	Nf6
30 Bd3	Kg7
31 Bd2	Ng8?!

Black ensures the loss of this endgame by playing as passively as possible. Trifunovic suggests the

active 31 ... Qb5! 32 Qxb5 axb5 33 Bxb5 Nxd5. It is true that, after 34 Bc4 Ne7 35 b5 Bd4! 36 a6 bxa6 37 bxa6 d5, the outside passed pawn supported by the two Bishops gives White the better chances, but Black also has a passed pawn and a generally free position; so White's win is not assured.

32 b5!

The creation of an outside passed pawn is still White's most promising approach.

32 ...	axb5
33 Qxb5	Qxb5
34 Bxb5	Ne7
35 Bc4	Bd4
36 b4	Kf8?!

Again very passive. There is still the opportunity to reach the type of position given after Black's 31st move: 36 ...c6! 37 dxc6 bxc6 to be followed by ...d5.

37 b5   Nc8?!

Here, too, the active move 37 ...Nf5! has to be better.

38 a6

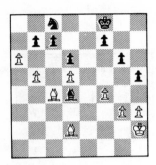

White has achieved his first objective, the outside passed pawn, whereas Black has done nothing but move backward.

38 ...   b6?

Why, oh why, such passivity? 38 ...bxa6 is mandatory. Black then has some chance of getting a passed pawn in the center and, with it, prospects for a draw. After the text, White gets a passed a-pawn for nothing, since White's b-pawn and d-pawn easily hold back the three Black pawns. With the text Black hopes that he can keep the position sufficiently blocked to prevent any penetration by White. In practice there is invariably a winning breakthrough, and White finds it readily enough.

39 f5!

The start of the loosening-up process. The position is won for White; only the specific winning route is uncertain.

39 ...	Bf6
40 h4	Kg7
41 fxg6	fxg6
42 Kg2	

The King should actually head for h3 - see move 46. However, since there is nothing Black can do to strengthen his position, this slight delay is immaterial.

42 ...	Na7
43 Kf3	Kf7
44 Bd3	Kg7
45 Kg2	Kf7
46 Kh3	Kg7
47 g4!	hxg4+

There is no way to prevent White's King from making progress. After 47 ...Kf7 Langeweg gives the following winning line: 48 gxh5 gxh5 49 Bg5! Kg7 (49 ...Be5? allows 50 Bd8) 50 Kg3 Be5+ 51 Kf3 Bf6 52 Kf4 Be5+ 53 Kf5, followed by 54 Bd8.

48 Kxg4	Kf7
49 Bg5!	Kg7
50 Bxf6+!	Kxf6
51 Kf4	

White will now achieve a zugzwang position, in which Black's Knight will have no move and Black's King will therefore have to give way to its colleague.

51 ...	Nc8
52 Bc4	Na7
53 Bf1!	Nc8

54 Bh3	Na7
55 Bd7	Ke7
56 Kg5!	

61 Kg7
Black resigns

The ultimate point of the previous maneuvers. If now 56 ...Kxd7 57 Kxg6 Ke7 58 Kg7! and the h-pawn wins, the closest variation being 58 ...c5 59 bxc6 e.p. b5 60 h5 b4 61 h6 b3 62 h7 b2 63 h8=Q b1=Q 64 Qf8 mate! Black's response is equally hopeless.

56 ...	Kf7
57 Kh6!	Kf6
58 Be8!	Ke7
59 Kxg6!	c5
60 bxc6 e.p.	Kxe8

Black's even a move behind the variation given after White's 56th move.

GAME 68

White: L. Espig
(East Germany)

Black: E. Vasiukov
(U.S.S.R.)

Played at Dubna (U.S.S.R.)
International Tournament, December 1973, Round 2.

Reti Opening

A crush. Vasiukov allows his opponent to build up a strong, secure center, and gets smothered by it. To contain damage in the center, Black is forced to create a fundamental weakness on the Queenside. White goes so resolutely for this weakness that Black decides that his only hope is a nebulous attack on the Kingside. The net result is only that Black's collapse is accelerated. An excellent practical example of "How to Defeat a Superior Opponent."

1	Nf3	d5
2	c4	d4
3	e3	Nc6
4	exd4	Nxd4
5	Nxd4	Qxd4
6	Nc3	

Thus far this followed Game 32, in which White played 6 d3. Usually that amounts only to a transposition of moves, but not here.

6 ...	Bg4?!

Leads to a considerably greater misplacement of the Bishop than of White's Queen. Black's correct equalizing method was given in notes to Game 32: 6 ...e5! 7 d3 c6 8 Be3 Qd6 9 Be2 Ne7! (on the way to f5).

7	Qa4+	c6
8	d3	Nf6?!

This hands the center over completely to White. Not quite satisfactory for equality, but considerably better, is 8 ...e5 9 Be3 Qd7 10 f3 Be6 11 Rd1! followed by 12 d4, with White better but not as much as in the game.

9	Be3	Qd8

Or 9 ...Qd7 10 d4 e6 11 f3 Bf5 12 0-0-0 Bd6 13 g4 Bg6 14 h4, with a clear advantage for White, as in Keres- Euwe, Nordwijk 1938.

10	d4	g6
11	h3	Bd7
12	Qb3	Qc7
13	Be2	Bg7
14	0-0	0-0
15	Rfd1	

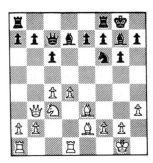

White's moves have been as simple as possible, but the net effect is overwhelming. White has a secure central superiority, and his pieces are placed in active, purposeful central direction. Even though Black has no fundamental weakness at the moment, he is in danger of slow death by asphyxiation. How did White's simple moves bring about such a commanding situation? Well, Black's moves were neither simple (witness 6...Bg4?!!) nor accurate (8 ...Nf6?! instead of 8...e5).

15 ...   Kh8?!

For want of a good plan, Black chooses one which is something like a cross between bad and meaningless. 15...e6, trying to inhibit White's d5 advance, has to be better.

16 Rac1   Ng8?!
17 d5!   c5

With control of the d5 square

lessened, Black's best approach is to keep the position as closed as possible. However, White is able to execute a different line-opening plan.

18 Qa3   b6
19 b4!   cxb4
20 Qxb4   Rac8
21 Nb5   Qb8
22 a4!

White's huge space advantage is unperturbed, and with a5 he threatens to force a fundamental weakness in Black's Queenside pawn formation; i.e., Black will be left with either a weak a-pawn or a weak b-pawn. Black tries to get some counterchances by offering to sacrifice the e-pawn.

22 ...   Nh6
23 Nd4!

But White correctly prefers to keep Black in a total bind. After 23 Qxe7 Bxb5! 24 cxb5 Nf5 followed by 25...Nxe3, the opposite-color Bishops give Black some drawing chances.

23 ...   Qd6
24 Qd2!   Nf5
25 Nxf5   gxf5?!

Objectively speaking, the normal 25...Bxf5 has to be better, though after 26 a5 White's positional advantage is major. With the text Black hopes (dreams is proba-

bly more accurate) for some play
along the g-file.

26	a5	Qg6
27	f4!	e6?!

Black's position is rather
hopeless; even so it's difficult to see
what his last move has to do with the
game.

28	axb6	axb6
29	Rb1	Rg8
30	Rxb6!	Bf6

The KB has no effective move
to clear the g-file, and White can
stop the routine mate threat routinely. Black's position is resignable.

31	Bf1	Rg7
32	Bd4	Bxd4
33	Qxd4	h6
34	c5!	Qh5
35	c6	Be8
36	d6!	

Passed pawns must be pushed!
Major material loss for Black is
unavoidable. If now 36 ...Rxc6, then
37 Rb8 is the strongest. Black's
reply is even less satisfactory.

36	...	Bxc6
37	Rxc6	Rxc6
38	d7	

Black resigns

White has a new Queen coming up.